GW01605913

# THE MONGOL CONQUESTS

## AD 1200-1300

AD 1200-1300

CENTRAL ASIA AND THE FAR EAST

AFRICA AND THE MIDDLE EAST

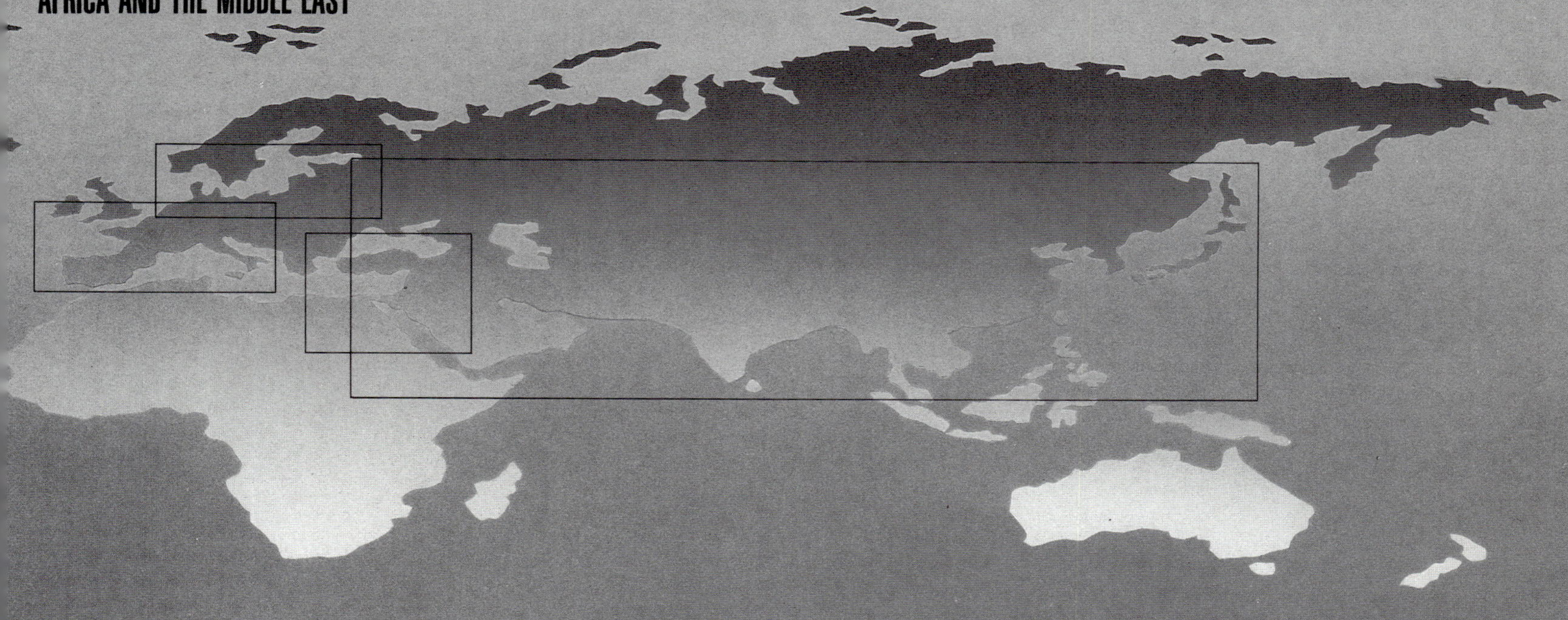

A CHILD'S FIRST LIBRARY OF LEARNING
VOYAGE THROUGH THE UNIVERSE
MYSTERIES OF THE UNKNOWN
TIME-LIFE HISTORY OF THE WORLD
FITNESS, HEALTH AND NUTRITION
HEALTHY HOME COOKING
UNDERSTANDING COMPUTERS
THE ENCHANTED WORLD
LIBRARY OF NATIONS
HOME REPAIR AND IMPROVEMENT
CLASSICS OF EXPLORATION
PLANET EARTH
PEOPLES OF THE WILD
THE EPIC OF FLIGHT
THE SEAFARERS
WORLD WAR II
THE GOOD COOK
THE TIME-LIFE ENCYCLOPAEDIA OF GARDENING
THE GREAT CITIES
THE OLD WEST
THE WORLD'S WILD PLACES
LIFE LIBRARY OF PHOTOGRAPHY
TIME-LIFE LIBRARY OF ART
GREAT AGES OF MAN
LIFE SCIENCE LIBRARY
LIFE NATURE LIBRARY

This volume is one in the Time-Life series
HISTORY OF THE WORLD.

# THE MONGOL CONQUESTS

## AD 1200-1300

BY THE EDITORS OF TIME-LIFE BOOKS

TIME-LIFE BOOKS, AMSTERDAM

**TIME-LIFE BOOKS**

EDITOR-IN-CHIEF (Europe): Sue Joiner
*European Executive Editor:* Gillian Moore
*Design Director:* Ed Skyner
*Assistant Design Director:* Mary Staples
*Chief of Research:* Vanessa Kramer
*Chief Sub-Editor:* Ilse Gray

**TIME-LIFE HISTORY OF THE WORLD**

SERIES EDITOR: Tony Allan

Editorial Staff for *The Mongol Conquests*
*Editor:* Fergus Fleming
*Designer:* Mary Staples
*Writer:* Chris Farman
*Researchers:* Caroline Lucas (principal), Marie-Louise Collard
*Sub-Editors:* Diana Hill, Christine Noble
*Design Assistant:* Rachel Gibson
*Editorial Assistant:* Molly Sutherland

Picture Department
*Administrator:* Patricia Murray
*Picture Coordinator:* Amanda Hindley

Editorial Production
*Chief:* Maureen Kelly
*Production Assistant:* Samantha Hill
*Editorial Department:* Theresa John, Debra Lelliott



ISBN 0 7054 0979 1


**CONSULTANTS**

**General:**
GEOFFREY PARKER, Professor of History, University of Illinois, Urbana-Champaign, Illinois.

CHRISTOPHER BAYLY, Reader in Modern Indian History, St. Catharine's College, Cambridge University.

**Western Europe:**
CHRISTOPHER GIVEN-WILSON, Lecturer in Medieval History, University of St. Andrews, Fife.

MICHAEL PRESTWICH, Professor of History, University of Durham.

**The Baltic:**
ERIC CHRISTIANSEN, Fellow of New College, Oxford University.

**Central Asia and the Far East:**
I.J. McMULLEN, Lecturer in Japanese, Oxford University.

D.S.M. WILLIAMS, Lecturer in History of Asiatic Russia, School of Slavonic and East European Studies, London University.

**Africa and the Middle East:**
ROBERT IRWIN, Author of *The Middle East in the Middle Ages.*

SPECIAL CONTRIBUTORS: Windsor Chorlton, John Cottrell, Ellen Galford, Alan Lothian, Deborah Thompson (text); Stephen Rogers (research).

Correspondents: Elisabeth Kraemer-Singh (Bonn); Maria Vincenza Aloisi (Paris); Ann Natanson, Ann Wise (Rome); Dick Berry (Tokyo).

# CONTENTS

# THE MONGOL HORDES

1

"I am the flail of God. If you had not committed great sins, God would not have sent a punishment like me upon you." The speaker was the Mongol leader Chingis Khan, and the year was 1219. He was addressing refugees in the principal mosque of Bukhara, in central Asia. But there were few of them to hear him. Earlier his soldiers had burnt the outer city and herded the inhabitants together to serve as a human shield for their assault on the citadel. All of the city's 30,000 defenders had been killed. Those civilians who did survive were stripped of their possessions and driven before the invaders at the launch of their next campaign.

For some 50 years, from the first decade of the 13th century onwards, the fate of Bukhara was shared by cities across the Eurasian landmass – from China and Korea in the east, through Persia, Iraq and Turkestan, to Bulgaria, Russia, Poland and Hungary in the west. The sumptuous palaces of Zhongdu (now Beijing) were razed; Samarkand and Baghdad, resplendent capitals of Islamic culture, were destroyed; Kiev, the most opulent city in all of Russia, was reduced to ashes. In those years, half the known world reeled under an onslaught of unprecedented ferocity.

Outside their empire the Mongols inspired universal dread. In the Christian West, the chronicler Matthew Paris called them a detestable nation of Satan. "Piercing the solid rocks of the Caucasus, they poured forth like devils from the hell of Tartarus. They swarmed locust-like over the face of the earth, and brought terrible devastation to the eastern part of Europe, laying it waste with fire and carnage." It was only by chance that the lands west of Hungary were saved from a similar fate.

Although spared Mongol invasion, the West was experiencing a metamorphosis almost as momentous. In Germany, Italy and Sicily, the Holy Roman Empire was riven by quarrels between pope and emperor. Amidst this discord blossomed the glittering Sicilian court of Emperor Frederick II, one of the most enlightened and cosmopolitan rulers of his day. But after his death in 1250, his empire disintegrated into a collection of principalities, which would not reunite for six centuries.

At the same time, the mass of feudal territories that comprised France and England were moving in the opposite direction. By the dawn of the 14th century the two nations had become recognizably their present shape, and were experiencing under strong monarchs the benefits of centralized governments, and in England the birth of democratic parliaments. In the frozen lands of northeast Europe, where the Mongols' yak-tail banner was seen as a demon "with a devil face and a long grey beard", a Christian order, the Teutonic Knights, was clearing the southern Baltic coastlands of pagan inhabitants. By the end of the century these warrior-monks had formed a rich, powerful military state in the lands of Prussia, Livonia and Estonia.

Muslims knew the Mongols as "the Accursed of God", and indeed, the old Islamic civilizations of Persia and Turkey were all but extinguished by their ferocity.

**Shooting backwards from his mount at full gallop, a Mongol hunter demonstrates the mobility and firepower that made the steppe warriors unequalled on the battlefields of Asia and Europe. In combat, every Mongol carried two bows made out of bone and sinew on a wooden frame, one for short-range work, the other with a reach of over 300 metres. His quiver could hold as many as 60 arrows, some armour-piercing and some fitted with whistling heads for signalling. He could bend and string his bow while in the saddle by putting one end between his foot and the stirrup, and he could shoot accurately even at speed, timing the release of the arrow to come between the paces of his horse.**

Only in Palestine were they successfully thwarted — by the Mamluks, a dynasty of Turkish-born warrior-slaves who would make Palestine the centre of Islamic culture and their empire the most powerful in the Middle East. And in Japan, another emergent warrior class, the samurai, also successfully defied Mongol expansion, having earlier pushed imperial rule to one side and instituted a reign of military feudalism.

Nevertheless, the Mongols carved out in under fifty years the largest empire the world had seen. Behind this lay the military genius and inspiration of Temujin, a chieftain who rose from obscurity to be proclaimed Chingis Khan, "Lord of the Earth". Driven by a sense of divine mission, he forged the Mongol nation out of disparate nomadic peoples, creating an army with potential to conquer the world.

At the time of Temujin's birth, in the early 1160s, the Mongol world was confined to the immense central Asian plateau, varying from 900 to 1,500 metres above sea level, bounded by the Altai and Tianshan mountain ranges in the west, and by the Great Khinghan peaks in the east. The land was divided by nature into three terraces: the vast northern plain of Outer Mongolia merging into the great forests at the fringe of the Siberian tundra; a central region dominated by the Gobi Desert, some 1,900 kilometres wide; and the southern grasslands of Inner Mongolia.

East of the grasslands was the Buddhist kingdom of Xixia, founded in about 990 by Tangut nomads from Tibet. Yet farther east lay China, divided into two realms — in the north, the empire of the Jin dynasty, created in 1115 by the conquering Jurchen, a seminomadic forest people from Manchuria; and in the south, the 200-year-old Song empire, perhaps the world's most advanced civilization.

Between the Mongols and China rose the Great Wall, a fortified serpent of stone stretching nearly 2,400 kilometres from the eastern coast at Shanhaiguan to Jiuquan

**In 1207 the forces of Chingis Khan burst out of their Mongolian homeland, and within half a century had created the largest empire the world had ever seen. At their greatest, Mongol territories encompassed all Russia and almost the entire land mass of Asia. The Mongol conquests were divided after Chingis' death into four separate khanates — the Ilkhanate of Persia, the Golden Horde in Russia, the Chagatai khanate in central Asia, and the lands of the Great Khan, comprising the Mongolian heartland coupled with China. Mongol armies also penetrated eastern Europe, India and the jungles of Southeast Asia; only in Palestine and Japan was their advance halted.**

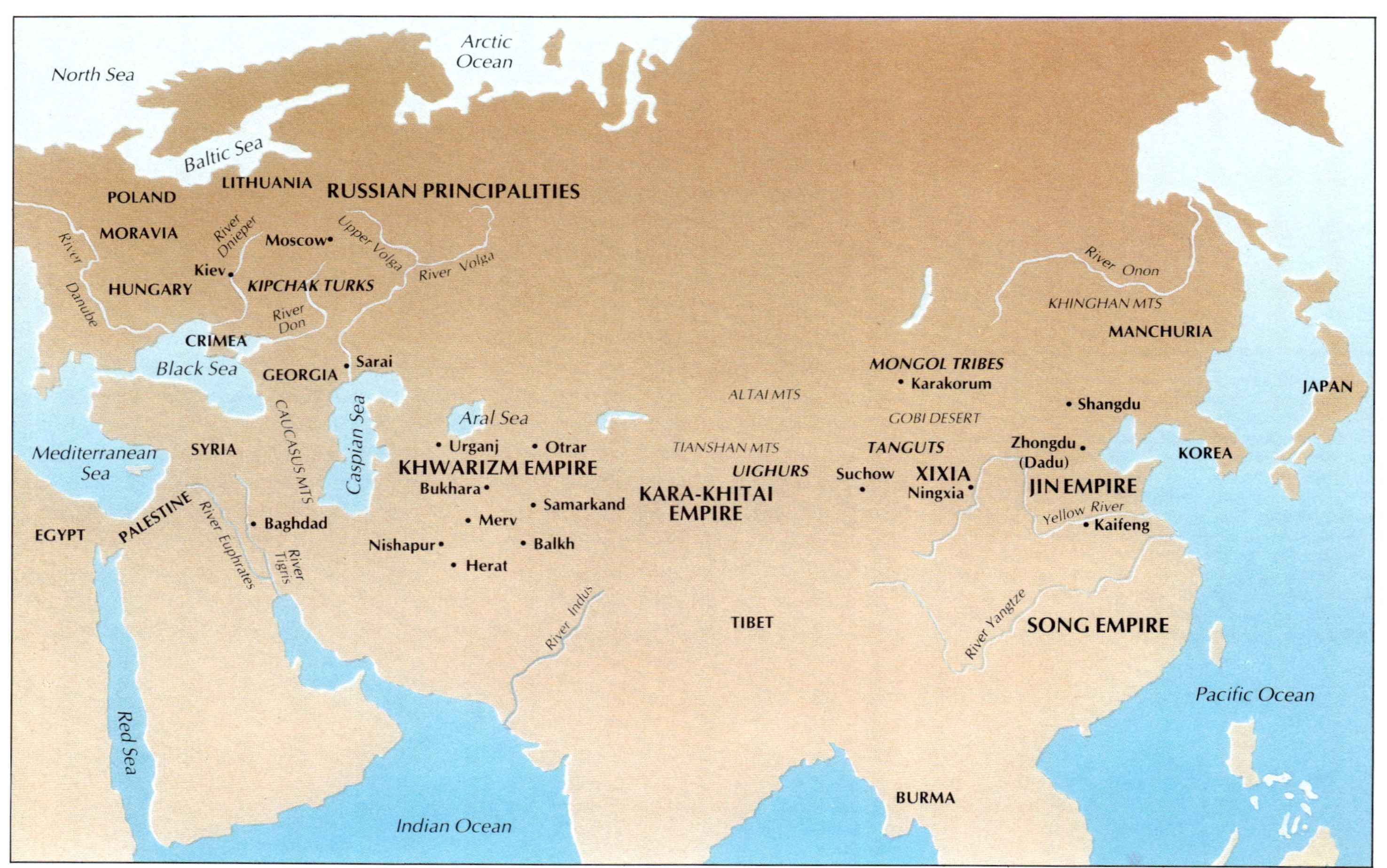

near the Gobi Desert. Strategically, the wall was only as strong as the armies that manned it; at times, invaders had surmounted it without force of arms, relying instead on political guile and the treachery of Chinese commanders. Symbolically, however, the wall never weakened. Dynasties rose and fell, but to the Chinese it remained the last outpost of civilization. Beyond it lay the lands of the barbarians, deemed by the Chinese to be totally lacking in culture and artistic refinement.

Compared with the Chinese, the Mongols were certainly barbarous. While the Song and the Jin built palatial cities and prospered from an agriculture-based economy, the Mongols were tent-dwelling nomads whose primitive life style was dictated by harsh climatic conditions. The greater part of their lives was spent on horseback. They eked out a living by driving cattle, sheep and goats to the north for the brief growth of vegetation in the summer, and then moving south at the onset of the long, hard winters. The desert and steppelands could barely support them, and warfare between different groups was a natural part of their struggle for survival.

Numbering perhaps two million, the Mongols were not so much a race as a confusion of tribes, each with a ruler known as khan, and each comprising numerous clans whose members honoured a common ancestor. They had been united once. At the dawn of the 12th century, a great Mongol state had been formed by Kabul Khan of the Bojigin clan. But this unity had evaporated following defeat in wars against the Jin. By the 1160s, the Mongols were again hopelessly divided, with tribes and clans pursuing feuds passed down from generation to generation.

Temujin, as a descendant, possibly a great-grandson, of Kabul Khan, was born into a clan with a tradition of power. According to legend, his birth was auspicious because he entered the world gripping a clot of coagulated blood in his fist. In his early years, however, he seemed doomed to obscurity. He was nine years old when his chieftain father, Yesugei, was poisoned by members of the Mongol Tatar tribe in continuance of an age-old feud. Subsequently his clan abandoned Temujin, together with his mother and five younger brothers and half-brothers. For a time, they endured abject poverty in the harsh region of the upper Onon River, subsisting only on berries and such small creatures as marmots and dormice.

The 13th-century *Secret History of the Mongols* is the only native source of information about Temujin. Compiled in 1240, possibly by a Mongol chief justice, it tells of Temujin's ancestry and early life, emphasizing his courage by recounting various boyhood adventures. The chronicler did not say precisely how the family's fortunes were revived, but the first step must have been the acquisition of horses and livestock from sympathetic clansmen. For all Mongols, their herds provided the essentials of life: food, drink, clothing and makeshift housing in the form of felt. But herding these flocks would have been impossible without the help of the horse. In both peace and war the Mongols' success depended on their wealth of horses and their skill in breeding, training and riding them. All young Mongols, boys and girls alike, were raised to be accomplished riders: it was not unusual for children to be tied on to the backs of ponies before they had learnt to walk.

As a chieftain's son, Temujin would have received early initiation into horsemanship; also, from the age of three, he would have been taught to handle a bow and arrow, eventually learning to fire at a gallop while standing in the stirrups – a technique that was to make the Mongol cavalry the deadliest in all Asia.

Temujin badly needed proficiency in such fighting skills, having inherited several feuds with other Mongol clans, most notably with the Merkits, from whom his

Mongol nomads, such as the two pictured conversing here, eked out a bare existence from the surrounding steppe. Their food consisted primarily of mutton, beef or wild game, plus curds, butter and cheese from the milk of their herds and horses; their favourite drink, koumiss, was an alcoholic beverage made from fermented mare's milk. Their animals also provided the raw materials for making clothes, saddles, stirrups, bow cases, quivers, and even homes – felt, produced by beating and oiling animal hair, was an essential item in building the circular Mongol tent called a yurt.

father had forcefully acquired his future wife. The Merkits were to take revenge many years later by snatching Temujin's bride, Bortei, and giving her to one of their own warriors. When Temujin finally succeeded in tracking down the abductors he killed every one of them, and went on to defeat the entire clan. Nine months afterwards, Bortei gave birth to a boy. His paternity was uncertain, but Temujin named him Jochi and accepted him as his son.

By now, as a renowned warrior and born leader, Temujin had built up a large following. At the head of an army more than 20,000 strong, he set about destroying his enemies with a combination of outstanding generalship and utter ruthlessness. He followed his victory over the Tatars by executing every Tatar male taller than the height of a cart axle. After defeating the rival Taichi'ut clan with massed cavalry charges, he had the enemy chiefs boiled alive. His aim was to destroy traditional divisions and unite the Mongol world under his control, and he sought to achieve it by eliminating rivals capable of challenging his authority.

By 1203, Temujin had achieved complete mastery of central and eastern Mongolia. Over the next three years he completed his conquest of the steppelands by marching west to defeat the great Naiman tribe. In addition, he consolidated his position by capturing a warrior chief named Jamuka, who had formed tribal coalitions to challenge Temujin's leadership. Jamuka was Temujin's blood brother, a close friend since teenage days when he had allied himself with Temujin against the Merkits. But there was no concession to sentiment on his capture. Temujin ordered his men to crush Jamuka to death by piling rocks upon his chest. Not one drop of blood was to be shed; otherwise, or so Temujin believed, his blood brother's spirit might escape the body and return to haunt him.

Like the majority of the Mongols, Temujin was deeply religious. The god he and his people worshipped was known as *Mongke Koko Tengri*, the "Eternal Blue Sky", the almighty spirit who controlled the forces of good and evil that emanated from the North Siberian plain. According to the Mongols' animistic creed, powerful spirits lived in fire, running water and the wind; these spirits were to be treated with the greatest respect. Thus it was a grave offence – punishable by beating, sometimes by death – to thrust a knife into a fire, to urinate into a stream, or to launder clothes or even wash out food vessels with running water.

The Mongols offered prayers to the idols of the various gods and spirits, most commonly to an image of the earth goddess Nachigai, believed to be mistress of grass, crops and herbs; and every clan had its own animal spirit or totem (the Blue Wolf was the legendary ancestor of Temujin's family). They also believed in oracles, dreams and visions, as interpreted by shamans, who served as prophets, spiritualist mediums, astrologers, wizards and witch doctors.

The Mongols venerated the spirits of their ancestors; and it was the sacred duty of each child to learn the names of his forebears, to strive to be worthy of them and to ensure their memory lived on. It was from such childhood indoctrination that Temujin came to be driven by a sense of divine mission, by an unshakable belief that it was his destiny to emulate Kabul Khan by uniting the Mongol tribes. In 1206 he fulfilled that mission. On the banks of the Onon River, at a *kuriltai,* or general assembly of all the chieftains of the steppelands, he was proclaimed Chingis Khan – Khan of Khans, or "Universal Ruler" of all the Mongol peoples.

At the age of 45, Chingis Khan had become more than the supreme ruler of the Mongol nation. Because of his achievements, he was, so the presiding shaman declared, the representative on earth of the Eternal Blue Sky, a veritable visitation from heaven, and it was popularly accepted that his destiny was to conquer and rule the world. The very definition of his divine status denied the existence of sovereign states equal to his. All were expected to recognize the supreme authority of Chingis Khan. They could pursue their own forms of religious worship, but any that offered resistance to his demands were seen to be defying the will of God.

Chingis Khan has been recorded as saying: "The greatest joy a man can have is victory: to conquer one's enemy's armies, to pursue them, to deprive them of their possessions, to reduce their families to tears, to ride on their horses and to make love to their wives and daughters." Yet he was by no means only a destructive force. He was also a military organizer of genius, and by Mongol standards an administrator and lawmaker of the first magnitude. He not only built the most efficient war machine of his time, but also within his own homeland created order and unity out of chaos: all internecine feuding abruptly ended. Old tribal loyalties were replaced by allegiance to a single people and a single ruler. A new pyramid of power, with Chingis and his kin at its apex, was established by the appointment of some 95 senior governors who, with lesser commanders beneath them, were responsible for law enforcement, taxation and conscription within their domains.

At the same time, Chingis ordered the recording of all legal judgments, to form a body of case law for the guidance of judges. These judgments dictated extremely high moral standards within the Mongol world, forbidding, among other things, blood feuds, adultery, sodomy, theft, the bearing of false witness, betrayal, sorcery, disobedience of a royal command and bathing in running water – the last a reflection of the Mongols' animist beliefs. In most cases the punishment for infringement was death. More lenient was the decree that no man was to be persecuted for his religion, provided that he acknowledged the ultimate authority of the great khan.

Chingis' new, disciplined Mongol nation was totally geared for war. It was not based on settled agricultural communities, but on nomadic groups of hunters divided into military-style units of one hundred, one thousand and ten thousand.

Warriors by nature, these men were unencumbered by material possessions and never needed to allow time for the planting and harvesting of crops. And a history of constant feuding made warfare an integral part of their lives.

When the Mongols were not engaged in warfare, they were practising for it. Chingis Khan once stated, "When the Mongols are unoccupied by war, they shall devote themselves to hunting. The objective is not so much the chase itself as the training of warriors, who should acquire strength and become familiar with drawing the bow and other exercises." Thus, every winter, all able-bodied Mongols were obliged to make themselves available for a great hunt, conducted over an area of several thousand square kilometres, and involving many thousands of men. This annual event not only provided a reserve of meat for the harsh months to follow, but served as an elaborate military rehearsal; the hunters were deployed in regimental formations, and individuals were assessed on their performance.

For an outstanding young hunter-warrior, the supreme accolade was promotion to the great khan's Imperial Guard, an elite, full-time corps of more than 10,000 men. In battle, the Guard was always deployed in the centre and used for the final thrust. Its members were so highly esteemed for their military skills that each one was considered qualified to take command of any fighting unit in an emergency.

Therein lay a key aspect of the Mongols' military might. Beyond the immediate royal family, promotion was by merit alone, and that merit was judged by martial ability. Important, too, was Chingis Khan's rare talent for delegating authority. His own sons – Jochi, Ogedei, Chagatai and Tolui – were well trained for command and his chosen generals were men of outstanding ability and unswerving loyalty.

Within one year of his elevation to emperor, the Great Khan had amassed an army of many tens of thousands, all strictly disciplined, expertly trained and admirably equipped for open warfare. In 1207, driven to expansion by the inadequate pastures of their homelands and by their inbred love of war, the newly organized Mongol hordes burst out of the steppes. Fierce and merciless, they swept with the force of a typhoon across the Tangut kingdom of Xixia. Next they struck directly across the Gobi Desert, lured eastwards by the fabulous riches of the mighty Jin empire and its imperial capital, Zhongdu.

Ahead of them lay the limitless rice plains of one of the richest agricultural regions in the world, whose great cities boasted artistic and scientific wonders of the most advanced civilization of the time. But the Mongol horsemen, steeped in their nomadic tradition, gave no thought to the many advantages of occupying such a bountiful land. Life in permanent settlements was alien to them. They conquered for conquest's sake, for a harvest of immediate booty.

However, the Mongols were far from being ignorant savages, limited to brute force alone. In open warfare they were tactically brilliant, dividing their armies for three-pronged advances and making use of the feigned retreat before launching counterattacks. They were shrewd in negotiating alliances with non-Mongol tribes bordering the Jin empire, and they made artful use of spies, neutral merchants and dissatisfied Chinese officials to gather intelligence. Moreover they were quick to strengthen their war machine with new materials and techniques acquired from their enemies. Most importantly, with the aid of captured Chinese engineers, they gained the means of laying siege to cities: great rock-catapulting machines such as the mangonel and the trebuchet; a giant crossbow mounted on vertical stands; and gunpowder that could be fired in bamboo-tube rockets from a longbow.

Initially, however, lack of siege-machines was the Mongols' one major weakness. In the kingdom of Xixia they had been long delayed by the resistance of the fortress capital Ningxia. Likewise they were brought to a halt by the challenge of the Great Wall. For two years Chingis waited menacingly in the mountain region of Jehol to the north, while the Jin emperor stalled him with gifts. The Great Khan demanded more, and he received more: 1,000 young men and girls, 3,000 horses, quantities of gold, jewellery and silk. Then, on learning that the imperial court had made a new headquarters at Kaifeng on the Yellow River, he ordered an all-out attack.

The Mongol hordes broke through the Great Wall by sheer force of numbers, and at appalling cost to both sides. In May 1215, they stormed the walls of Zhongdu, leaving the imperial capital in ruins – its palaces stripped bare, every building razed to the ground, and almost the entire population exterminated. In the words of the Mongols' own *Secret History* it was a "glorious slaughter"; its monument, as described by later travellers, was a mountain of human bones and horse skeletons.

Of the imperial officials remaining in Zhongdu, only a few survived the carnage. Among them was one Yeh-lu Ch'u-ts'-ai, a 25-year-old noble of Mongol descent, who so impressed Chingis with his dignity and loyalty to the Jin that the Great Khan offered him a position in his service. The young scholar-mandarin accepted and had soon become one of Chingis' chief advisers, exerting a moderating influence on the Mongol leadership. He discouraged needless destruction, advised against

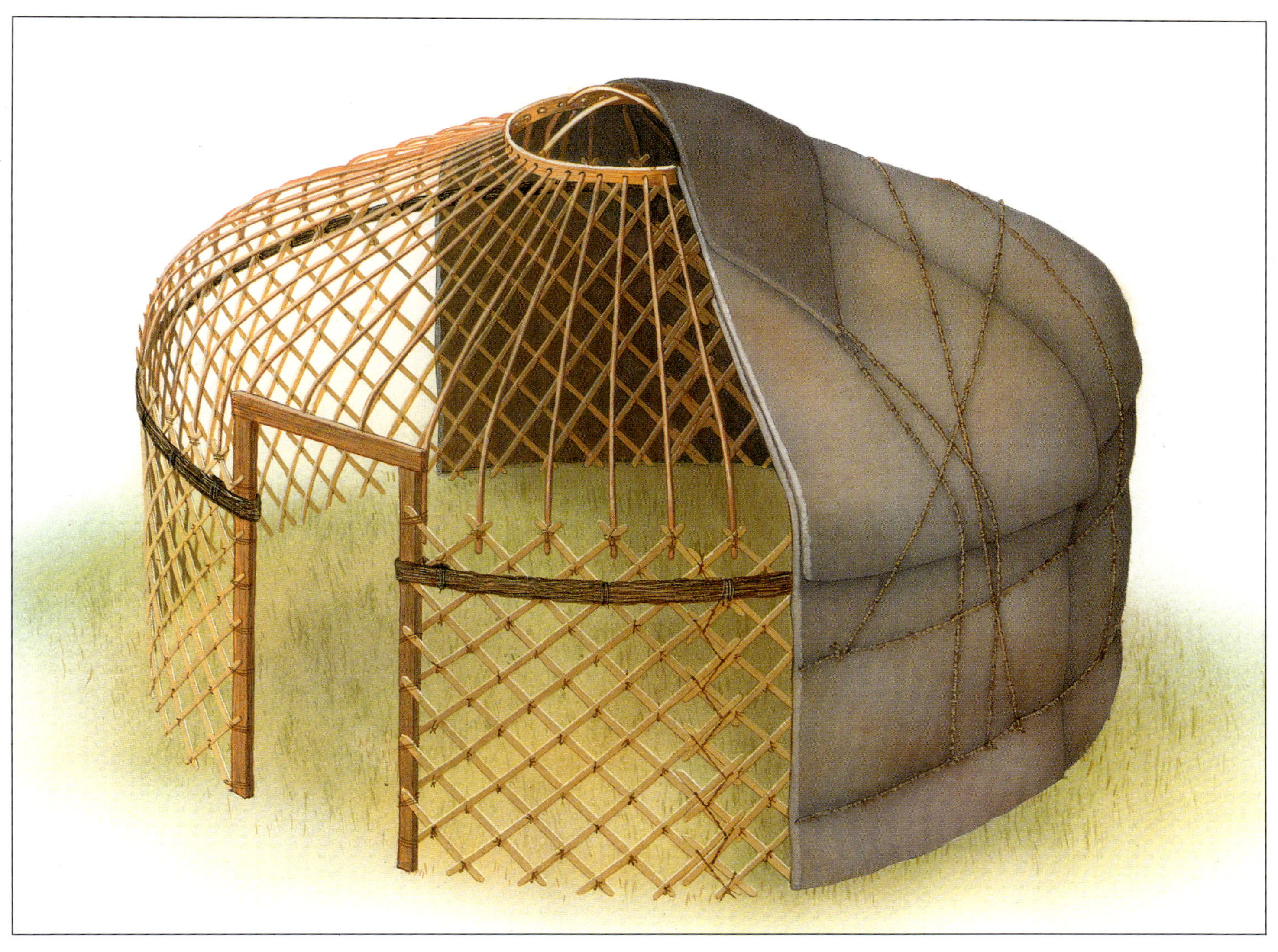

**The typical Mongol yurt, as depicted here, was about 4.5 metres in diameter, made from willow poles and latticework lashed together with rawhide and then covered with layers of greased felt. The layers varied in number according to the weather; the outermost was often whitened with lime or powdered bone. Inside, the floors were covered with felt, skins or rugs, and horns were fixed to the latticework for hanging meat and weapons. Opposite the entrance, which always faced south, the head of the household sat on a couch behind a central hearth, with his womenfolk to the east and men to the west. Most yurts could be put up quickly and carried by pack horses, but those of great commanders were sometimes so large that they were kept permanently erected and were transported on huge wagons drawn by oxen.**

Mongol cavalry moved in huge separate columns, often many kilometres apart, their advance coordinated by a sophisticated signalling system of flags, smoke and burning torches. In battle a huge camel-mounted kettle drum was used to sound the charge, while a yak-tailed banner was waved to signal the commander's orders.

Every soldier was amply equipped for battle, carrying bows, quivers, a wicker shield covered in thick leather, a lasso and a dagger strapped to the inside of his left forearm. He also had a large hide saddle-bag – a receptacle for food, spare clothes and tools – that could be inflated to act as a lifejacket, as shown in this illustration of a Mongol army fording a river. The light cavalryman, armed with a small sword and two or three javelins, wore a quilted tunic, or else a cuirass of lacquered leather strips. His heavier counterpart, clad in mail and a cuirass made either of oxhide or iron scales covered in leather, wielded a scimitar, a battle-axe or a mace and a lance equipped with a hook for dragging enemies from the saddle.

The whole column was followed by enormous, well-organized support units – ox-drawn carts transporting equipment, food and fodder; Chinese technicians to operate siege machines; engineers to build or repair bridges; shamans to give spiritual guidance and medical aid; officials to catalogue the booty; and a host of women workers who not only prepared food and equipment, but also took part in mopping up operations, such as slitting the throats of enemy wounded.

## AN ARMY ON THE MOVE

A sceptred commander views the progress of battle from a pontoon bridge formed of chained boats. Although it shows only one of the opposing sides, this Persian illustration is believed to depict the Mongol capture of Baghdad, straddling the River Tigris. Such victories were initially made possible by the Mongols' use of Chinese siege machines, specially modified to be carried in pieces on pack horses. After the fall of Samarkand these engines were enhanced by the application of advanced Khwarizmian mechanics. Catapults *(bottom, left)* were fitted with counterpoises that increased their 100-metre range to over 300 metres. Such artillery was also used in open battle: on April 11, 1241, the Mongols crossed the River Sajo in Hungary behind a rolling barrage of fire bombs from a battery of seven catapults.

plans to turn the cultivated fields of North China into grazing land, and showed how the Mongols might profit through both taxation and trade if agriculture and the mining of salt and various metals continued to flourish.

Although Chingis Khan heeded much of this advice, he himself never again set foot in China, withdrawing to his tented headquarters in Outer Mongolia. Over the next 17 years it was his general, Mukali, who gradually brought the whole of North China under Mongol domination. Chingis himself turned his attention westwards, to campaign against the border empires of the Islamic world.

In 1217 his general Jebe subdued the neighbouring kingdom of Kara-Khitai, sandwiched between Tibet and Lake Balkhash, which had fallen under the rule of a fugitive Naiman chieftain. Subsequently the Mongols established trading relations with their new western neighbours in the state of Khwarizm, a Turkish-dominated empire that included Turkestan, Persia, much of Afghanistan and part of northern India. Possibly the Mongols might have once more turned eastwards had it not been for extreme provocation by Shah Muhammad, ruler of Khwarizm. In 1218, Muslim traders travelling with a huge caravan under the protection of Chingis were robbed and murdered by the Khwarizmian governor of the frontier town of Otrar. Perhaps the governor saw the caravan as a cover for a spying mission (a common enough Mongol ploy) or he may have been motivated by greed. In any event, the Great Khan demanded his extradition. Shah Muhammad not only refused but also, in defiance, beheaded a Mongol ambassador sent to his court at Samarkand.

It was this action that impelled the Mongols into western Asia, stirring up a tidal wave of such irresistible fury that it swept on into eastern Europe. In pursuit of his vengeance, Chingis conscripted all Mongol men from the ages of 17 to 60, and he himself rode against Khwarizm at the head of some 200,000 men, including about 10,000 siege-engineers from China The great mechanized catapults constructed and operated by these men now proved indispensable. In Khwarizm, no army dared to face the Mongol cavalry in open combat, and resistance was centred on the fortified cities, notably Bukhara, Samarkand, Nishapur, Merv, Herat, Balkh and Gurgan. But none of them survived the wrath of Chingis Khan. In a war lasting only three years, literally millions of men, women and children were put to the sword.

It was in this war against Shah Muhammad that the Mongols earned a reputation for infinite savagery. While they punished cowardice and rewarded courage among their own, this policy was reversed for all foreigners. The prolonged and heroic resistance of any city ensured only that the Mongols' vengeance was that much greater. They stormed one great city after another, massacring the inhabitants or driving them ahead as human shields for subsequent sieges. When forces commanded by Chagatai and Ogedei finally captured the offending governor of Otrar, they killed him by pouring molten silver into his eyes and down his throat.

Indeed, the Mongols calculatingly used slaughter and carnage as a means of demoralizing the opposition. The civilian inhabitants of defiant cities were sometimes rounded up like cattle to be massacred by troops who were required to bring back sacks containing a designated number of ears as proof of having fulfilled their quota. After the fall of Nishapur, all the survivors were decapitated, the skulls of men, women and children being piled into three separate pyramids. Even dogs and cats were killed; the city simply ceased to exist. Throughout the land, the stories of Mongol atrocities were legion; and historians of the time recorded astounding death tolls: 700,000 at Merv; 1,600,000 at Herat; 1,747,000 at Nishapur. If these

figures were exaggerated, it was entirely to the satisfaction of the Mongols, who usually sent ahead agents to foster panic in their targeted cities.

Meanwhile, generals Jebe and Subedei led an army that pursued Shah Muhammad as far as the Caspian Sea; he died there of pleurisy on an offshore island. On their way, the generals overran northwest Persia, routed a 10,000-strong army sent out by King George IV of Armenia, and then drove north, defeating the Georgians, the Kipchak Turks of the Volga steppes and the Bulgars of the upper Volga. By 1223, the Mongols had become firmly entrenched in the Ukraine and the Crimea, where, despite numerical inferiority, they successfully resisted all counterattacks.

At this point, the Mongols temporarily ended the westward thrust that had brought them victory over the armies of 20 different states. Now, Chingis concentrated on a new, urgent objective: the suppression of the Tanguts of Xixia, who had defied his call to arms against Khwarizm and were now in open revolt. It was his last military campaign. In 1227, after a succession of victories, he was waiting for the Tangut king to pay him homage when he developed a high fever and died.

It was just 20 years since Chingis had first led the Mongols out of their barren homeland. In that time, he had broken the power of Islam in central Asia and had destroyed the mighty Jin empire. He had believed that it was his divine destiny to conquer the world. Now, on his death, that mission fell to his descendants.

Chingis had already divided his empire into subordinate khanates to be ruled over by his sons and grandsons, under the supreme authority of Ogedei, his favourite child. However, it was two years before a *kuriltai* was held in Mongolia to formally elect Ogedei as great khan. Then the Mongol war machine swung back into action with the same devastating effect as before.

In the first few years of Ogedei's reign, the Mongols completed the conquest of North China, subjugated Korea, declared war on the Song rulers of southern China, and campaigned across northwest Persia, northern Iraq, Armenia and Azerbaijan. Then, in 1236, eastern Europe was made the primary target of an army numbering 150,000. This great force was under the nominal command of Chingis' grandson Batu, though largely reliant on the tactical genius of the veteran general Subedei. Its purpose was to secure the inheritance of Batu, who, after the death of Chingis' son Jochi, shared the northwestern of the four khanates with his brother Orda. The latter received western Siberia, while Batu inherited a vaguely defined region beyond the Volga. Mongol authority in the region remained to be fully asserted.

Batu's horde drove north and west, defeating the Bulgars of the middle Volga region and the Cumans of the southern steppes, before invading Christian Russia. In a lightning winter campaign, they overwhelmed Rostov, Moscow and Vladimir, before pausing in 1238 to recoup their strength. In December 1240, they captured and destroyed Kiev. They then defeated a Polish army at Liegnitz in April 1241, devastated Moravia and Silesia, and, turning south, took all of Hungary.

The Mongols now seemed poised to sweep across the divided Christian states of central and western Europe. But in December 1241, the European offensive was abruptly halted. The great khan Ogedei, his health long impaired by excessive drinking and licentiousness, had died at Karakoram, the capital he had established in western Mongolia. It was time to elect a new khan, so all the Mongol leaders were summoned to a *kuriltai*. The invading hordes streamed back to the steppes.

For a short while Ogedei's son Guyuk ruled as great khan, but in 1251 the title passed to Mongke, another grandson of Chingis. In eight years, under Mongke's,

# A HARDY COMPANION

Prized throughout Asia for its courage and stamina, the Mongolian horse was his master's most valued possession, in both peace and war. Some 14 to 15 hands high, thickset, with broad forehead and short legs, the Mongolian horse roamed wild in huge herds of 10,000 or more, from which Mongol tribesmen captured their chosen mounts using nooses attached to the ends of long, springy poles.

Treated with the utmost care, the steeds were broken young, never ridden until three years old, and wherever possible kept rested on marathon journeys by the use of numerous remounts. Chingis Khan laid down strict rules for their welfare, one of which, for example, forbade a mount to be led with a bit in its mouth.

It was the qualities of such steeds and the ingenuity with which they were used that gave the Mongols their military superiority. Although Mongol armies were often quite small, their manoeuvrability in battle could make their numbers seem doubled. And the rate at which they advanced could take even the most wary foe by surprise. When on the move, each soldier had at least three horses following behind him, and by regularly changing mount he could ride at speed for days, eating in the saddle or pausing when sustenance was scarce to slit a vein and drink the blood of his weakest animal. Batu Khan's vanguard was said to have advanced into Hungary at the rate of 100 kilometres a day.

Warfare aside, horses also played a prominent role in ceremonies and folklore. Although a weak horse might be eaten, one that had been ridden in battle could never be killed for food. Some Mongols worshipped mounts of rare speed and stamina, eventually preserving their skins and skulls as sacred relics. Indeed, according to the Western missionary John of Plano Carpini, a great chieftain was customarily buried alongside a mare, a stallion and a foal so that he might breed horses in the afterlife.

Seen through the eyes of a Chinese miniaturist, a Mongol hunter and his horse stand, short, stocky and inseparable, by their felled quarry.

In a late 13th-century Japanese scroll, the soldiers of Kublai Khan are shown clad in luxurious Chinese tunics and bearing Chinese musical instruments. Despite the adoption of such foreign customs, however, the warriors are still mounted on Mongolian horses.

A horse and groom feel the bite of North China's winter wind, as depicted by Zhao Mengfu, Kublai Khan's leading painter. Some Chinese artists refused to serve the Mongol conquerors; those who did found that their patrons seldom asked for anything other than equestrian portraits.

In this Persian miniature two clashing forces are represented in Mongol armour. Here the artist has depicted slimmer, faster horses, which were the result of crossbreeding between Mongolian and Arab steeds.

A khan and his chief wife prepare to dine, their guards and courtiers arranged according to Mongol etiquette, with men on the khan's right and women on his left. The Mongols never lost their liking for the traditional boiled meats and koumiss, which they consumed in copious quantities. But they did also develop tastes for the luxuries that they encountered among their conquered subjects. During the invasion of Khwarizm, for example, Chingis Khan became particularly fond of Persian wines from Shiraz.

shrewd leadership, Mongol rule spread both east and west. Under his brother Kublai, the Mongols advanced deep into Song China. And with another brother, Hulegu, at their head they completed the conquest of western Asia, all but annihilating the Assassins, a fanatical Muslim sect which had terrorized the Middle East for 160 years. Most notably, they destroyed Baghdad, the rich capital of Iraq. Among the two million deaths reported by the 14th-century historian Maqrizi was that of the caliph, the religious head of the Muslim world.

In 1259 Mongke died of dysentery while he was campaigning in China. His death was as great a blessing for the Muslim Middle East as that of Ogedei had been for Christian Europe. At the time, Hulegu had advanced through Syria, and was planning to attack Egypt, a rich and powerful country ruled by the Mamluks, warrior-slaves who had recently seized power. At the news of the Great Khan's death, he at once hurried eastwards to attend the traditional *kuriltai* in Mongolia, leaving behind a much depleted force, primarily of Mongol-led Turks, to continue the campaign. The result was military disaster. On September 3, 1260, at Ayn Jalut near the River Jordan in Palestine, the 10,000-strong Mongol force was engaged in battle by the army of Qutuz, the Mamluk sultan of Egypt. It was outnumbered, outmanoeuvred and completely routed. Subsequently the Mamluks annexed Syria, driving the Mongols back across the Euphrates.

The Battle of Ayn Jalut destroyed the Mongols' reputation for invincibility. In addition, it marked the end of their expansion towards the Mediterranean. Nevertheless, they continued to dominate central and western Asia, which yielded a rich booty of army recruits — in particular the nomadic Turks, who fitted well into the ruthless Mongol mould. And 19 years later in the East, Kublai's ultimate victory over the Song brought the entire Chinese nation of some 90 million people under their rule.

When Mongke died, the empire began to disintegrate into almost independent states that fiercely pursued their own interests. Hulegu and his successors, the Ilkhans, held sway over Persia. From their capital, Sarai, on a tributary of the Volga, the descendants of Orda and Batu controlled the Kipchak khanate — later called the Golden Horde — from Batu's gold-embroidered tent, exacting tribute and military support from almost all of Russia. And in Samarkand the descendants of Chingis' second son Chagatai ruled the central Asian steppes as the Chagatai khanate.

Meanwhile, control of the Mongolian heartland and of China was disputed between two of Mongke's brothers: Kublai and Arik-Boge. It was to take four years of civil war before Kublai finally won in 1264. Although designated great khan, he was never to have the universal sovereignty over the entire Mongol people which Chingis enjoyed. Both the Chagatai khanate and the Golden Horde were openly opposed to him. This time it was not merely tribal and family feuds that divided the Mongols. Fundamental religious and ideological differences were emerging between traditionalists, who favoured the old ways of the steppes, and progressively minded rulers like Kublai in China and the Ilkhans in Persia, who modified their life style to suit their changed circumstances. It was a fatal dichotomy.

The new great khan of the Mongols was cast in an entirely different mould from his predecessors. Where they had been rough, unlettered warriors, he was literate, cultured, politically astute and adaptable. Chingis had been immutably bound to the nomadic life, and regarded his beloved Asian steppes as the permanent base of the great khans. Kublai, however, aspired to create a new, more sophisticated Mongol civilization outside the inhospitable homeland of his ancestors.

Born in 1215, four months after his grandfather had devastated the Jin capital of Zhongdu, Kublai grew up in an environment influenced by Chinese ideas. His education was largely the responsibility of a Confucian scholar, Yao Ji. During years of campaigning against the Jin and the Song, he became increasingly Chinese in his tastes and manners, to such a degree that he felt China to be his natural home.

In 1256 Kublai commanded the building of his North China summer palace at Kaiping, later renamed Shangdu. Four years later, after his election as great khan, he chose a site just northeast of ruined Zhongdu for the building of his winter capital. By 1270 it had become a city of great splendour — a vast complex of palaces, courtyards, gardens, man-made hills and artificial lakes teeming with fish.

It was not until 1279, some 70 years after Chingis' first invasion, that Kublai completed the conquest of China. The final victory was delayed partly because Mongol cavalry-style methods were not suited to the paddy fields of the tropical south; also because the enemy was more numerous, tenacious and advanced than any in western Asia. Kublai, however, did not wait for total victory before affirming his authority. In 1271, when the last vestiges of Song power were confined to the southeast, he proclaimed himself first emperor of the Mongol Yuan dynasty, and thereafter lived in a style of dazzling opulence and refinement totally belying his nomadic origins. His palace walls were plated with gold and silver and decorated with figures of dragons, beasts and birds. He was surrounded by counsellors and courtiers, both Chinese and Mongol; guarded by rotating shifts of 3,000 warriors

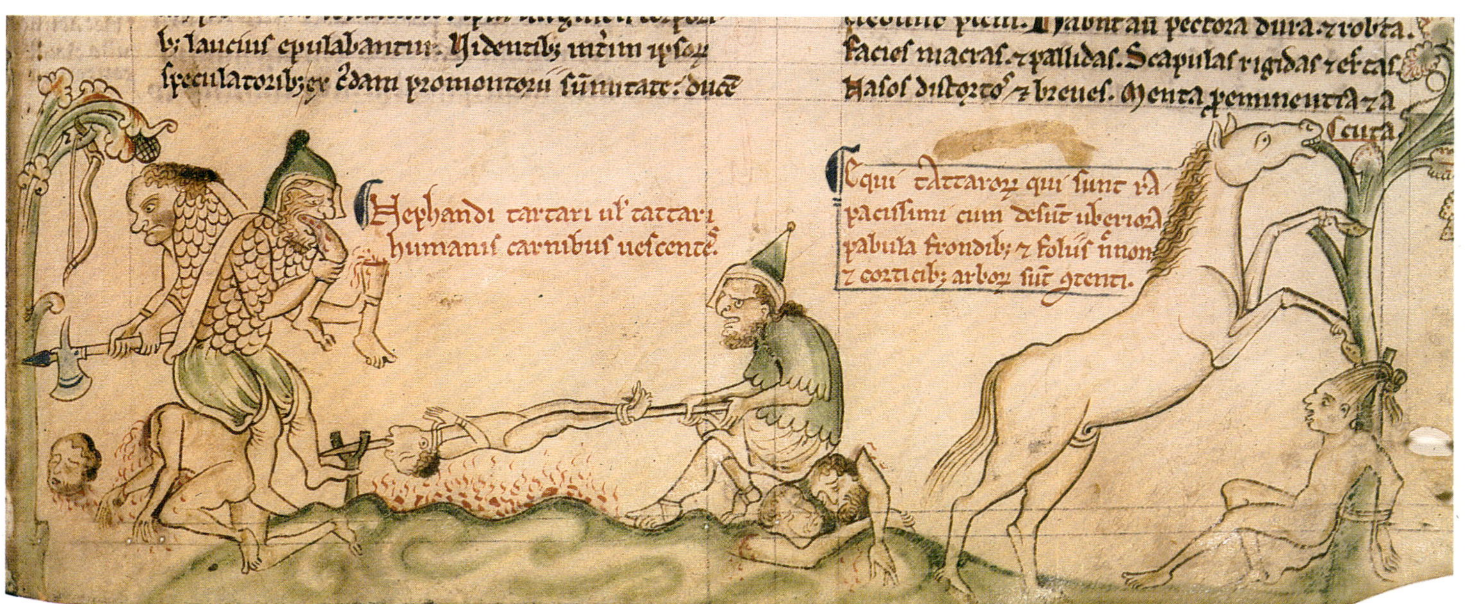

**Leering Mongols devour their victims in an illustration from *Chronica Majora*, by the 13th-century English chronicler Matthew Paris; to the right, a horse feeds off a tree. During the invasion of Poland and Hungary, panicking Europeans believed every fanciful tale of Mongol atrocities which, so priests proclaimed, had been visited on man as God's punishment for the sins of the world. One terrified monk, Ivo of Narbonne, wrote from Austria, "Virgins were raped until they died of exhaustion; then their breasts were cut off to be kept as dainties for their chiefs".**

**More realistic reports were written by friars John of Plano Carpini and William of Rubruck, the first Western emissaries to visit Mongolia. But even Friar John wrote of a land of which he had heard tell where "every male had the shape of a dog".**

from his 12,000-strong personal guard; and attended by countless concubines who, in their turn, were served by eunuchs. He gave audiences to ambassadors and merchants from all over Asia and beyond, and held feasts with up to 6,000 guests.

This great khan of the Mongols saw himself in traditional Chinese terms: as the proclaimed Son of Heaven, issuing edicts from the very centre of the world in the Middle Kingdom, to which all peoples of the earth owed tribute. By identifying himself so closely with the Chinese world, Kublai fanned the fires of revolt within Mongolia, and eventually was forced to send an army to regain the old capital of Karakoram. His forces triumphed, but to no lasting effect. Kublai Khan would never reside in Karakoram; nor was he willing to station his troops permanently in the steppes. China had become far more precious to him than all the far-ranging domains of the Mongol empire, and even more valuable than Mongolia itself.

**On a hunting expedition, Kublai Khan, clad in a magnificent ermine coat, is accompanied by a woman dressed in the Chinese fashion. Although he adopted the life style of the Chinese court, Kublai never lost his Mongol passion for the hunt. The Great Khan did not stint his enjoyment, travelling in high style and employing trained lions, leopards and eagles in addition to huge numbers of mastiffs and falcons. Nor were others to miss out on the fun: Marco Polo recorded that between the months of December and February, Kublai ordered all the people within 100 kilometres of where he was staying to devote their time to hunting and hawking.**

The West had made several overtures to the Mongols with, amongst other things, the aim of converting them to Christianity. Most notable among these ventures were the missions by two friars — John of Plano Carpini and William of Rubruck. That of the former, in 1245, was the first recorded European exploration of Asia. It failed in its purpose, however; the khan assumed that the pope was merely offering homage. That of William fared no better: he mourned his failure to convert Mongke in 1254 with the words, "Had I had the power of Moses to work miracles, perhaps I could have convinced him". In 1266, however, a further opportunity presented itself almost by chance. In that year, Kublai received at his court two Venetian merchants, who had been forced off their intended route by wars. Their names were Niccolo and Matteo Polo.

Kublai Khan was so impressed with the two Europeans that he made them a startling proposition. Let the pope, he said, send 100 men learned in religion and the arts to his court. If these savants could prove the superiority of Christianity over other religions, then he and all his subjects would be baptized. The Khan assured the Polos that there would then be more Christians in his realm than in all their part of the world. The two Venetians travelled back to the West, but were unsuccessful in this project; and when, in 1275, they returned to Kublai's court, they could deliver to him only some papal letters and, as requested, some holy oil from Jerusalem. With them, however, they brought a companion: Niccolo's 20-year-old son, Marco Polo.

Kublai, it seems, took an immediate liking to this bright young Venetian, and employed him for 17 years as a special envoy, sending him on missions throughout the Mongol empire. Those journeys, together with his intimate acquaintance with the court of Kublai, provided Marco with the material for *A Description of the*

The capering antics of this 37-centimetre-high pottery actor recall the many theatrical entertainments on offer at Kublai Khan's court. Chinese drama flourished under the Mongol rulers' patronage, and districts with as many as a dozen theatres grew up in most principal cities. Simple entertainments with singers and dancers evolved into fully constructed plays which tackled serious subjects and used colloquial dialogue. Court-room stories became particularly popular. Prestige was added to the profession by scholars who, no longer guaranteed a career in the Khan's civil service, took to writing comedies and tragedies that became the foundation of Chinese classical drama.

*World*, the story of his travels as dictated to a professional romancer, which gave an invaluable first-hand picture of Mongol-ruled China and its Emperor.

Kublai Khan, as Polo described him, was a man of medium height, well-proportioned in build, and with "a pink and white complexion like a rose, fine black eyes and a handsome nose". He had perhaps over 100 children, but only the boys were noted: 25 sons by numerous young concubines, and 22 sons by four legitimate wives, each of whom had her own household with no fewer than 300 beautiful girls in attendance. Beyond the bedchamber, Kublai's pastimes were hunting and feasting. He rode to the hunt on the backs of four harnessed elephants in a richly timbered howdah, accompanied by trained leopards and hounds and the hawks of some 10,000 falconers. He observed many feast days, most notably New Year's Day, when his 5,000 elephants were paraded, and his birthday, when he dressed in beaten gold and dined with 1,200 nobles clad in similar finery.

The young Marco Polo was overwhelmed by the opulence of Kublai's life style. He marvelled at the splendours of Dadu and Hangzhou, the greatest cities he had seen. He was amazed by everyday things he had never seen before – porcelain, asbestos, a "long-burning black stone" (coal), and the common use of paper money, "made from bark collected from mulberry trees". But in truth, his impressions only emphasized how far Chinese civilization was in advance of Europe. Few of the wonders he observed could be attributed to Kublai Khan and the Mongols.

Among those few was a super-efficient communications system. New roads, radiating from Dadu to the farthest corners of the Mongol empire, greatly boosted international trade, making China more accessible than ever before. Internal transport was much improved by extending the Great Canal – built in the fifth century BC to connect the Yangtze and Yellow rivers – until it stretched some 1,600 kilometres from Hangzhou to the capital in the north. There was also a remarkably swift mounted courier service, operated via some 10,000 palatial post houses, each set about 40 kilometres from its neighbours and stabling hundreds of horses.

Marco Polo lavished praise on Kublai for these developments. He stressed, too, the Emperor's generosity in distributing free grain to "people who are poverty-stricken because of illness or other misfortunes which prevent them from working". But his view of China was one-sided. To the Chinese themselves, already used to the benefits of their civilization, Kublai's reign was in many respects a disaster. Although the Great Khan was the first Mongol ruler to fully recognize the importance of agriculture and trade, his 23-year rule brought progressive impoverishment for the Chinese peasantry. His efforts to expand the productivity of the land were a dismal failure, and in his encouragement of commerce he favoured non-Chinese interests to such a degree that profits from foreign trade drained out of the country.

The Mongols themselves showed little talent for government. Yeh-lu Ch'u-ts'-ai, the adviser of Chingis and Ogedei, had warned: "The Empire was won on horseback, but it will not be governed on horseback." The great khans heeded his words, but were incapable of setting up efficient administrations of their own. In China, they retained the local ways of administering the country through an elite class of bureaucrats. It was a sensible expedient. But now the system operated with unusual inefficiency, largely because the number of Chinese officials was limited, and all important offices were allocated to Mongols and privileged foreigners.

In addition, Kublai never abandoned the shamanistic beliefs of his Mongol ancestors. In Dadu, as Marco Polo noted, he maintained some 5,000 full-time

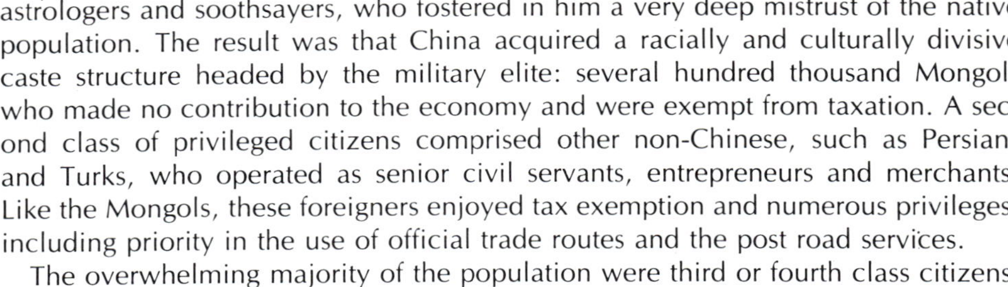

**Issued by Kublai Khan to a military commander, this seal would also have been accompanied by a *paiza*, a metal tablet bearing a symbol of authority which could easily be recognized by illiterate soldiers. The seal's impress reveals writing in the script known as 'Phags-pa, an early attempt to unite Mongol lands linguistically. As the Mongols had no alphabet, and the steppe Uighur script that they used did not truly represent Mongol sound, Kublai Khan commissioned a Tibetan lama to devise a script which would represent not only Mongol but also Chinese and the other major languages of the empire. The lama succeeded, yet his new alphabet never gained popular acceptance, and the Uighur script continued to be used.**

astrologers and soothsayers, who fostered in him a very deep mistrust of the native population. The result was that China acquired a racially and culturally divisive caste structure headed by the military elite: several hundred thousand Mongols who made no contribution to the economy and were exempt from taxation. A second class of privileged citizens comprised other non-Chinese, such as Persians and Turks, who operated as senior civil servants, entrepreneurs and merchants. Like the Mongols, these foreigners enjoyed tax exemption and numerous privileges, including priority in the use of official trade routes and the post road services.

The overwhelming majority of the population were third or fourth class citizens, with former subjects of the Jin taking marginal preference over the Song Chinese, who were treated as the lowest of the low. They regarded their alien rulers as barbarians, and yet they were the ones treated as inferiors both by custom and law, being forbidden, for example, to learn the Mongol language, or to marry a Mongol. They were not allowed to walk the streets after dark, nor to possess weapons.

Kublai further exacerbated the economic inefficiency of Mongol rule by engaging in costly wars that brought only modest gains. His aim was to establish his Middle Kingdom as the true centre of the world. In its pursuit, he sent armies on inconclusive, often disastrous, campaigns against Japan and other kingdoms in the territories now known as Thailand, Burma, Vietnam, Malaysia, Java and the Philippines.

Mongol military expertise, so dependent on cavalry, had little value in the Southeast Asian jungles. Nor were the Khan's men any more successful in two great naval expeditions against Japan. The last, in 1281, ended with tens of thousands of Mongols either enslaved or killed. Kublai never avenged this humiliating defeat.

He died, aged 79, in 1294. Although he had failed to emulate his grandfather Chingis in uniting the Mongol peoples, his achievements had been considerable. His Chinese conquests brought about the reunification of a country that had been divided for 350 years. But although his Yuan dynasty survived another 74 years, it was never powerful enough to seek new conquests. Its decline was hastened by rivalries between Kublai's descendants, by the growing arrogance and oppressiveness of the Mongol nobles, by the greed and corruption of the landowning Chinese aristocracy, and by inflation which rendered paper money worthless. Civil war was made inevitable by the combination of crippling taxes and a series of floods and other natural disasters.

A number of rebel groups rose up to defy their alien masters. The most powerful of these was led by the peasant-born Zhu Yuanzhang, a former Buddhist novice, who gradually gained control of the rural south. In 1368, a huge peasant army swept over the north, taking the capital of Dadu in the face of token resistance. The anti-Kublai conservatives in Mongolia had been proved right. After decades of exposure to the silk-cushioned court life of China, a new generation of Mongol warriors had emerged: soldiers not only poor in discipline but even lacking the traditional appetite for war. Subsequently, Zhu Yuanzhang proclaimed himself first emperor of the new Ming dynasty. Mongol rule in China had not even lasted 100 years.

The rot was not restricted to China. From the late 13th century onwards the whole Mongol empire went into rapid decline. Quarrelling factions and weak hereditary leaders destroyed Chingis' dream of Mongol unity; the once proud Mongol armies lost discipline and dedication when their purpose switched from conquest to occupation; and in China and Persia especially, Mongol power was eroded by surrender to the subtle influences of infinitely more advanced civilizations.

In the Ilkhanate of Persia, the Mongols devastated the land to such a degree that they were ultimately compelled to make use of a Persian bureaucracy to revive the shattered economy. Here, even more rapidly than in China, the conquerors became submerged in the culture of the conquered. Faced with the threat of the powerful Mamluk rulers in Egypt and Syria, it became politically expedient for the Ilkhans to adopt the Islamic religion. The first to do so, ruling from 1282 to 1285, assumed the Muslim name of Ahmad and took the title of sultan. During the reign of his successor, however, Buddhist and Christian influences prevailed, bringing with them economic chaos in the form of bureaucratic corruption, ruthless exploitation of the peasantry, and rampant inflation that was fuelled by the use of paper money. Order was restored in 1295, but on Islamic terms. In that year the Ilkhan Ghazan proclaimed his adherence to Islam, heralding an unbroken succession of Muslim Ilkhans until, in 1335, the male line of Hulegu's heirs came to an end. The khanate of Persia had lasted for only 80 years.

**Made in China for a high-ranking officer, this silver-inlaid Mongol helmet was of the same design as the iron or leather headgear worn by all Mongol cavalrymen. Like the hats and helmets of all the Khan's soldiers, it would have originally been adorned with two red ribbons hanging down the back from the top.**

The Mongols' rule in Russia and central Asia was considerably more enduring, mainly for the reason that these lands had a less developed tradition of centralized government, making the Mongols' administrative inexperience less disadvantageous. Compared to Persia and China, these were primitive societies, where the conquerors had no need of sophisticated governmental machinery. The power of the sword was sufficient to harvest tribute and taxes.

The khanate of the Golden Horde prospered at the expense of Russia's disunited native principalities. Princes of the various local dynasties were allowed to remain on their thrones as long as they journeyed to pay tribute and do homage at Sarai. The system operated without significant resistance for a period of more than 130 years, and continued in existence, although on a diminishing scale, for some two-and-a-half centuries. Indeed, it was not until the 18th century that the last independent Mongol state in the Crimea was overrun by the Russians.

In the meantime, the Chagatai khanate was fatally weakened by years of inter-Mongol conflict between the traditionalists in the east, and those in the west who had adopted the Islamic faith and in many cases the Persian language. Finally, in 1369, a new leader emerged: a soldier who seized power in Samarkand and later asserted his authority over nearly all of the Mongol lands in both the Chagatai and Golden Horde realms. Commonly called "Timur the Lame", he was destined to become infamous throughout

# A Traveller's Tale of Wonders

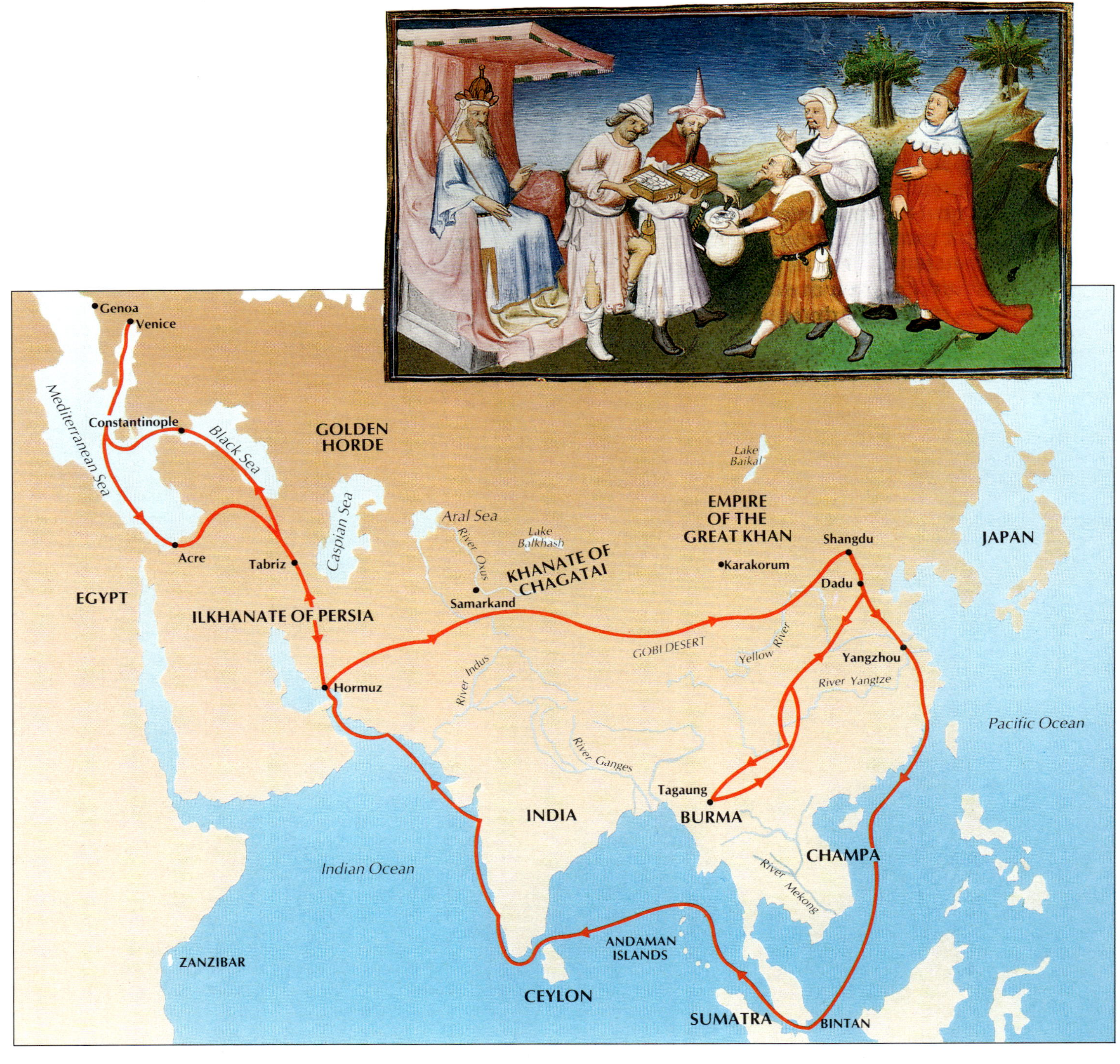

Europe as Tamerlane, the scourge of all central and western Asia. The rise of Timur signalled the end of the Mongol empire proper. By the dawn of the 15th century, the conquerors from the steppelands had become so integrated with the conquered that they almost ceased to exist as a separate race. In Russia they had merged with Turks, Slavs and Finns to create a new Turkish-speaking race loosely known as Tatars. In central Asia they had become indistinguishable from the masses, who were predominantly Turkic or Persian. The devastating force unleashed by Chingis Khan in 1207 had swept across Eurasia and finally burnt itself out.

At its height the Mongol empire stretched from the Pacific Ocean in the east, to Russia's Dnieper River in the west, from the Arctic Ocean in the north to the Strait of Malacca in the south. In their conquests of Persia and China, the Mongols had gained control of the two most advanced civilizations in the world. Yet in carving out this colossal realm, they contributed virtually nothing to methods of organized government or the advancement of arts and sciences. Indeed, they had nothing to give their conquered peoples except a keener appreciation of the methods of war.

As military conquerors, however, the Mongols were catalysts for many changes, amongst which were the alteration in strength and distribution of the world's leading religions – Islam, Christianity and Buddhism. Under the Mongols, Buddhism took far stronger hold in eastern Asia, especially in China where it was viewed sympathetically by Kublai and his descendants. Islam suffered a shattering blow with the sack of Baghdad, only to flourish anew with the Cairo of the Mamluks as its new capital. Meanwhile, under the aegis of a flourishing Persian culture, the Muslim religion was adopted by a majority of the Mongols and spread far and wide in their western territories. And although this represented a lost opportunity for Christianity, the western half of Christendom had escaped Mongol conquest. With its natural development undisturbed, the West was eventually able to flourish, while the Mongol-influenced East was held back by a heritage of tyranny.

In addition, the vastness of the Mongol empire allowed, for the first time, an intercontinental traffic in goods, knowledge and ideas. For a while in the mid-13th century, the main arteries of Asia and Europe were opened by the Pax Mongolica, a terror-enforced peace so effective that merchants and missionaries under the nominal protection of the great khan could journey east and west in relative safety. Representatives of all nations and religions were received at the court of the great khan in Karakoram. In Kublai Khan's Dadu, travellers could encounter a mingling of papal envoys from Rome and Buddhist priests from India, of craftsmen from France, Italy and China, of merchants from Persia, Java and Ceylon.

Asia was crisscrossed by caravan routes, and China was thrown open to the world by both land and sea. Each year, so Marco Polo recorded, 20,000 cargo ships sailed up the Yangtze, bringing diamonds and pearls from India; ginger, cotton and muslin from Ceylon; black pepper, white walnuts and cloves from Java. More significantly, the westward flow of eastern artefacts, knowledge and expertise worked in favour of a Europe that was far behind China in the arts and sciences.

Ultimately, the barbarian rule of China caused a backlash of xenophobia. Under the fiercely nationalistic Ming, China isolated itself more then ever. By then, also, the great trans-Asian trade routes had been closed by political upheavals in the last years of the Mongol empire. But no matter. The wonders and wealth of the Far East were no longer a secret, and the West would not be denied them forever.

**Travelling overland through Persia and the Gobi Desert with his father, Marco Polo arrived at the court of Kublai Khan in 1275. For the next 17 years he acted as Kublai's envoy, travelling on fact-finding expeditions as far afield as Burma and southern China, and possibly even acting as governor of the city of Yangzhou.**

**Polo eventually returned to Venice in 1295, voyaging via Champa (present day Vietnam), Sumatra, Ceylon and India. With him he brought not only a fortune in precious stones, but also a series of notebooks, in which he had recorded detailed observations of all he had seen, and reports of lands as distant as Zanzibar and Japan. Later, during a brief imprisonment by the Genoese, he dictated the story of his travels to a fellow prisoner. After Polo's release it was published as *Divisament dou Monde*, "A Description of the World". The prologue claimed that Polo had travelled more widely than any man since Creation; indeed, he revealed a world that was almost wholly unknown to western Christendom, and some parts of his route would not be travelled by Europeans for another 600 years.**

**The wonders that he described captured the popular imagination, and the book was reprinted many times. From one 14th-century version came the picture *(above, left)* depicting the Khan's men exchanging paper money – an unknown commodity in the West – for bullion. The idea of paper being valued as much as silver seemed to many westerners to be fantastic, as did other reports such as that of rocks which were burnt for fuel – coal. Indeed, it is related that Polo was asked on his deathbed, in 1324, to retract his invented fables. His reply was that he had barely told half of what he had seen.**

# RISE OF THE SHOGUNS

2

On a spring morning in the year 1185, so the chroniclers claimed, the sea in the narrow Strait of Dannoura, between the Japanese islands of Honshū and Kyūshū, turned red with blood. Pounding war drums echoed off the coastal cliffs; shouted commands and the screams of the wounded all but drowned out the relentless clattering of arrows hitting armour as the warships of two rival clans met in battle. The prize they sought, apart from each other's destruction, was domination over the archipelago of rocky, volcanic islands, off the eastern flank of Asia, which formed the isolated realm of Japan.

The contending armies were led by the Taira and Minamoto, the mightiest of Japan's warrior clans. Numerically, the Minamoto forces were superior, with a fleet twice or possibly three times as large as the Taira's. But the Taira troops were far better at naval warfare, or so their commanders reassured them: the Minamoto might be good cavalrymen, but they had little experience of sea fights. In addition the Taira possessed what they saw as the moral advantage. For behind the fighting fleet stood ships carrying the cream of the Japanese nobility, connected by birth or marriage to the Taira clan. In their midst was the emperor himself, the seven-year-old Antoku, with his mother and grandmother, both Taira, who carried the imperial regalia — the Sacred Seal, the Sacred Mirror and the Sacred Sword — the triple emblems of imperial power since time immemorial. But even with such impressive patronage, a Taira victory could not be guaranteed. Soothsayers on both sides had seen omens — a mysterious white banner drifting in the sky, the sudden appearance of a school of dolphins — suggesting that heaven might favour the Minamoto.

The omens did not lie. The Minamoto bided their time, taking only defensive action, until the tide turned in their favour. Then they bombarded their enemy with hurricanes of arrows; Minamoto warriors boarded one Taira ship after another, slew the sailors and seized the helms. Escape was well-nigh impossible: the heavy seas and the high cliffs lining the strait made landing difficult, leaving would-be fugitives at the mercy of Minamoto grappling hooks.

Even to the imperial party, defeat now seemed inevitable. But Antoku's Taira grandmother would not allow herself, the royal child or his imperial regalia to fall into the enemy's hands. She dressed herself in a gown of dark-grey mourning, and instructed Antoku to press his palms together and recite his prayers. Then, enfolding Antoku in her arms, she seized the Sacred Sword and plunged into the sea. Following this example, the boy-emperor's mother weighted down the sleeves of her kimono with stones and flung herself overboard, together with a host of other courtiers — male and female — who preferred death to humiliation.

The boy-emperor sank below the waves and quickly drowned, but not all his elders succeeded in joining him. Minamoto boatmen plied their grappling hooks to

**Glaring ferociously at potential evildoers, this woodcarving of *Kongō Rikishi*, or "Thunderbolt-Wielding Strongman", originally stood guard at the portals of a Buddhist temple. As an official state religion, Buddhism was already widespread in Japan when the military came to power in 1185. In the following century the ranks of its adherents swelled dramatically, as an increasing number of sects offered simple paths to enlightenment for prince and peasant alike.**

catch the ladies by their long black hair, and hauled them, painfully and unceremoniously, to safety. The Sacred Seal and the Sacred Mirror were also recovered: the Taira lady who had tried to jump overboard with the mirror in her arms was stopped by a Minamoto arrow that pinned her gown to the deck. But the Sacred Sword was lost forever, and no number of prayers at the country's greatest shrines, nor forays by the most skilled and courageous divers, could bring it to light.

The sword's disappearance marked an irrevocable alteration in the fortunes of its owners, and indeed, of all Japan. The victory of the Minamoto at Dannoura radically transformed nearly every aspect of national life: the way the country was governed, the identity and nature of those who wielded power, the system of values espoused by the rulers, the distribution of wealth, and even the ways of worship. The days of unchallenged imperial rule were over: now the warriors of the provinces, who prized martial discipline over courtly etiquette, and bravery in battle over patrician pedigrees, controlled the destiny of this island kingdom.

Separated from the Asian mainland by the dangerous currents of the Sea of Japan, the islands of Japan lay 200 kilometres from their nearest neighbours, with the easternmost parts some 800 kilometres from the continental landmass. Although the country comprised innumerable islands, most of the people lived on the major

**Japan entered the 13th century as a powerful nation under the hegemony of a military government, or shōgunate, ruling from the town of Kamakura. The shōguns nominally took their authority from an emperor, residing with his court in the ancient city of Kyōto, 480 kilometres to the west, although in fact the monarch's duties were mainly ceremonial. Centred on the three major islands of Honshū, Kyūshū and Shikoku, the Japanese population enjoyed a period of stability under the shōguns in which the country prospered and merchants plied a lucrative trade with mainland Asia. However, the cost of meeting two unsuccessful Mongol invasions, launched from Korea in the latter half of the century, proved too much: by 1333 the Kamakura shōgunate had fallen, and the country was once more at war with itself.**

southernmost cluster of Honshū, Kyūshū and Shikoku. The terrain of Japan was spectacularly beautiful, with steep mountains – reaching up to 3,776 metres above sea level – deep gorges and fast-flowing rivers that poured into innumerable rocky bays. Yet, for all its beauty, it was an inhospitable landscape: the very earth underfoot was unsteady, lying precariously on fault lines, prey to earthquakes, volcanic eruptions and tidal waves. Most of the land was unreceptive to agriculture; despite concerted efforts to clear new territory and painstaking terracing of the lower mountain slopes, less than one sixth of the total area could be cultivated.

Compensation for these difficulties came in the form of a climate ideally suited to rice cultivation. Seasonal winds came with almost clockwork regularity, bringing heavy rains in the summer and drier, cooler weather in the winter. These conditions, together with plentiful sunshine and subtropical temperatures for much of the growing season, were perfect for rice. No other grain gave so high a yield in so restricted an area – an important advantage where farmland was so scarce. Other crops, such as millet, barley, wheat, soya beans and various vegetables were grown but, essentially, the Japanese – whether prince or peasant – lived on rice.

Rice was the basis of the entire economy. The coasts supported small fishing communities, whose catch might be traded for a share of the precious grain from the hinterland, but the vast majority of the population were peasants, living on the food they grew. Farming land was divided up into large manorial estates, generally held by the aristocracy, by the imperial house itself, or by the great temples and monasteries. These landowners were remote figures, based mainly in the capital, Kyōto, whose sole link with the land was the receipt of their quota of its yield, in rice or in cash. Estates were actually run by powerful local landlords – members of warrior clans such as the Taira and Minamoto. As stewards and overseers, they organized the manors and collected the crops for the proprietors. But they were more than hired managers: in troubled times they took up arms and led troops to defend their territories; in more peaceful periods they ruled the countryside, dispensing justice and enforcing the law. They were a formidable power, whose influence and authority far outstripped that of the absentee landowners in Kyōto.

Antoku's predecessors had ruled this land for possibly a thousand years. For the last 400 of these, the Heian period, the fountainhead of power had been Kyōto – home to the imperial court and the inbred network of aristocratic families who dominated it. But by the 12th century, the aristocrats had become dependent on two great clans, the Taira and Minamoto. In the capital, these warriors shielded the emperor and kept the peace; in the countryside, they quashed rebellions, pacified outlying provinces, and defended the rural manors whose income sustained the urban nobility in their opulent, leisured lives at court. These patrician paymasters relied on the warriors for protection, although they treated them with contempt. But before the century had ended, the control of Japan would slip altogether from the perfumed hands of the nobility into the rougher palms of the military.

By the mid-12th century the imperial court at Kyōto was no longer the sole hub of the Japanese political universe. The emperor himself had become a figure of largely ceremonial significance, whose ritual functions were so time-consuming that it was the normal practice for any monarch seeking effective political involvement to abdicate. The ex-emperor would then set up his own separate, fully staffed court and hold sway from behind the scenes. Meanwhile, his successor, who might be of extremely tender years, would preside as the official monarch. Coexistence was not always a peaceful affair; rivalries between different court factions would often boil up into power struggles between the old emperor and the new.

About these twin poles of government developed a cumbersome bureaucracy. Senior posts remained firmly in the hands of often incompetent hereditary office-holders, and promotion was not so much a matter of merit as of patronage. The lives of all members of this rank-obsessed hierarchy were ruled by rigid etiquette, which governed everything from the permissible size and shape of their carriages to the fabrics and colours of their gowns.

In contrast, Japanese spirituality reflected an easy tolerance: Buddhism, which declared that any man could attain enlightenment by destroying fear, hatred and

**In a picturesque incident from the civil war that was waged in Japan during the latter half of the 12th century, Minamoto cavalrymen attack the fleet of their Taira foes in the shallow strait of Fujito, off the southern coast of Honshū. The conflict between the two rival factions climaxed at the Battle of Dannoura in 1185, which ended in complete victory for the Minamoto. During the following century, tales of the clan struggles became national legend. Part of an oral tradition later committed to paper using a recognizably modern Japanese script, these accounts formed the basis for the 700-metre long *Heike Monogatari* scroll, from which this detail is taken.**

delusion, had arrived by way of China from India, and been adopted as a state religion in the eighth century, but its adherents never presented it as the one true faith. In Japan it coexisted comfortably with other traditions, such as Shinto, in which a random collection of ancient native deities, representing mountains, valleys, localities and the forces of nature, were worshipped in modest shrines with the simplest of ceremonies. People saw no contradiction between honouring these native gods, making pilgrimages to Buddhist shrines and paying deference to the moral codes of Chinese Confucianism — a formalization of ethical and behavioural rules, that espoused harmony and respect for superiors.

But it was the great Buddhist temples and monasteries that dominated the religious establishment. Their abbots were actively engaged in politics, their monks and nuns were often members of the nobility — even emperors — who had opted to lead a religious life, and their considerable land-holdings made them prodigiously wealthy. To protect their interests, the religious houses had private armies, consisting of warrior-monks whose spiritual service was based partly on their skill with a sword. These troops were volatile: if they felt the prestige of their monastery was compromised, or their revenue endangered, they would not scruple to march on the capital nor to fight secular soldiers or the monks of other houses. Buddhist strictures against shedding blood did not appear to enter into their theology.

The wilful warrior-monks were just one indication of a country that was gradually drifting out of the court's control. The roads were dangerous, the haunts of impoverished soldiers who lived by robbery and theft. On the seacoasts, piracy was rife. And the countryside was dominated by strong local lords and their bands of well-armed horsemen. Provincial officials, originally appointed by the court, did little to restrain the chieftains and their clansmen: they were more interested in garnering local wealth and prestige than in carrying out their public duties.

The leaders of these provincial warrior clans boasted princely origins. By ancient custom, all descendants of the imperial house, except eldest sons or direct heirs to the throne, lost their noble status after six generations. For the ex-nobles, military life offered a means of making their way in the world: of such stock were many of the Taira and the Minamoto. Generations of soldiering had removed their courtly polish but given them a different kind of pride: they were samurai (literally "one who serves"), fighting men, who lived by a code of discipline, self-sacrifice and courage. While their followers were not necessarily their kin, they were attached by ties of loyalty as powerful as bonds of blood.

For some time, the Taira and Minamoto had coexisted in wary rivalry, gathering patronage at court, and furthering their own material and political interests in the countryside. But a succession of brief yet savage internal conflicts had made the two clans enemies. In the 1150s the court had split into two warring parties, enlisting Taira and Minamoto to fight each other on their behalf. The Taira won, so crushing the Minamoto that few believed they could ever rise again.

The victors quickly established themselves in Kyōto as virtual dictators, packing key offices with their own kinsmen and dispatching their followers to govern the provinces. Forsaking their spartan military life, they insinuated themselves into the innermost circles of court society: no doubts about their new prestige remained when the daughter of their chief became the emperor's consort and, in due course, mother to his successor. Their arrogance became a byword; one of their clan was heard to say that anyone who was not a Taira was simply nobody at all.

But while the Taira leaders revelled in the soft life of the capital, the Minamoto forces began to regroup in the provinces of eastern Japan, under the formidable Minamoto Yoritomo. A contemporary portrait of Yoritomo reveals a man of grave demeanour, determined jaw and intelligent, unsmiling eyes. Born in 1147, he had ample reason to hate the Taira. At the age of 12, he had accompanied his father, a Minamoto leader, into combat against the Taira. The Minamoto were defeated, his father killed by a traitor in his own ranks, and the boy was captured and subsequently exiled to the eastern province of Izu. There he found a benefactor, and eventually, a father-in-law, in Hōjō Tokimasa, a local warlord who, although connected to the Taira, was friendly to the Minamoto. With Tokimasa's support he was able to gather an army of some 300 men, and in 1180 he once more marched against the Taira, to aid an imperial prince who had risen against their stranglehold.

But the rebel forces were defeated by an overwhelmingly superior Taira army at the Battle of Ishibashi Mountain, and Yoritomo fled east, by sea, to the remote peninsula of Awa. Distant and difficult of access, Awa offered a secure base from which Yoritomo began to regroup, re-establishing contact with the old Minamoto followers, and gaining support among other warrior families opposed to the Taira.

As his strength grew, Yoritomo needed a more accessible base of operations, and, on the advice of his new allies, he chose the small coastal town of Kamakura. Strategically, the site made sense: some 480 kilometres east of Kyōto, it was far from the reach of the Taira and the imperial court, easy to defend, and surrounded by lands belonging to Minamoto loyalists. Historically, too, there were Minamoto connections: Yoritomo's ancestors had built a shrine there a hundred years before.

Yoritomo set out from Awa with a few hundred followers on horseback. But as he travelled west towards Kamakura, more and more allies flocked to join him. Even disaffected Taira supporters fell in behind him: one warlord, so the chroniclers say, brought an army 60 times as large as Yoritomo's own. When Yoritomo entered Kamakura in the autumn of 1180, he had 27,000 men at his command. Those lords who cast in their lots with Yoritomo did not necessarily do so through any belief in the greater virtue of his cause. They were more likely to be motivated by sheer self-interest, and the realization that Yoritomo's star was now in the ascendant.

Before the end of 1180, Minamoto troops had defeated a Taira force in battle, and wiped out a formerly powerful provincial family that, in spite of its Minamoto connections, stood against the clan. But Yoritomo was in no hurry to plunge into all-out war. His first priority was to bring strength and unity to his cause. To this end, he forgave old enemies, and welcomed former opponents, even Taira, into his following. He used his influence to reconcile ex-rivals who now found themselves side by side in the Minamoto camp. Those of his supporters with no blood-ties to his house were turned into honorary Minamoto; where possible, these bonds were cemented by marriage, or by adoption into families within the clan.

The new vassals had a clear understanding of their obligations to their lord. In times of war, they rendered military service; during peacetime they were required to stand guard at Yoritomo's headquarters, act as his escorts and attendants when he travelled or took part in religious ceremonies, accompany him on hunting trips, and participate in all manner of martial contests, from archery competitions to trials of horsemanship. At Kamakura, military skills were not allowed to rust.

Yoritomo's followers also made more material contributions to the Minamoto cause. They were expected to present generous gifts to the lord and his family on great occasions, offer hospitality in their country houses, and contribute timber to Yoritomo's construction projects, horses for his cavalry, and funds for various good works, such as a roof repair to their leader's favourite shrine.

Yoritomo recompensed his warriors for their efforts. The best rewards within his gift were land-rights — a share of the rice crop from one of the ever growing number of rural estates under Minamoto control, or a stewardship on a manor, with an automatic entitlement to a healthy portion of all profits from the land.

All Yoritomo's efforts, he said, were dedicated to protecting imperial interests. Those who served him also served the emperor. But at the same time he demanded his adherents' unswerving personal loyalty. A man whose father had been murdered by a traitor, he would brook no infidelities: soldiers caught deserting were beheaded on the spot, and anyone whose devotion seemed lukewarm became the

Ceremonial robes and an elaborate coiffure lend gravity to the stern-eyed figure of Japan's first warrior ruler Minamoto Yoritomo, as captured on silk by a 12th-century courtier-artist. A charismatic leader who defeated the rival Taira clan with the aid of his able brother Yoshitsune, Yoritomo was ruthless in his search for power: in 1185 he declared his brother a rebel, and eventually pursued him to his death. Following his victory at Dannoura, Yoritomo ruled the country from his headquarters at Kamakura, and in 1192 was awarded the supreme title of *Seitaishōgun*, "Barbarian-Subduing Generalissimo". He died seven years later at the age of 52.

target for his imprecations and accusations. "He has the eyes of a rat," murmured Yoritomo of one suspected waverer. "Rarely might one find a more villainous lieutenant." To enforce this loyalty and keep order amongst his burgeoning army of followers, Yoritomo set up a military management office, known as the *Samurai-dokoro*, or Warriors' Bureau. It controlled the assignment of ranks and duties, kept military discipline, and supervised the activities of the Minamoto vassals.

Between 1181 and 1183, Yoritomo gradually built up his administration at Kamakura and consolidated Minamoto control over the eastern provinces. The Taira, lacking influence in that part of the country, could do little to stop him. At the same time, he was winning increasing support in Kyōto from those nobles who looked to the Minamoto to rid them of Taira hegemony. With these in mind, Yoritomo proposed that the policing of Japan be divided, with the Taira named Protectors of the West, where their own influence was strongest, and his own clan given the protectorate of the east. The imperial court seemed amenable to the idea, but the Taira spurned it.

By the end of that year, however, the Taira were on the run. Aware that Minamoto support was growing and that their enemies at court were gathering strength, they left Kyōto en masse to seek greater safety in their western strongholds, taking with them their most important kinsman, the child-emperor Antoku, and the imperial regalia, the Three Treasures of Japan. The ex-emperor, Go-Shirakawa, who nursed bitter grievances of his own against the Taira, declared them outlaws, and sent Yoritomo to put them down. As a rueful Taira clansman observed, "Every single warrior in the east must have answered Yoritomo's call to arms".

The pursuit of the Taira was carried out under Yoritomo's younger brother, Yoshitsune, whose military exploits made him a hero of folklore and literature for centuries to come. It was Yoshitsune who led the forces that crushed the Taira at Dannoura. Meanwhile, Yoritomo continued to develop his administration at Kamakura. In 1184 the *Samurai-dokoro* was joined by a bureau for running civil affairs in clan territories, and a legal department for settling land disputes and seeing that justice was done on all Minamoto manors.

By the time the Minamoto won their decisive victory at Dannoura, Yoritomo had become the acknowledged defender of the imperial house, the man who would cleanse the land of Taira corruption. He was given supreme authority over the armed forces, and used the exigencies of winning and keeping the peace as the justification for extending his control. The country was soon being controlled by a military elite consisting of Minamoto vassals, whom Yoritomo had appointed as land stewards in charge of former Taira manors and as constables to police the provinces.

The court felt comfortable with Yoritomo, and he, in turn, felt comfortable with the court. Although his own upbringing had been in the stern martial tradition of his clan, he had spent his earliest years amongst courtiers. Unlike his often

# A WARRIOR'S ESTATE

As military retainers of the feudal lords who governed large domains in Japan, the samurai pledged themselves to defend their master's territory. In return for this service they were often granted their own lands, occupying substantial houses set on self-supporting estates.

High-ranking samurai dwelt in secure stockades that were well equipped for both peace and war. As in the typical example shown here, stables, storehouses and the living quarters of servants and lesser warriors stood grouped round the samurai's personal residence, which was thatched in reeds and equipped with extensive verandas. The walls of the buildings were constructed of expensive white cedar, and panelled with translucent paper screens. A plot within the compound provided space for a grove of maple trees and for cultivating vegetables. Food was cooked and eaten outdoors or in open-sided sheds. Water would have come from a nearby spring, beside which a small shrine might be erected.

In times of peace, the samurai's warriors practised the martial arts of archery and swordplay within the fenced enclosure in front of the houses, while labourers tilled the surrounding land. This tranquil compound, however, was also a defensive fortress, constantly guarded, and protected by a moat, stout fences and steep banks of earth planted with trees. When under attack mud was spread on the roofs to protect them from incendiary arrows, and archers were hurried to the raised platform above the single gateway.

Skilled in the use of bow and sword, the samurai was a fearsome fighting machine whose loyalty lay first and foremost with his lord. To protect himself he wore an elaborately efficient suit of armour. Over a light silk robe, with baggy pantaloons and sleeves, the warrior donned a single garment made of metal scales and plates, laced together with cords and suspended from the body by leather straps. For easy movement, the right arm was left unprotected, and the armour below the waist was divided into a loose, four-part skirt. On his head the samurai sported a flared helmet, designed to intimidate the enemy as much as to deflect the blows of a sword. Compact, easily mended, and only about 11 kilograms in weight, such armour was unparalleled for lightness and flexibility.

illiterate fellow warriors, he valued scholarship, and recruited many of the ablest court officials for his own staff at Kamakura. He appreciated the niceties of court etiquette, understood its traditions and was always punctilious in adhering to its procedures. He also had a reputation for fairness and justice: the smooth running of his own legal bureau had not gone unnoticed. With such effective administrative and judicial structures already in place, it seemed only sensible for Yoritomo to extend their reach beyond his own vassals, to embrace the country as a whole.

Both Kyōto and Kamakura stood to gain from this sharing of power. Freed of the humiliating yoke of Taira control, the imperial house was no longer compelled to restrict appointments and promotions to that clan's puppets. With peace restored in the countryside, nobles grew rich from the increased rice production of their estates. The monks of the great shrines and temples also approved of Yoritomo's respect for their rights; they too had been victims of the Taira, with their rice-lands expropriated and their sanctuaries burnt. The provincial warrior clans were equally enthusiastic. They felt secure under a strong government run by men of their own kind, and greater centralization was a small price to pay: with order restored, they had less need to render military service, and could get on with the more attractive business of clearing new land and increasing their estate revenues.

Yoritomo's prestige grew in proportion to his power. A contemporary historian, the abbot Jien, described his glorious entry into the capital, on a ceremonial visit from Kamakura: "Everyone had waited expectantly for his arrival. But because it was raining on the day Yoritomo planned to enter the capital, he stopped over at a place outside the city. Then, when he entered the capital on the seventh day of the month — the rain having stopped, just as he wanted — his soldiers came riding into the city three abreast. Over 700 horsemen preceded him, and more than 300 were grouped behind him. Riding a black horse, and wearing an apron of deer's summer fur over a glossy tricoloured robe of dark blue, light blue and red, he was an impressive figure. After entering Kyōto, he paid his respects to Retired Emperor Go-Shirakawa, and called at the imperial palace. In the eyes of Go-Shirakawa, no one was the equal of Yoritomo . . ." Other witnesses remarked that Yoritomo drew greater crowds, and engendered more excitement, than any public appearance by a retired or incumbent emperor. And it was felt to be no more than his due when, in 1192, he was honoured with the title of *Shōgun*, or in full, *Seitaishōgun*, Barbarian-Subduing Generalissimo.

His moment of glory was relatively brief: he died only seven years after the title was conferred. But the *bakufu*, (literally, "tent headquarters"), the system which Yoritomo had created to govern his vassals at Kamakura, and the legitimate status and power that he had won for the warrior caste, would survive long after him, shaping the politics and culture of Japan for centuries to come.

On Yoritomo's death, real power in Kamakura passed into the hands of his widow, Masako. Like many highborn women of the age, she had taken religious vows after her widowhood. But her official renunciation of the world and its illusions did not stop her from taking an active part in government, and she equalled, if not surpassed, her late husband in ruthless efficiency. Her son Yoriie, nominal successor to the shōgunate, was a weak reed: she provided the power behind the throne and set up a council of 13 ministers — including her father, Hōjō Tokimasa, Yoritomo's old benefactor — to help her govern. She and her father soon hatched a conspiracy

to remove Yoriie from the shōgunate. Their alliance disintegrated, however, when Tokimasa, without informing his fellow plotter, had Yoriie assassinated. When Tokimasa was revealed to be plotting against her second son, Sanetomo, as well, Masako and her brother, Hōjō Yoshitoki, joined forces to drive out their father, and made Sanetomo, his intended victim, the new shōgun. He did not win universal approval. The monk-historian Jien disparaged him as "foolishly careless, indulging himself in learning, and disgracing the offices he held".

But public approval was immaterial. The real power remained in the hands of Masako. On Sanetomo's death in 1219, she set up another underage member of her own family as puppet shōgun, and made her brother the official regent, to run the Kamakura government on the child's behalf. After her brother's death, the regency would become a hereditary post, passing to his own heirs, and remaining in the hands of the Hōjō family for more than a century. Some chroniclers found the irony amusing, recalling that, although the Hōjōs were in the Minamoto camp, they were actually of Taira blood.

The intricate political structure of Kamakura Japan was now in place. The titular head of state was the emperor, whose court functions were largely ceremonial. Behind him stood the retired emperor, whose freedom from ritual responsibilities allowed him to devote more attention to furthering the interests of the imperial house. Meanwhile, many administrative responsibilities were officially in the hands of the shōgun, presiding over the military establishment at Kamakura. Yet he too was in fact a figurehead: the regent was the real power in the land.

Not all parties were satisfied with the arrangement. Relations between Kyōto and Kamakura soured. In 1221, the retired emperor Go-Toba began to raise and train an army of his own, with a view to restoring the dominance of the imperial house. The provincial monasteries, with their large troops of warrior-monks, sympathized with his cause. With this force behind him, he denounced the Hōjō regent as a rebel and called upon the whole country to rise up in support.

The *bakufu* responded swiftly. A large army made the long march west to Kyōto, and suppressed Go-Toba's uprising in a matter of weeks. The regent then banished the emperor, the retired emperor and various members of the imperial family to remote islands, where, in true aristocratic tradition, they passed the time composing poetry. Ex-emperor Go-Toba wrote:

*Sorry not to see*
*Some people and sorrier*
*To see some others,*
*In my inmost self I feel*
*The World has lost its savour.*

Back in Kamakura, the regent did not pause for any such lyrical reflection. He was busy stamping out the last traces of dissent, exiling or executing the nobles who had taken part in the disturbances, and seizing their manors.

These lands fell into the regent's hands at an opportune moment. The military government was responsible for maintaining a growing population of warriors, many with little or no title to their own lands; to keep their loyalty, the regent could now reward them with stewardships of the confiscated manors. The vassals were not given the properties outright, but they enjoyed a generous share of the profits:

for every 4.5 hectares under their stewardship, they were awarded half a hectare they could call their own, with no need to share out its income. On the other four hectares – whose yields were shared among the cultivators of the land, overseers, and the feudal masters in Kamakura or Kyōto – the stewards could impose a tax.

The regent scrupulously followed the policy, laid down by Yoritomo, of gaining the exiled emperor's permission for these arrangements. A little diplomatic arm-twisting may have been needed, but court resistance had been thoroughly broken. And to prevent any future misunderstandings, a branch of the *bakufu*, backed by a large armed force, was installed in the former Taira headquarters in the capital.

Culturally, the two establishments inhabited very different worlds. The Kamakura society was based on traditional martial values: self-discipline, loyalty, honour and austerity. By courage and devotion to duty, the samurai brought credit to his clan. When he went to war, the ghosts of his ancestors stood at his shoulder: the fighting man proudly inscribed his name and origins on the shafts of his arrows, and loudly recited his pedigree as he stepped on to the battlefield. "I who say this," declared one, as he flung a challenge to the foe, "am a descendant of the Emperor Kammu in the tenth generation, grandson of the Minister of Justice Tadamori, second son of the governor of Aki, Kiyomori. My name is Motomori, my age is 17."

In the middle of the 13th century, a member of the regent's own family, the Hōjō, wrote a manual of good conduct, entitled *Family Instructions*, for the guidance of his son, who was about to take up a post in Kyōto as a deputy of the military government. It enjoined him to avoid bad companions, to fear all gods, to obey his lord and his parents without question, to be generous to the needy and cautious in his dealings with strangers, to avoid showing fear, and to practise his horsemanship and other martial skills on a regular basis. "The warrior," wrote the father, "must always bear in mind his moral duty. A good heart and the faith of a warrior are like the two wheels of a carriage."

The love of luxuries and an undue interest in clothes were to be avoided too. Everyone in Kamakura remembered their first shōgun's reaction to an extravagantly dressed vassal: Yoritomo had borrowed the man's own sword, used it to lop off the rainbow-coloured skirts of his robe, and excoriated him for squandering his wealth on silken garments instead of spending it for the good of his underlings.

The aristocrats in Kyōto had no such scruples. Aesthetics obsessed them. They poured the wealth of their manors into exquisite costumes; they expressed their emotions and arranged their assignations in allusive verse inscribed in beautiful calligraphy. Expeditions to view the full moon, to admire the autumn leaves or to observe the first blossoms of spring occupied their abundant leisure hours. Court life consisted largely of a round of ceremonies, religious rituals, official banquets and poetry competitions. Much behind-the-scenes activity went into the allocation of court privileges and promotions, and the acquisition of the visible symbols of rank that went with them. Lady Nijo, a 13th-century courtier, proudly quoted the emperor's declaration of her status: "Nijo has publicly been granted permission to wear thin silk gowns and white pleated trousers anytime. She has even been given permission to board her carriage at the palace door."

The aristocrats privately called the Kamakura warriors "the Eastern Barbarians". But even the most supercilious courtier could not deny that Kamakura provided an effective administration. Pragmatism was the order of the day: untrammelled by

# SOUL OF THE SAMURAI

Everything that was important to the warrior in 13th-century Japan was symbolized by his sword. Awesome weapons requiring strict training and a meticulous etiquette for their use, swords were also revered emblems of the samurai code of honour, bravery and respect.

The creation of a blade was imbued with all the ritual of a religious ceremony. Swordsmiths abstained from animal food, sexual intercourse and intoxicating drink for several months while working on the weapon. They then donned ceremonial costume for the final forging that created the razor-sharp edge of the perfect blade.

All disputes and problems were resolved by the sword, and the warrior lived and died by its laws. Strict decorum was involved: it was an offence to touch or step over another man's weapon, and to lay one's own on the floor and kick its guard in anyone's direction was tantamount to a challenge to the death.

Fashioned in traditional "rice-cake" shape, this silver gilt guard adorned the blade of the ceremonial sword shown below. The swirling bird design on the guard, possibly indicating spiritual longing, underlines the sword's purpose as a religious offering.

Worn suspended from two woven chains, this richly decorated sword was specially commissioned by a Kamakura warlord family for dedication to the Mishima shrine in the Izu peninsula. Many such blades never saw combat, but were placed in temples for worship or offered up as thanks for winning an important battle or fulfilling wishes.

In a fragment of a screen depicting the Battle of Rokuhara during the civil war of the late 12th century, a warrior pulls back the head of an enemy to slit his throat with a short sword. Worn cutting edge up through the samurai's sash or belt, the short sword was indispensable for the rapid manoeuvring of close-quarter combat. Such weapons were produced in great numbers during the late 13th century, after the Mongol invasions of Japan had proved the unwieldy nature of the traditional long blade.

centuries of precedent and protocol, the *bakufu* ruled by trial and error. Decisions were made collectively, by the Council of State, which was presided over by the regent. Their discussions were held in secret, and the results of their deliberations were presented as unanimous decrees.

The policies devised in Kamakura were translated into action by the agents of the *bakufu*. Its inspectors traversed the country to supervise the military constables who policed the provinces, and oversee the land stewards who controlled the manors. The conduct of these local officials was examined, their accounts were thoroughly scrutinized, and any corruption severely punished. The central administration took charge of revenue-gathering, and varied the tax rates according to the success or failure of the rice harvest. When disputes over land or water rights could not be settled locally, Kamakura stepped in to adjudicate.

The military administration, though never lenient, strove to be fair. In 1232 the Council of State issued a document known as the *Jōei Formulary* – a collection of rules, recommendations and legal wisdom. The *Formulary* was based on principles that Yoritomo and his clan had followed for dispensing justice to their own vassals. Several decades of experience had proved their worth, and the *bakufu* now chose to extend these benefits to the country as a whole, to the feudal estates of the Kyōto aristocracy, as well as those of provincial lords. Even the lowliest peasant, wading through his rice paddy, had a hope of just treatment. He now had rights which he had never had before: he was no longer tied to a particular parcel of land; he could sell his holdings and move to new districts being cleared for cultivation.

With the constant flow of traffic between Kyōto and Kamakura, a degree of cross-fertilization was inevitable. Career-minded scholars and administrators, stultified at court, came to Kamakura to make better use of their talents in the *bakufu*. There they learnt that not all men of action were philistines. A prominent figure in the shōgunate during the mid-13th century, for instance, was Hōjō Sanetoki, a military leader who was also a passionate bibliophile. His vast store of Japanese and imported Chinese texts contained many treasures, including thousands of rare works he had had copied at his own expense. He placed the collection in a favourite temple in Musashi province, and organized a system to let readers consult or even borrow volumes for their own use, creating the most famous library in Kamakura.

A cautious respect began to replace the ancient mutual contempt between the soldiers and cultured courtiers. As the Kamakura warriors established themselves as the ruling class, a new literary genre developed that glorified the deeds of their ancestors and extolled samurai values of loyalty, courage, honour and obedience. These martial epics originated in the tales of the old Taira-Minamoto conflicts recited aloud by storytellers with musical accompaniment. Eventually written down and embellished by scholarly compilers, prose romances such as these provided a new mythology, a cultural encyclopedia for an era dominated by military men.

Indeed, the samurai were fast learning how to read and write. China had always been the source of religious and secular learning: for centuries literacy had been the exclusive province of a leisured elite that had the time and tutors necessary to master the complexities of Chinese script, with its thousands of characters. But a greater use of the considerably simplified syllabic script, evolved in the early Heian period, now made it easier to read and write Japanese. Nevertheless, the historian Jien still felt the need to apologize to his readers for using their native language, not Chinese, in his chronicle: "Since this book has been written in Japanese it will sound common. But meaning may be deeply embedded in Japanese words . . ."

The younger generations of the warrior caste began to lose their contempt for the sybaritic patricians of Kyōto, and to develop a taste for luxury: craftsmen prospered as never before, with the widening market for fine textiles, ceramics and lacquerwork. Sculptors, carving the wooden statuary that wealthy patrons liked to bestow upon temples, displayed fresh exuberance: their gods and demons were no longer abstractions but actual personalities, with faces expressing all human emotions and naturalistic bodies revealing superhuman power. Painters created vibrant, realistic picture scrolls of the lives of heroes and sages, the histories of shrines or episodes from the newly popular military romances. Dignitaries, of both imperial court and *bakufu*, commissioned portraits of themselves, their carriages and favourite horses.

**Created in 1306 to hold the ashes of a Zen Buddhist monk, this pot was one of many such items made at Seto in eastern Japan. The town's artisans rose to prominence in the 1230s, using Chinese technology to fashion the region's fine white clay into glazed stoneware that was prized both for its durability and its distinctive green "autumn-leaf" glaze. Fuelled by demand from the newly wealthy warrior class, Seto became the country's foremost pottery producing area. Indeed, the goods produced there were traded so widely throughout Japan that the word *Setomono*, "Seto things", became the accepted term for pottery.**

An emerging mercantile class catered for the increased demands. In the countryside, smiths and other artisans no longer worked just to meet the needs of a private manor; they sold their wares, in company with itinerant traders, at markets, held thrice a month in settlements that soon became small commercial centres with resident craftsmen and permanent shops. In provincial capitals and in Kamakura itself, merchants also gathered; in 1251 the Hōjō regent set up a specific commercial district, and gave the merchants living there the exclusive rights to hold markets.

In town and country alike, traders and artisans began to band themselves into trading associations or guilds, known as *za*. In Kamakura alone, for instance, there were *za* for merchants of silk, of rice, charcoal, fuel, fish, salt and horses, as well as for those who worked in woodcarving and joinery. These bodies flourished under the patronage of powerful protectors – members of the Kamakura government, local landlords, Kyōto aristocrats, or the abbots of important temples – who helped their protégés to acquire monopolies, exemptions from taxes and other commercial privileges.

Foreign trade also flourished. Links established between Japanese Buddhist monks and religious centres on the mainland helped forge a more comfortable relationship with South China under the Song dynasty. The Chinese themselves were quick to take advantage of advances in shipbuilding and navigation techniques and to brave the China Sea with large cargoes of brocade, incense and medicines, which they exchanged for gold from the newly opened mines of northern Japan. Copper coins from the Song dynasty became common, and by the middle of the century the markets were beginning to operate on a cash economy instead of barter.

Alarmed by the growing materialism among their vassals, military leaders passed various sumptuary laws. Undeterred by fines or other penalties, the warrior class's appetites grew ever closer to those of the old metropolitan aristocracy. But as this new group of potential consumers swelled in numbers, so too did the pressure on Japan's precarious agrarian economy: more people were demanding ever more luxury goods, but the rice lands that would ultimately pay for these purchases could yield only a finite amount of income. New lands might be cleared when there was sufficient labour, but the demand for rice and basic commodities far outstripped the limited quantities these islands could provide.

Economic stresses were not the only difficulties facing the Hōjō regents. A massive earthquake shattered the Kamakura region in 1257, followed two years later by widespread plague and famine. It was said that the streets of Kyōto were filled with the bodies of the dead, and that the peasants in the countryside were subsisting on roots and fistfuls of grass. To ameliorate rural suffering, the *bakufu* ordered its land stewards to give back the taxes they had gathered, and to refrain, temporarily, from collecting any more. With so many dead, there was a shortage of able-bodied men to work the land and perform other necessary labours. Criminals were released from custody, and even murderers given amnesty, to supply the manpower. Kyōto seemed to verge on anarchy. Graffiti appeared on the walls of the imperial palace:

*At the New Year, ill omens . . .*
*In the land, disasters . . .*
*In the capital, soldiers . . .*
*In the palace, favouritism . . .*
*In the provinces, famine . . .*
*In the shrines, conflagrations . . .*
*In the riverbed, skeletons . . .*

Temples and monasteries throughout the land were enlisted to conduct marathon prayer sessions to beseech a return of Heaven's favour. But these institutions also added to the burdens of the *bakufu*. The great landowning monasteries quarrelled frequently – with each other, with the nobility, and even with the imperial house over territorial rights and privileges, and over payments due for religious services rendered. To reinforce their arguments, they sent out their fierce battalions of warrior-monks: the army of one monastery marched on Kyōto more than 20 times in the course of the 13th century. Whenever possible, the *bakufu* stood back and let these conflicts take their course until the monks' grievances had been answered or their honour satisfied. During the famine period, however, when the imperial court appeared to be in serious danger from a brigade of very angry monks, Kamakura was compelled to intervene. It took several hundred soldiers, dispatched by the *bakufu*, to force the holy warriors back to their cloisters.

If the monks were restive, it was only a symptom of the dramatic changes taking place in the religious life of Japan. Years of clan warfare and disruption had given the common people a hunger for hope and consolation. The corrupt and arrogant clergy, more interested in enriching their own temples and furthering their personal interests at court, offered little comfort to a peasant whose rice crop had been expropriated by soldiers or to a woman raped by bandits. And as political power shifted from the patricians to the samurai class, new popular forms of Buddhism began to emerge. No longer were the Buddha's teachings obscured through theological disputation and arcane scholarship. The spread of a simplified Japanese script made the basic tenets of Buddhism much more widely accessible: life was painful and transient, the world a kaleidoscope of shifting illusions. Through self-discipline and compassion for all fellow creatures, the seeker would eventually achieve enlightenment, and escape forever the wearisome round of deceptions and unfulfilled desires. New sects arose, and old ones revived, offering their own paths to nirvana for anyone, prince or peasant, who cared to follow them.

Salvation, said the adherents of one of these creeds, the Pure Land Sect – formed in 1175, and named after the paradise to which its followers hoped to go – did not require a lifetime of rigid asceticism, constant meditation or a retreat from the world. It was attainable by anyone who faithfully repeated the name of the Amida Buddha, the Lord of Boundless Light, as he or she went about the tasks of daily life. Even women, previously denied all hope of salvation until they underwent successive rebirths as a man, could achieve enlightenment in their present existence if they assiduously repeated the *Nembutsu* prayer: "Homage to Amida Buddha." All classes of society embraced the practice: it was reported that the ex-emperor Go-Shirakawa uttered the prayer several million times, and died with it on his lips.

The orthodox Buddhist clergy were scandalized. So simple a faith would render needless all temples, priests and ceremonies, and so they launched into a violent persecution of the upstart creed. In 1201, they persuaded the emperor to take their part. The leader of the sect was exiled, and some of his most prominent disciples beheaded. The utterance of the *Nembutsu* prayer was banned. But the hope the Pure Land Sect offered was so potent that these measures ultimately proved fruitless. The sect went through various schisms and modifications, but survived – with its basic premises intact – to become a permanent part of Japan's religious life.

More rigorous in its demands, but equally influential, was the form of Buddhism known as Zen. Like the Pure Land Sect, it rejected ritual and scholarship as roads to salvation. Enlightenment – the virtual transformation of a human being into a Buddha – was achieved by a simple monastic life of meditation and hard physical labour. It could come at any time, in a sudden, ecstatic flash of light; intellectual effort, reason, philosophizing had nothing whatever to do with it. The Zen master devoted much energy to kicking, beating and shouting at his disciples to purge them of self-deception and shake them into a state of higher consciousness.

The warrior class, with its own tradition of self-discipline, found this approach particularly sympathetic. They could appreciate a religion that emphasized and rewarded individual effort, especially one that did not make literacy a prerequisite for spiritual success. Monks from more conventional religious establishments put several Zen monasteries to the torch, but in spite of official hostility, the young sect flourished under the protection of the samurai.

Although their respective advocates believed themselves to be in sole possession of religious truth, neither Zen nor Pure Land Buddhists wanted to eradicate other branches of the faith, as did a third force, the Lotus Sect, founded by the monk Nichiren. Combative in spirit and colourful in his invective, Nichiren had begun his religious life as a traditional scholar, steeped in classic Buddhist literature and theology. Like proponents of the Pure Land Sect, he too preached that salvation was accessible to all, and that the key to enlightenment lay within a particular sacred text, in this case the Lotus Sutra, an ancient Indian Buddhist scripture. It was not, however, necessary for the faithful to read or understand this text, as long as they followed the path of righteousness and, most important, repeated a certain prayer: *namu Myōhōrengekyō* ("salutation to the Lotus Sutra").

Nichiren was convinced that a new, reformed and truly national Buddhism was the only way forwards for the Japanese people, and he excoriated all other versions of the faith as pernicious influences that drained the lifeblood of his compatriots

# A NEW SPIRIT IN SCULPTURE

Carved in wood, an arch-browed attendant to one of Buddhism's ten Kings of Hell prepares to record the fate of a sinner. According to the tenets of the Pure Land Sect, Hell was one of six realms into which man could be reborn.

The military shōgunate that ruled Japan during the 13th century imposed a peace in which the nation's culture flourished. Nowhere was this more evident than in religion. The Buddhist faith, transmitted to Japan in the sixth century, spawned sects which appealed both to the ruling military class and to a wider population seeking easier ways to enlightenment. One such was Zen, whose rigorously monastic doctrines reached Japan from China at this time; others were the Pure Land Sect, a movement which promised rebirth in a western paradise after death, and the Lotus Sect, fiercely nationalistic in tone.

This spiritual ferment was felt in the arts, and above all in sculpture, which attained a peak of craftsmanship and expressivity. Working under the influence of the new beliefs, Kamakura sculptors toiled to produce masterpieces that reflected a tender realism; dark-centred crystals were even used to give life to the eyes. The idealized forms of earlier Japanese carvings were replaced by a natural sincerity emphasizing the individual personality.

Bearing a mysteriously wrapped object, possibly an offering, in his hands, the saint Muchaku, attendant to the Buddha, mirrors the suffering of humanity in his eyes. Carved in 1208, the statue was the work of Unkei, one of the greatest artists of the time.

and allowed the state to wallow in its corruption. He denounced all his religious opponents as "the greatest liars in Japan", condemning Zen as "a doctrine of fiends and devils" and the Pure Land *Nembutsu* prayer as "a hellish practice". Only when his compatriots abandoned all these heresies would the country thrive. He himself would spearhead national regeneration: "I will be the pillar of Japan. I will be the eyes of Japan. I will be the great vessel of Japan."

Preaching in the streets of Kamakura, three years after the great earthquake of 1257, during a period of plague, near anarchy and famine, Nichiren found a receptive audience. The troubles in the land, he asserted, were punishment for years of religious corruption. If Japan did not embrace the one true faith worse horrors would follow. His warning was specific: a foreign army would invade Japan.

Displeased by the presence of such a troublemaking priest, the Hōjō regency banished Nichiren from the city. Undeterred, he carried his gospel through the eastern provinces, winning many adherents from among the samurai. Nichiren had his supporters even within the *bakufu*, and in 1263 he was allowed to return to Kamakura, where he did not refrain from constant criticism of the government. He was tried for high treason, escaped execution – possibly through the intercession of influential friends – and was banished once more. But only a few years would pass before the Hōjō regents would be faced with an alarming fulfilment of Nichiren's prophecy: a formidable enemy was massing to the west.

For more than 300 years Japan, inward-looking and isolationist, had exchanged no official missions with its massive neighbour, China. But even without state envoys, communications of a less formal nature had persisted. Chinese merchant ships plied the sea, carrying exports to Japan and ferrying back the monks and students for whom the mainland was still the fountainhead of religious and secular learning. Korea, adjoining China and separated from Japan by a much narrower stretch of water, was similarly neglected by the Japanese rulers, although the westernmost vassals of Kamakura occasionally plundered its vulnerable coasts.

But in the middle of the 13th century, Japanese isolation came to a sudden and unwelcome end. In 1264, Kublai Khan, grandson of the Mongol conqueror Chingis Khan, became great khan of the Mongols, and established his capital at Beijing. Bowing before superior might, Korea rapidly became a vassal-state to the Khan. Kublai then cast his eyes eastwards.

In 1268 he sent an emissary, bearing a letter addressed "To the King of Japan". The Japanese officials who received the communication sent it, without hesitation, to the shōgun at Kamakura rather than to the emperor. In his missive, Kublai Khan proposed that Japan buy his friendship with tribute – and suggested that the only alternative was war. Over the next few years, the Khan peppered Kamakura with similarly veiled threats: the *bakufu* did not deign to reply.

Kublai bided his time until November 1274. In that month, a Mongol army, carried in Korean ships, made its way across the strait that separated the southern tip of Korea from Japan's southwestern island of Kyūshū. Chroniclers estimated that some 15,000 Mongol troops, supported by an equal number of Koreans, and carried in 450 warships, landed in Hakata Bay.

The local chieftains, together with the *bakufu*'s own land stewards and law officers, dispatched urgent messages to Kamakura and banded together to hold off the invaders until reinforcements arrived. For two days they battled successfully against unequal odds. They were vastly outnumbered and terrified by the Mongols' strange new weapons – burning projectiles that exploded with an earsplitting bang. The rules of warfare were about to be changed forever: gunpowder, previously the preserve of Chinese firework-makers, had come to the attention of the military.

The defenders suffered many losses, but fought valiantly until sundown of the second day. With every expectation of resuming the engagement in the morning, the Mongols returned to their ships to wait out the hours of darkness. But during the night a typhoon blew up and, within a matter of hours, devastated the invasion force. Those Korean vessels not shattered by giant winds and waves were driven out to sea, and some 13,000 Mongol lives were lost.

To guard against further invasion, the Kamakura leaders hurriedly raised vast numbers of troops, built new ramparts and strengthened defences. Responding to the call to mobilize, local lords and chieftains, especially on the vulnerable western island of Kyūshū, required all their vassals to submit lists of their men, arms and other resources. An aged warrior named Saikō, for example, sent an inventory of his rice lands and described the members of his household:

> *Saikō, aged 85, cannot walk.*
> *Nagahide, his son, aged 65. Has bows and arrows and weapons.*
> *Tsurehide, aged 38. Has bows and arrows, weapons, corselet, horse.*
> *Matsujirō, aged 19. Has bows and arrows, arms and two followers.*
> *Takahide, aged 40. Has bows and arrows, weapons, corselet, horse and one follower.*
> *These are at His Lordship's orders, and will serve faithfully.*

Despite an initial hesitancy, the imperial court too, by the end of 1280, began to appreciate the implications of the Mongol threat. The emperor placed all revenues from royal estates at the *bakufu*'s disposal, and ordered prayer sessions, offerings and other placatory rites at the country's shrines. Religious services were held by day and night, nobles and priests joined together in vigils, and crowds gathered at the shrine of the ancient Japanese war-god. The emperor and ex-emperor deposited letters in the tombs of their own ancestors, begging the intercession of the dead on behalf of their realm. Not to be outdone in zeal, the Hōjō regent Tokimune was said to have copied out certain sacred texts in his own blood.

Kublai Khan, busy conquering southern China, which still resisted him, waited for several years before resuming hostilities. Twice he sent letters to Kamakura, demanding that Japan become a vassal-state. The *bakufu*'s response was the same both times: the letters were destroyed, and the Mongol envoys beheaded.

Finally, in June 1281, the long wait ended. A force of 150,000 Mongol, Chinese and Korean troops landed on Kyūshū. This time the Japanese were ready. Their newly formed navy of small vessels was swift and light enough to attack and harry the cumbersome Chinese troop ships. And the Japanese, defending an imperilled homeland, fought with an intensity unmatched by a Mongol force consisting largely of southern Chinese and Korean conscripts. Yet the defenders' will was not matched by experience: apart from those in the west, Japanese warriors had seen little active service since the revolt of ex-emperor Go-Toba, nearly 60 years before.

The battle continued for 50 days. Then, once again, a great wind came roaring out of heaven. For two days, massive storms pounded the jagged Kyūshū coastline.

On land, trees were uprooted; at sea, enormous waves engulfed the Mongol ships. Those that were not swallowed up were rammed together, and Japanese archers easily picked off the frantic soldiers as they clung to their splintered vessels. The Mongols beat a desperate retreat, and only a fragment of the Khan's forces survived to carry the news of their failure back to China. According to the Japanese chroniclers, four fifths of the invaders perished.

Japan exulted. Its people gave thanks for the typhoon that had saved them, calling it *kamikaze,* the Divine Wind, and claiming it as positive proof that they were favoured by the gods. Celebrations notwithstanding, the *bakufu* did not relax its vigilance: for 20 years, Kamakura kept its warriors on full military alert. Only in 1300, six years after Kublai Khan's death, was the danger said to be over.

But the aftermath of victory was chaos. Kamakura's treasury was empty: there was little money to pay the vassals who had defended the land during the war and through the years of wary peace that followed. In this instance, triumph was not accompanied by conquest: there were no rebels' rich estates to be confiscated, no spoils of war to be awarded. The priests, no longer engaged in round-the-clock prayers for peace, grew petulant: they claimed that they were far more deserving of reward than the warriors, for had not their chants brought forth the heavenly wind?

There was little the *bakufu* could do to meet these demands. The entire country was impoverished. The expenses of maintaining troops had been ruinous. Kyūshū

**His horse spurting blood, Japanese general Takezaki Suenaga collapses under a hail of arrows in this detail from a scroll depicting the attempted invasion in 1274 by the forces of Kublai Khan, Mongol emperor of China. Faced with superior numbers, the Japanese forces also had to contend with advanced weaponry: the shell exploding over Suenaga's head is the first known depiction of the use of gunpowder in artillery. Such advantages availed the invaders little in the face of stout resistance and a devastating typhoon — dubbed *kamikaze*, or Divine Wind, by the Japanese. Suenaga survived to commission the scroll, most of which focuses on his own heroic deeds; it is believed that the proud general himself added the red arrow piercing his helmet after the scroll was completed.**

had suffered great loss of life during the invasion, and its war-lords had used their own resources to build up the coastal defences. Throughout the country, farming had virtually stopped: such rice as there was had been taken to feed the army, and many able-bodied men had been taken off the land to join the troops. A historian of the period reported that "during the last few years, owing to the Mongol attacks, in both east and west warlike arts have not been neglected, but agriculture has practically been abandoned by the peasants and the landholders".

Discontent spread. The only way the *bakufu* could compensate its vassals for their expenditures would be to take the money from one deserving group to pay another. Those who did not receive sufficient recompense were forced to mortgage their estates to pay their accumulated debts. For a short period, the *bakufu* tried to ban any sale or mortgage of its vassals' estates, but those who had money to lend – and those who needed it – found ways to circumvent the law, and the ruling was soon rescinded. In Kyōto, there were nobles who were no friends of the Kamakura regime. They made common cause with the unhappy military vassals, and gradually began to subvert the *bakufu*'s influence.

The Hōjō regents were losing their grip. The spartan simplicity that had characterized the early days of Kamakura rule had now well and truly vanished. The law courts, once admired for their fairness and efficiency, became as cumbersome and corrupt as any organ of the old pre-Kamakura imperial bureaucracy. The regime did not come to an abrupt standstill, but even the most dedicated members of the *bakufu* knew that they presided over a government in decline.

For the first three decades of the 14th century, military government still ruled in Kamakura. But by 1333 its enemies had forged a coalition: disaffected provincial warlords conspired with members of the nobility and faction-ridden imperial and ex-imperial households to raise an army. The force marched on Kamakura, captured the city, and burnt it. The last Hōjō regent, with 200 of his loyal followers, committed ritual suicide rather than surrender, after the tradition of that warrior class their predecessors had elevated to new heights of dignity and power.

But the last Hōjō regent's death did not end the shōgunate. For 50 years Japan was rocked by a power struggle between the aristocracy and the provincial warriors, until in the 1390s the Ashikaga clan won control. Once more the country was ruled by a *bakufu*, this time from Kyōto, and once more the imperial court was relegated to the shadows. Military rule in Japan had come to stay.

# SLAVE SULTANS OF EGYPT

3

Shortly after sunrise on the morning of September 3, 1260, an insistent thunder of drums filled the air in the five-kilometre-wide Palestinian valley between Mount Gilboa and the hills of Galilee. An Egyptian army was advancing down the Plain of Esdraelon towards Ayn Jalut, the "Spring of Goliath", where waited the world-conquering Mongols, triumphant from a series of bloody victories that had brought them all of Iraq and Syria. The Mongols' next goal was the conquest of Egypt, which would ensure the entire Islamic civilization of the Middle East was theirs.

When the two armies clashed, the Mongol confidence seemed well founded; their first furious charge swept the Egyptian advance guard aside, overrunning its left flank. But the Egyptians rallied. Their sultan Qutuz rode out before his troops, removed his helmet so that all could recognize him, and crying "O Muslims! O Muslims! O Muslims!" led his army headlong into the Mongol ranks. The impetus was overwhelming: the Mongol leader Kitbugha was killed, and his troops driven into headlong flight, to be pitilessly slaughtered by the pursuing Egyptians. After the battle Qutuz dismounted, offered two prostrations to Allah, then sent Kitbugha's severed head back to Cairo as proof of victory.

Ayn Jalut was the battle that marked the limit of Mongol expansion in the Middle East. Although the steppe warriors returned five times to Syria during the next 50 years, they never again threatened Egypt itself. In addition, the victory was a turning point that saw the emergence of a new power in the region: the Mamluks, Turkish slave-warriors who for the next two-and-a-half centuries — a bloody era of coup and counter-coup — would rule over all Syria and Egypt. They would stem the Mongol tide, destroy the remaining Christian enclaves set up by the Crusaders of the 12th century, and raise Cairo to a position pre-eminent in the Muslim world.

The empire the Mamluks controlled had previously been run by the Kurdish Ayyubids, who in 1171 had deposed the Fatimid rulers of Egypt and founded their own dynasty under the leadership of Saladin. By the first half of the 13th century, Ayyubid rule extended beyond the borders of Egypt over Syria, the Yemen and parts of Iraq. The Ayyubids' realm was a prosperous one. On the banks of the River Nile and in its fertile delta, the rich alluvial silt produced by annual floods yielded a bountiful harvest of wheat, cotton and rice. The drier lands of Upper Egypt provided good grazing for Bedouin herds. And in Syria, the cities of Aleppo and Damascus grew wealthy from a bounty of fruit and olives. Whatever commodities the empire lacked — such as iron and copper — were obtained from the Western merchants who flocked to the bustling port of Alexandria at the mouth of the Nile.

Despite its riches, the Ayyubid empire was far from stable. In Iraq its rule was contested by the hostile Islamic dynasty of the Abbasids; in Syria rival Ayyubid factions disputed the sovereignty of Saladin's successors; and along the coast of

**Carousing subjects of the Mamluks, Egypt's Turkish ruling elite, are depicted in this miniature taken from a Mamluk version of *Maqamat*, a popular collection of picaresque tales by the 12th-century writer, al-Hariri. Following their rise to power in 1260, the Mamluks imposed an austere military regime in Egypt and Syria. Despite the Islamic ban on alcohol, however, many towns offered relief for private imbibers. Native Arabs could find wine and beer in taverns that were usually run by Christians and often attached to monasteries. The Turkish sultans and soldiers preferred koumiss, an extremely alcoholic beverage that was made from fermented mare's milk.**

The inexorable westward sweep of the Mongol hordes came to a halt in 1260, at Ayn Jalut in Palestine, when a Mongol army was defeated by an Egyptian force in a battle that redefined the boundaries of the Middle East. From that year Egypt and Syria were controlled by the Mamluks, Turkish slave-warriors imported from the central Asian steppes. By the end of the century the Mamluks further consolidated their territories by crushing the Western Crusader states of Jerusalem, Antioch and Tripoli. From their twin capitals of Cairo and Damascus, they dominated a rich empire that lay at the very hub of world trade.

Palestine the Christian Crusader states were a constant threat to security. Since the First Crusade had arrived from the West in 1098, Muslim and Christian forces had been engaged in an endless struggle for possession of what each regarded as their religion's holiest places. At the beginning of the 13th century the Christians, or Franks as they were known to the Muslims, were still established in the states of Tripoli, Antioch and Jerusalem — excluding the Holy City itself, which had been taken by Saladin in 1187. Both Christians and Muslims profited greatly from the trade brought by these coastal enclaves, and in the lower strata of society members of both religions went about their everyday life in comparative peace. But, in spite of this uneasy coexistence, the situation was always extremely volatile, and when a particularly warlike batch of crusaders arrived, or when a Muslim ruler saw an opportunity to exploit some Christian weakness, blood was inevitably spilt.

Nor were the Christians the only religious threat. The Ayyubids were Sunni Muslims, who saw the caliph in Baghdad as their spiritual leader. However, there still remained in Egypt and Syria a few small communities who clung to the Shiite faith of the Ayyubids' predecessors, the Fatimids, denying the authority of the caliph, and believing in a line of hidden redeemers, who would one day return to claim the caliphate. In the towns, where they could be easily controlled, the Shiites were tolerated, but in remoter parts they were seen as a serious threat to civil order and were often repressed by the military. The greatest menace, however, was that presented by the Assassins, a group of Shiite extremists who had terrorized the inhabitants of Syria, Christian and Muslim alike, since the early 12th century. To the Ayyubids, the heretical Assassins were an even graver danger than the Frankish Crusaders.

To maintain order in their volatile empire, the Ayyubids, like other Muslim rulers since the ninth century, made extensive use of imported slave-warriors who had been acquired as tribute, booty or by purchase. Saladin himself replaced the African infantry of the Fatimids with a 500-strong Turkish corps, which he dressed in distinctive yellow uniforms. His successors continued the practice, and by the reign of the last great Ayyubid sultan, al-Salih Ayyub, Mamluk warriors had become the mainstay of the Egyptian army. Foremost among them were the sultan's own personal elite corps, the Bahris — so called because they were garrisoned on an island in the River Nile, Bahr al-Nil, just outside Cairo.

With few exceptions, Mamluks were members of the Turkish Kipchak tribe recruited from the

Crimea and southern Russian steppes. Islamic law sanctioned the enslavement of heathen, non-Arab peoples, but for military service the Turks were prized above all others; trained to ride and draw a bow almost as soon as they could walk, they were natural warriors. According to the ninth-century Arab author of an *Epistle Concerning the Qualities of the Turk,* "They care only about raiding, hunting, horsemanship, skirmishing with rival chieftains, taking booty and invading other countries. Their efforts are all directed towards these activities, and they devote all their energies to these occupations. In this way they have acquired a mastery of these skills, which for them take the place of craftsmanship and commerce and constitute their only pleasure, their glory and the subject of all their conversation. Thus they have become in warfare what the Greeks are in philosophy."

A newly purchased Mamluk learnt all aspects of the military arts, concentrating especially on improving his native skills with the short Turkish bow, and mastering cavalry tactics such as the feigned retreat, which had drawn many enemies into fatal traps. Conversion to Sunni Islam was an integral part of his education, and he would probably be taught to speak, and possibly read and write, Arabic. Removed far from home and family, he developed strong bonds of kinship both with his fellow recruits and his master, whom he might address as father. Although the word *mamluk* signifies "something that is possessed", he was treated not as a menial but as a valuable part of his master's extended family. While his master lived, the Mamluk's duty first and foremost was to him alone. An important Mamluk might act as his equerry, cupbearer or falconer. If he was ambitious, well-favoured and belonged to an important household, he could aspire to even higher office, for once he had embraced Islam, he was effectively emancipated, and no formal obstacles barred his advancement. It was not inconceivable that he would be named heir if his master was childless. If the warrior belonged to the Bahri elite, he might entertain hopes of elevation to the rank of emir, commanding an army in the field.

In the mid-13th century, however, a short, broad-chested Bahri by the name of Baybars al-Bunduqdari, was to raise Mamluk status to an even higher level. His destiny was to be far more than a mere emir: he was to become sultan of all Egypt and Syria. Born in about 1220, Baybars was a member of a Kipchak tribe that had fled from the Mongols into the Crimea, where he had been taken into captivity, then sold at the age of about 14 in the slave market of Aleppo. Although Turks were generally prized for their beauty, Baybars was disfigured by a cast in one eye, and for this reason he had been purchased for the relatively low price of 800 dirhams – an estimated two kilograms of silver – by an Egyptian emir. His master was subsequently disgraced and forced to hand over his Mamluks to the sultan al-Salih Ayyub himself, who recognised the youth's intelligence and fighting skills, and placed him in the guard section of his Bahri troops. Within a few years Baybars had become the deputy of the Bahri commander Aqtay.

Having used his Bahri Mamluks to good effect against the Crusaders and hostile Ayyubid kinsmen in Syria, al-Salih Ayyub encouraged his son Turanshah to maintain the relationship. In a letter written shortly before his death in November 1249, he bemoaned the poor quality of his regular troops and urged Turanshah to treat the Bahris with generosity. "I strongly recommend them to you," he wrote, "I owe them everything." And indeed Turanshah himself owed a debt of thanks to the Bahris, who had successfully defeated a Crusader army at Mansura in February

# A MANUAL OF MARTIAL INSTRUCTION

Taught to read and write as part of their training, Mamluks studied both the theory and practice of combat in military manuals such as the one from which the illustrations on these pages are taken, *The End of the Quest Concerning the Techniques of Horsemanship.* Its title notwithstanding, the book covered more than just horsemanship: it contained sections on archery, sword and lance play, strategy, tactics, ambushes, inspection parades, the employment of poisonous smokes and chemicals, the use of fireproof clothing, the treatment of wounds, the law regarding the division of booty, and even the practice of magic to gain forewarning of unseen military dangers.

Such works placed particular stress on thorough training, which was vital if the Mamluk cavalry was to function successfully in battle formation, and particularly if it was to perform its favourite tactic of the feigned retreat and rally. Exercises were regularly carried out on the open concourses of hippodromes at both Cairo and Damascus, where warriors would give public demonstrations of their prowess; Sultan Baybars would daily visit the Cairo site at noon to inspect the progress of his troops. Mamluk warriors would also hone their skills on hunting expeditions through the Syrian countryside, pursuing quarry that included lions, panthers, wild boar, hyenas, wolves, deer and gazelles.

Four beardless novices, their lances shouldered, gallop in simulated combat round a hippodrome pool.

A warrior demonstrates the effectiveness of an iron shield in countering Greek fire. A Byzantine invention widely used in medieval warfare, the composition of the incendiary is no longer known.

A lancer stabs a bear on a hunting trip. Mamluks valued the chase as a method of training; such expeditions sometimes gave cover for surveying borders of neighbouring Crusader states.

Swordsmen practise their art. Strengthened by repetitive exercise, a Mamluk warrior could slice through lead bars or heaps of clay a thousand times a day, using a sword of up to two kilograms.

1250, leading to the subsequent capture and ransom of the French king, Louis IX. But Turanshah had his own slave household, which included black Sudanese soldiers as well as Turks. After his father's death, he set about appointing his own men to key posts, ignoring the resentment of the Bahris. They were particularly incensed by the promotion of Sudanese to the influential posts of Master of the Royal Household, and Master of the Royal Guard. However, Turanshah confidently disregarded their pique: a contemporary Arab historian recorded that when warned of a possible rebellion, he drew his sabre and began chopping the tops off candles, shouting, "So shall I deal with the Bahris!"

They struck first. On May 2, 1250, a group led by Baybars burst into his tent and tried to cut him down. He managed to escape, but on hearing of the coup attempt, the rest of the Bahris hunted him down to a wooden tower by the Nile. Forced out by fire, Turanshah managed to reach the river before his assailants finally killed him. Then the Bahri commander, Aqtay, cut him open, plucked out his heart and took it, dripping, to the captured French king, Louis, who was still negotiating the terms of his release. "What will you give me now that I have killed your enemy?" he demanded. "Had he lived, you can be sure he would have killed you." The Crusader lord who reported the gory incident noted that Louis (who was finally released five days later) maintained a dignified silence.

Following Turanshah's death, Egypt saw a decade of manoeuvring for power, during which the Ayyubid empire began to collapse. In Egypt Mamluk and Ayyubid factions jostled for control of puppet sultans. In Syria, rival Ayyubid princes had united to form their own separate state. The Bedouin tribes of Upper Egypt were in rebellion. And in Cairo the streets were terrorized by the Bahris. Under Aqtay and Baybars, they acted as a law unto themselves, creating disorder, robbing citizens, and – one chronicler noted with alarm – raiding the women's public baths. Cairo, it was said, would be better off under the Franks than these rowdies.

However, relief for the townsfolk came in 1254 when a non-Bahri Mamluk emir named Aybak – who had briefly held power four years earlier, only to be pushed to one side – killed Aqtay and forced most of the Bahris, including Baybars, to flee to Syria. Those who remained were arrested and their wealth confiscated. With the Bahris out of the way Aybak felt confident enough in his own strength to reclaim his former position, and in September 1254 he declared himself sultan of Egypt.

Aybak did not enjoy his throne long. Four years previously he had married Shajar al-Durr – al-Salih's widow and former harem slave, who had herself ruled for a short while. Coming to suspect that he intended to replace her as chief wife, in 1257 she had him strangled in the bath by her servants.

Shajar al-Durr, however, profited little, for Aybak's supporters soon came seeking vengeance. Chroniclers relate that she held out for several days in the Red Tower of the Cairo citadel, grinding her jewels to dust so that no other woman might wear them. At last, forced by hunger to quit her sanctuary, she was beaten to death by the clog-wielding concubines of her late husband, and left for the dogs to eat. And in November 1259 the throne was seized by Aybak's Mamluk officer, Qutuz.

Qutuz had barely secured his position against internal rivals, when the country was threatened by a looming menace from outside: the Mongols. By mid-century the vast Mongol empire built up by Chingis Khan had been divided into four parts, the southwestern share being allotted to the Ilkhan dynasty, based in Persia. In 1258, the Ilkhan Hulegu, grandson of Chingis, had struck westwards, taking amidst terrible bloodshed and devastation the city of Baghdad, seat of the caliph, who was himself among the dead. Two years later the Mongols stormed into Syria; Aleppo fell in January 1260, Damascus in March. The Mongol army, which according to some accounts numbered more than 100,000 men, seemed unstoppable.

Confronted by so formidable a foe, even the turbulent Mamluks put aside their quarrels and prepared for a showdown. They were saved by an unexpected twist of fate; after taking Damascus, Hulegu heard news of the death of the then great khan in distant China. Immediately he set off eastwards to defend his position in the succession dispute, taking the bulk of his army with him. He gave command of the remaining 10,000 to 20,000 troops to Kitbugha, a Mongol who had adopted the Christian faith. Believing in the intrinsic superiority of his warriors, Kitbugha rather overplayed his hand. That summer a Mongol embassy arrived at Cairo demanding that Qutuz submit to the Ilkhan. The Mamluks, however, aware of Hulegu's departure, were not accommodating. The Mongol ambassadors were halved at the waist and decapitated. Their heads were nailed to the Zuwaila Gate of Cairo.

On July 25, 1260, Qutuz rode out of Cairo to take command of a combined army that may have been 100,000 strong. His forces were swelled by refugees from Syria, among them Ayyubid princes outraged at their losses, and more importantly Baybars, to whom Qutuz had guaranteed safe conduct in return for Bahri support against the Mongols. Even though the Egyptians outnumbered the Mongols 10 to one, they could not be certain of victory; for all their martial valour, the Mamluks were still only a small elite, and most of the army consisted of poorly equipped troopers and undisciplined Bedouin cavalry. Nevertheless, Baybars, as commander of the advance guard, easily defeated his opposite number at Gaza, then waited for the main Egyptian force and with it advanced up the coast of Palestine.

The Mamluks' route took them through the Crusader principalities. Although the Mongols had shown themselves to be sympathetic to Christianity, the Frankish leaders were distrustful of this new Oriental power, and chose to grant Qutuz free passage and furnish his army with supplies. It was while resting with their somewhat nervous Frankish hosts outside Acre that the Mamluks heard of Kitbugha's arrival in Galilee. Qutuz wheeled his army southeast, sending Baybars ahead with the advance force. And at Ayn Jalut the fate of the Middle East was decided.

The Battle of Ayn Jalut confirmed the Mamluks not only as the dominant force in the Middle East, masters of both Egypt and Syria, but also as champions of the faith, the last and most powerful bastion of Islam. As Qutuz followed Kitbugha's head back to Cairo, he had every reason to bask in the glory of his success. However, beside him rode a smouldering Baybars. After the battle, in which he had played an important part, Baybars' request that he be given the governorship of Aleppo or Palestine had been brusquely refused. And on October 23, his anger became bloodily manifest. While camped near to Gaza, Qutuz was slain by a group of Mamluk emirs in league with Baybars; by the account of one court chronicler, it was Baybars himself who struck the lethal blow. The ensuing debate over Qutuz' successor was ended, according to another chronicler, when one of the senior emirs declared, "He who kills the ruler should himself be ruler".

Few rulers were as ruthless as Baybars, a man of ferocious energy uninhibited by any notion of honour or scruple. During his stay at Acre, he had noticed the weakness of the Frankish stronghold and suggested to Qutuz that they capture it before tackling the Mongols — a suggestion that Qutuz, thankful for the help of the Franks, had dismissed. But at the same time Baybars was a realist, who took care to promote the interests of the Mamluks who had acclaimed him sultan. "When it pleased God to grant the advent of the sultan's reign," wrote his biographer, "he gathered the fugitives, and brought in those who were afar; he promoted those who lacked advancement, and gave office to those who had been set aside. He returned to them the possessions, wealth and favours of which they had been deprived. He appointed the deserving to emirates, and promoted the competent."

Not all his appointees were Bahri Mamluks. In many cases he was obliged to leave Qutuz' powerful supporters in office, which may have contributed to the nightmares that allegedly disturbed his sleep and the stomach upsets that troubled his digestion. So, in order to forestall a possible coup, he set up an elaborate espionage system under the control of a Mamluk official whose other functions included the supervision of the postal service and of foreign affairs. Not content with that, Baybars made it his habit to spring surprise visits on his officers and walk the streets of Cairo in disguise to discover what was being said about him. What he heard could not have been flattering. The ordinary citizens disliked the Mamluks in general because of their bullying, swaggering behaviour; and they well remembered Baybars for his leading role in the disturbances of the early 1250s. Baybars wooed them by reducing taxes, with only limited success; brave as he was, it was a couple of months before he dared ride through Cairo in public procession.

In Mamluk eyes, Baybars had earned the throne by virtue of his personal ability and the acclamation of the leading men of the realm. Nevertheless, perhaps remembering his slave origins, he sought a more formal method to legitimize his position. One way was to revive the caliphate, the supreme expression of Sunni

## The Metalsmith's Intricate Art

**As Mongol armies swept through Persia in the 1250s, Egypt and Syria played host to a horde of Muslim refugees. Among the newcomers were Persian goldbeaters and Iraqi smiths, under whose influence the art of metalworking reached new heights throughout the Mamluk empire.**

**Commissioned by the wealthy Turkish elite to produce high-quality luxury items, these craftsmen vied with each other to make ever larger and more impressive pieces, most commonly of brass inlaid with precious metals. Using mineral ore that was imported chiefly from Europe, artisans cast the decorative objects, then carved grooves and hollows into which were hammered inlays of gold, silver or niello — a sulphur compound mixed with silver, lead or copper. Abstract arabesque patterns and calligraphy featured prominently in their decoration, and although some Muslims disapproved of artists portraying living things, the shapes of men, animals and monsters were also used to adorn the finished masterpiece.**

Inlaid with gold, silver and niello, this costly brass penbox was possibly commissioned by a high-ranking official in the Mamluk chancery. Carried under the waistband, it would have contained all the tools of a scribe's trade — reed pens, threads for cleaning the reeds, ink, and sand for blotting.

Muslim unity and legality. Theoretically, the caliph was the figurehead to whom all sultans owed their allegiance, and from whom they derived their right to rule. Since the last Abbasid caliph had been killed by the Mongols, Baybars was obliged to find a new spiritual leader. He discovered a man who claimed to be an uncle of the last reigning caliph and brought him to Cairo, where his name was mentioned in public prayers and stamped on the state coinage. To Baybars' anger, however, the caliph proved less pliant than he had imagined, so he dispatched him on a deliberately under-equipped expedition to retake Baghdad from the Mongols. The caliph and his followers were slaughtered almost to a man. The Sultan lost little time in investing a new caliph who also claimed Abbasid kinship, and placed him under dignified house arrest, only bringing him out on ceremonial occasions.

But while the caliph remained innocuously in the background, Baybars' chief religious counsellor, Shaykh Khadir al-Mihrani, revelled iniquitously in his position. A professed mystic, he had fled his native Iraq to evade a noble who wished to castrate him for sleeping with his daughter. In Aleppo, he aroused the wrath of his conquests' male relatives and moved to Damascus, where Baybars, then still an emir, fell under his influence. As sultan, Baybars came to rely on the advice and predictions of Khadir, who used his position to divert money intended for the Sultan into his own coffers. In 1263, some of Egypt's most powerful men pressed for his trial on the grounds of embezzlement, unlawful fornication and sodomy. Found guilty, he escaped the death penalty by prophesying that the Sultan's death would follow closely on his own, and was sentenced to life imprisonment.

Among Khadir's unsavoury acts was the instigation of pogroms and riots against Jewish and Christian subjects — ostensibly as part of the jihad, or holy war, that Baybars declared on all unbelievers, but in reality for loot. Under the Fatimids and

**Adorned with a double-headed eagle, this brass and silver pomander would have contained strongly scented ambergris. Similar, though slightly smaller, spheres were produced for use as handwarmers, containing trays of burning charcoal that was supported on gimbals.**

the Ayyubids, Jews and Christians had lived in relative peace with their Muslim masters, and many had become important and wealthy members of the administration. Now, under the Mamluks, their position took a distinct turn for the worse. The Christians in particular were associated with the Mongols, who not only used Christian auxiliaries in their army, but when sacking cities often spared Christians in preference to Muslims. And both Jews and Christians aroused popular jealousy for their prominent civil posts. Often this ire manifested itself in protests and lynch mobs. At such times, the Mamluks chose to appease the majority, rather than to protect the threatened minorities. The Christians were forced to wear blue turbans and belts, the Jews yellow; both were forbidden to ride horses or mules in the towns; and churches and synagogues were sacked or shut down. Many Christians were dismissed from their offices for refusing to convert to Islam. However, both religious communities managed to survive, despite this persecution, because the Mamluks relied heavily on their bureaucratic skills and wealth.

Aside from the persecution of Jews and Christians, Baybars extended his jihad to Muslims, expressing his religious zeal in campaigns to purge immoral behaviour – which he defined to include prostitution, hashish eating, beer drinking and wearing immodest dress. The main targets of his holy war, however, were military, rather than spiritual foes – the Mongols, the Crusader magnates of the Levant, and the Assassins, who still terrorized Syria. Besides these enemies of Sunni Islam, Baybars was also determined to smash the power of the surviving Ayyubid princes in Syria.

During his 17-year reign he went a long way towards achieving all these goals. By a combination of force and treachery he brought the Ayyubids to heel and subdued the Assassins. He did not entirely dissolve the order, however; from now on they were to work for him. In addition, in a series of bloody campaigns he reduced

**One of the masterpieces of Islamic art, this basin's gold and silver inlay depicts Mamluk emirs and royal servants out hunting. The sultan himself is not shown – possibly because the political instability of the time prompted the artist to omit a potentially short-lived ruler.**

the Crusader presence to a few footholds on the coast. His most telling victory, and his most brutal, was the sack of Antioch in 1268, which fell after more than 150 years of rule by the Norman house of Hauteville. When his army breached the walls and poured in, he ordered the gates to be shut so that none of the inhabitants could escape. Most were massacred in the streets; the rest were taken for slaves – so many that the bottom virtually dropped out of the market. Four years later, when the English prince Edward landed at Acre to campaign in Palestine in conjunction with the Mongols, Baybars employed an Assassin disguised as a native Christian to stab him with a poisoned dagger. The Prince was seriously ill for some months, and left Palestine as soon as he had recovered, never to return.

For all his ferocity, Baybars was an astute diplomat. In 1261 he made an alliance with Berke Khan, leader of the Mongol Golden Horde. Based in Russia, the Golden Horde had inherited the northwestern quarter of Chingis' empire, but after a dispute over the succession of the Great Khan in Mongolia, had become increasingly hostile to the Ilkhan Mongols; more importantly, for Baybars, they controlled the Kipchak steppe where most Mamluks were recruited. To ensure the safe passage of slaves through the Bosporus, Baybars also struck an agreement with the ruler of Byzantium, Michael VIII, who controlled the route. And he came to a mutually profitable arrangement with the Genoese, the main slave-shipping agents, and with the Venetians, the Sultan's chief suppliers of war materials.

While strengthening his position abroad, Baybars also found the time for internal consolidation, reorganizing the army, rebuilding the navy, strengthening forts, digging canals and improving the major harbours. Superb communications were the key to control of his empire. His two capitals, Damascus and Cairo, were linked by a mounted postal service that took only four days to relay mail the 650 kilometres that separated them. From all the cities and towns of his empire mail reached Cairo twice a week, and urgent news was dispatched by carrier pigeons. Flying in relays between homing lofts, the birds delivered most messages within a day. Whenever a carrier pigeon – perfumed if it brought good news – arrived at its loft in the citadel, Baybars was notified immediately, even if he was at the dinner table or on the polo field. The speediest pigeons with the best pedigrees could fetch up to 700 gold dinars, about three kilograms of gold – more than Baybars had cost his first master.

With his empire running so efficiently, Baybars felt confident enough to launch his most ambitious campaign. It was to be his last. Early in his reign, he had been requested by the exiled sultan of Rum to help him win back his realm, which had been a Mongol protectorate since 1243. In the spring of 1277, Baybars took up the invitation, and invaded Asia Minor. He heavily defeated a Mongol army in the frontier region of Elbistan, then swung west and occupied Caesarea, where he had himself crowned sultan. His reign was short, though, for he was unable to enlist sufficient local support to take on a second Mongol army, sent by the Ilkhan to expel him, and he was obliged to retreat to Damascus, abandoning his new subjects to the wrath of the Mongols. That June he was taken sick after drinking koumiss – according to one account, a poisoned draught that he had intended for someone else. He lingered on for 13 days and died on June 20.

By its very nature, the Mamluk system discouraged hereditary succession. Mamluk status, after all, could not be inherited. Sons of emancipated Mamluks grew up to be Arabic-speaking Muslims, with Arabic rather than Turkish names. Although the military rulers regarded them more highly than native Egyptians, these sons were effectively assimilated into the local culture. They could pursue a military career if they wished, but only in the broad body of troops of free birth, whose senior officers were almost entirely Mamluk emirs. Moreover, it was virtually impossible for the son of a Mamluk to establish the military and economic base from which he could mount a bid for the throne; the sultan rarely consented to let him inherit his father's personal slave corps or his royal gift of *iqta,* a grant conferring the right to the income derived from a certain piece of land, but not ownership of the land itself. Many rulers naturally attempted to ensure the succession of their sons, but unless the sons were both strong and capable of mustering popular Mamluk support, their reigns were short-lived. In general, the Mamluk sultans were drawn from the ranks of first-generation foreign slaves.

Trained and educated in an environment where martial ability was everything, the Mamluks brought their barrack-room principles to politics. If a Mamluk aspired to supreme power, he had simply to make himself stronger than the incumbent sultan. As a result, factions formed like bubbles in a boiling pot, and often the pot would overflow in a bloody coup. The Mamluk political arena became littered with the corpses of deposed sultans, whose average rule lasted a mere five years.

Yet in spite of this quick turnover of rulers, the system in some ways promoted administrative stability. Politics and ideology scarcely ever entered into Mamluk succession struggles; rival candidates were not competing to change the system, only to control it. And while the Men of the Pen — native administrators who ran the day-to-day affairs of the country — might be discomfited by the violent methods of these Men of the Sword, they acknowledged with gratitude their firm government. Some even saw the benign providence of God in the coming of these aliens who had saved Egypt and Syria from the Mongols. In an age when most countries suffered the disruption of hereditary rule, which produced incompetent monarchs as often as it produced the great and the good, Mamluk society enjoyed the benefit of being a meritocracy — albeit a meritocracy dominated by the most ruthless.

Accordingly, it took just two years after Baybars' death for disaffected Bahri factions to overthrow the son he had appointed as his successor. In November 1279, following three months of political horse-trading, they chose as his replacement a senior and respected emir, Qalawun. Like Baybars, Qalawun was a Kipchak Turk; the two had been born around the same year, making Qalawun nearly 60 when he became sultan. He had not been enslaved until his late twenties, and as a result had never fully mastered Arabic. Tall, thick-necked and broad-shouldered, he was nicknamed al-Alfi, "the thousander" — a reference to the fact that he had cost his first master the exceptionally high price of 1,000 gold dinars. He had come into al-Salih Ayyub's possession during the last years of the Sultan's life, and fled to Syria with Baybars after the murder of their commander. More cautious than Baybars, he was just as ruthless, and equally unpopular with the Egyptians. When he finally dared to ride in procession through his capital, the crowds pelted him with offal.

Soon after ascending to the throne, he purged Baybars' private entourage, then launched an attack on Sunqur al-Ashqar, an emir who had taken advantage of the factional infighting following Baybars' death to declare himself ruler of Damascus. Sunqur's army was no match for Qalawun's, and after a heavy defeat on June 21, 1280, he fled to northern Syria. From there he apparently appealed for aid to the Mongol Ilkhan of Persia, one of whose tribeswomen he had married. The Mongols

# INSIGNIA OF IDENTITY

Although bitter foes, the Mamluks and Western Crusaders enjoyed a two-way exchange of trade and culture. One product of this mutual influence was the spread of distinguishing insignia to denote title or ownership. Originated by the Crusaders as a means of identifying different groups of heavily-armoured knights, these insignia then developed into Western heraldry – the hereditary use of distinctive devices on shields, surcoats and banners.

In Europe a complex system of rules developed on such matters as which colours could be placed upon others and how the shields could be divided and quartered. Colleges of heralds were established to adjudicate on such matters, and also to judge between individuals who claimed the same device as their own.

In the Middle East, Muslim warriors soon adopted the designs and the colours of Western heraldry. The fleur-de-lys, for instance, emblem of both French royalty and the Virgin Mary, was sported in the Middle East as the *faransiya*, or Frankish symbol, while lions and eagles, representative of power and dominion, adorned the property of Muslims and Christians alike.

Lance-bearing Christian forces face a Muslim army in an illustration of the Second Crusade in 1147 to 1148. The fleur-de-lys, sported here by the French king, Louis, was adopted almost at the same time by his opponent, the ruler of Aleppo.

In tournaments, as in war, a skilful knight could be identified by his heraldic device. But fighting aside, heraldry found acceptance in the West as a means of distinguishing titles and identifying property: seals bearing a noble's coat of arms carried all the authority of a signature; heraldic devices on tombstones indicated the identity of the incumbent; and a person's ancestry could be divined by close inspection of his arms.

A 13th-century miniature of a chivalric joust shows four knights and their steeds, all bearing distinctive rosettes — a device popular with both Muslims and Christians.

Used to authenticate deeds, this seal shows a knight whose shield displays the arms of Robert Fitzwalter, a prominent English crusader.

Made around the end of the 13th century, this casket bears the enamelled devices of its owner, the English earl of Pembroke.

As in Europe, Mamluk emirs and sultans used distinguishing insignia to indicate rank or title. Sometimes a Mamluk emir chose his own emblem, sometimes it was conferred on him by the sultan. Baybars, for example, granted a Mamluk who had distinguished himself at the siege of Antioch in 1268 the right to bear the arms of the city's defeated constable. Quite often a Mamluk's blazon reflected his official post at the sultan's court. Due to the non-hereditary nature of Mamluk succession, however, and a devastating invasion by the Ottoman Turks, the use of such insignia died out in the 16th century.

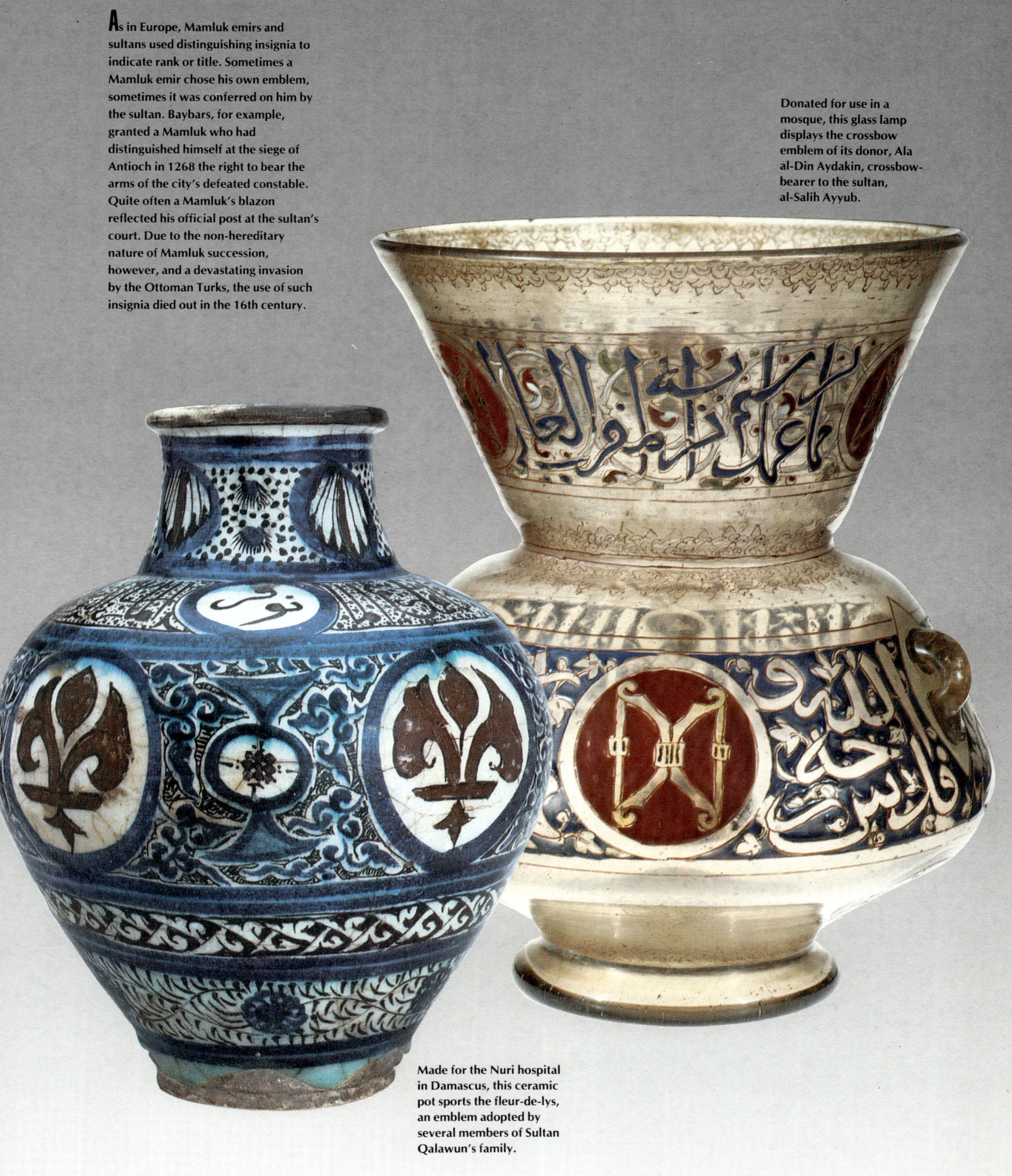

Donated for use in a mosque, this glass lamp displays the crossbow emblem of its donor, Ala al-Din Aydakin, crossbow-bearer to the sultan, al-Salih Ayyub.

Made for the Nuri hospital in Damascus, this ceramic pot sports the fleur-de-lys, an emblem adopted by several members of Sultan Qalawun's family.

were only too pleased to exploit the Muslim rift, and in 1281 the Ilkhan's brother rode into Syria at the head of 50,000 Mongols, in addition to 30,000 Armenian, Georgian and Turkish auxiliaries, with the full expectation of supplementing this force with Sunqur's Syrian rebels. While the population of Damascus prayed for deliverance from the Mongols, Qalawun camped outside the Syrian town of Homs, and waited for the invaders. Among his troops were those of Sunqur, who had been persuaded to change his allegiance with the promise of land in northern Syria.

In size and quality, the armies that faced each other outside Homs on October 29, 1281, were roughly equal. They also adopted a similar battle order; both sides placed their best troops in the centre and their auxiliaries on the wings. In the fray, the Mamluk right triumphed over the Mongol left, while the Mongol right inflicted a similar defeat on the Mamluk left. Amid all the confusion both sides imagined that they had lost the day. But at this critical moment, a senior Mamluk emir galloped to the Mongol centre, calling out that he was a deserter. Brought before the Mongol leader, he drew his sword and managed to wound him before being hacked down. Encouraged by this bravery, the Mamluks launched an all-out attack that broke the Mongols' nerve and scattered them in a hectic retreat across the Euphrates. By sunset, Qalawun was master of the field. But the cost had been very heavy. Although one chronicler was probably exaggerating when he reported that a mere 500 of Qalawun's horsemen had survived, the histories of the time were certainly littered with obituaries of dead officers and notable civilian volunteers who had perished in the bloody fray.

Qalawun's intention had been to drive the Crusaders out of the Holy Land after he had dealt with the Mongols, but first he had to rebuild his army. He did this so diligently that by the end of his 10-year reign his personal corps of Mamluks numbered as many as 12,000 – more than any other Mamluk sultan possessed either before or after, and possibly as many as one third of the total number of military slaves then in service throughout Egypt and Syria. It may have been Qalawun's pressing need for slaves, as well as a desire to keep the dominant Turkish element in check, that made him recruit Mamluks from beyond the Kipchak steppes – mainly Circassians from the eastern coastlands of the Black Sea. Most of these were organized in an elite corps consisting of 300 emirs and 3,000 other ranks stationed in the citadel and therefore known as the Burjis, or Mamluks "of the tower".

Although recruited from a different region, these new Mamluks fitted easily into the established military organization of the Turks. Indeed, so numerous were Qalawun's new recruits that they soon occupied every important post in the strict

**Arab traders haggle over the price of black slaves in a picture illustrating al-Hariri's *Maqamat*. Imported by North African slavers or captured in campaigns against Nubia to the south, such unfortunates were a common sight in Mamluk slave markets, where sultans and emirs purchased them as domestic servants or, less frequently, as military instructors or even harem guards. Gang warfare, which often broke out between such slaves and young Mamluks, was a major civic problem in medieval Cairo.**

Mamluk hierarchy. At the top were the members of the Sultan's personal corps, dominated by the two *naibs*, or vice-regents, who governed Egypt and Syria in his absence. Other senior officers of this guard included the Head Chamberlain, in charge of screening and presenting visitors; the Emir of Weapons, responsible for the armoury; and the Emir of the Stables. Outside the narrow elite of the household unit, there was a large body of emirs ranked according to the number of Mamluks under their command – from emirs of a hundred, down to emirs of five.

According to his rank, each Mamluk received certain perquisites from his master. Senior emirs who maintained their own Mamluk establishments were given grants of land tax at the sultan's discretion, donations of money and horses before a campaign, and gifts on the accession of a sultan who wanted their support. In turn, some of this money was passed on to the junior Mamluks as pay and rations.

More ostentatious signs of favour were also bestowed; government regulations laid down in detail the type of ceremonial uniform each rank was entitled to wear. Emirs of a hundred were invested with sumptuous robes of red and yellow satin, embroidered with gold thread and trimmed with fur. They wore turbans of muslin ornamented with strips of silk, and gold belts inset with precious stones, and they carried swords in gold-inlaid scabbards. An emir who had won royal approbation might be given a horse with an ornate harness and saddlery prepared by a special court official. Officers of lower ranks wore robes sewn from multicoloured bands and bordered with a gold fringe. The colourful uniforms distinguished all Mamluks from the civilian notables, who usually wore white or black.

Emirs with at least 40 men under their command had the right to maintain a small orchestra, consisting mainly of percussionists, to encourage their men on the battlefield – many Crusader chroniclers wrote of the terrible and intimidating cacophony made by a Mamluk army as it attacked. Nor was the racket restricted to wartime; as audible proof of his exaltation, the emir was entitled to have the band assembled to play outside his house at sunset.

Although Qalawun's own men filled all the important military posts, the threat of a coup was nevertheless ever present. Accordingly, Qalawun took pains to train his Mamluks thoroughly and promote them slowly, and he was careful to move his Syrian vice-regents from post to post to prevent them from establishing an independent power base. During Qalawun's visits to Syria, Egypt was governed by his son, acting with his vice-regent and according to stringent guidelines which were to form the basis for most subsequent Mamluk administrations. The whole of Cairo was patrolled by armed police, with special attention devoted to the area round the citadel, and local governors ensured that the populace travelled only by day. Troops dispatched to join the Sultan in Syria were sped on their way by the issue of special *laissez-passer* documents. The Bedouin of the Nile Delta were detailed to provide horses for use by the postal service, and regular contact with Damascus was maintained by pigeon post. In addition, the Christian merchants in Alexandria were locked in their caravanserais at night, and at midday on Fridays, to prevent a surprise coup while most Muslims were at prayer.

The cost of maintaining this administrative machinery and financing the army was vast, and to meet the expense the sultan looked to his three main sources of income: taxation, tribute and trade. The chief source of tax revenue was the *iqta*. In Ayyubid times, the revenue from one sixth of the cultivable land had formed the royal treasury, with that of five twelfths allotted for the maintenance of the

Mamluk emirs' establishments, and the rest going to the army of freeborn soldiers. By the early 14th century, the Mamluk sultans had more than doubled their share to over five twelfths, effectively concentrating the wealth of the state in their hands.

War booty and tribute from weaker neighbours also swelled the sultans' coffers. After the battle of Homs, for example, King Leo II of Armenia, an ally of the defeated Mongols, bought a peace treaty from Qalawun at the cost of an annual tribute of half a million Armenian silver dirhams, payable in advance, in addition to 25 horses, 25 mules and 10,000 horseshoes with nails — this last a desirable commodity in mineral-poor Egypt. Other clauses specified that Leo should release all Muslim merchants and prisoners, and that he should put no obstacles in the way of slavers bringing their youthful merchandise to the Sultan.

Similar considerations prompted Qalawun to issue a proclamation in 1288 giving safe conduct to the Genoese sea traders who shipped slaves from the Crimea and who shared with the Venetians the lucrative trade in spices that were purchased on the Egyptian market. Brought in by traders from countries such as Ceylon and India, spice was exported to Europe in vast quantities, along with commodities such as silk, linen and aromatic woods; in turn, the Egyptians imported copper, for resale at a handsome profit to the Indians. The huge prices and heavy duties that the Sultan imposed on spices contributed greatly to his financial resources, and the wealthy corporation of Muslim merchants who handled the trade provided a convenient source of money when he was short of funds.

Most of the sultan's income was earmarked for the military establishment. The stables alone cost a fortune to maintain. One 14th-century sultan had 7,800 horses, most of which were detailed for the use of his Mamluks, as well as 30,000 sheep, which helped provision the army, and large herds of camels, which were used as military baggage animals. However, this outlay was not at the expense of home comforts: pedigree racing camels sped ice from the Lebanese mountains to cool the sultan's drinks, and large sums were lavished on polo, hunting and hawking.

In addition the Mamluks heavily patronized the arts, and their era witnessed a flourishing of Islamic culture. Metalwork and glasswork both reached new heights, and on a far larger scale the Mamluks established many mosques, colleges, and retreats for Sufis — Islamic mystics, who commanded much popular respect. From Qalawun's reign, such buildings were usually built in local limestone, which withstood decay far better than the brickwork of their predecessors, and lent itself to carved decoration. Much of this building work was carried out by immigrants from Iraq and Asia Minor, who had fled from the Mongols and who, by the end of the 13th century, had helped push Cairo's population to about 500,000, making it the largest city outside China, and five times as populous as any in Europe.

Like Baybars before him, Qalawun continued to cherish the idea of driving the Crusaders out of the Holy Land. In 1289 he went some way towards that dream by exploiting differences between Venice and Genoa to take the busy port of Tripoli. The immense amount of booty he gained thereby served to spur his ambition, and in the last years of his reign he set his sights on Acre, the last of the Franks' capitals, and their greatest port. To protect his flanks during the attack on Tripoli, Qalawun had made a treaty with Acre, designed to last 10 years, 10 months and 10 days — but a pretext for breaking it came to hand in August, 1290. In that month a rabble of newly arrived Italian Crusaders ran riot through the city, killing everyone they took to be a Muslim. When the Sultan's envoys arrived and called for the guilty men to be sent to Cairo, some counsellors advised that all the Christians held in Acre's gaols should be handed over to them. Public opinion would not allow it, however, and the ambassadors returned to Qalawun empty-handed.

Qalawun was delighted, and at once mobilized his army to avenge the outrage. He was to be denied the satisfaction; on November 5, 1290, while camped outside Cairo, the 70-year-old sultan was taken ill with a fever. He died five days later.

It seemed to the inhabitants of Acre that they were saved. Given the factionalism of the Mamluks, it was probable that their energies would be diverted to the succession struggle — especially since Qalawun's eldest son and heir had died shortly before his father, leaving as the likely claimant a younger brother, Khalil, whom the Sultan had openly disliked. Rumour had it that Khalil had poisoned his brother, and Qalawun had repeatedly refused to sign the decree appointing the young man as his heir, insisting, "I will not set Khalil over the Muslims".

Within two days of Qalawun's death, however, Khalil had seized the throne, dashing the Crusaders' hopes and confounding the wishes of Qalawun. He had planned well in advance and amassed considerable support through his martial prowess. Even by Mamluk standards he was noted for his horsemanship, archery and skill in the conduct of war. Khalil spent the winter of 1290 securing his position in Egypt by eliminating the most serious of his rivals, and distributing their wealth to other potential opponents. Meanwhile, preparations for the assault on Acre continued under his officers. In total, nearly 100 siege engines had been constructed by the time the Sultan led his army out of Cairo in March.

By April 6, 1291, the siege was prepared. Though the chroniclers probably exaggerated the Mamluks' numbers, talking of some 60,000 cavalry and 160,000 infantry, the Islamic army dwarfed the defence forces, which amounted to no more than 1,000 knights and sergeants, about 14,000 foot soldiers, and 30,000 to 40,000 civilians. Even so, a Mamluk victory was not a foregone conclusion, since Acre occupied a peninsula with its back to the sea and its one landward side protected by a triple line of walls and strong towers. Moreover the defenders, who represented nearly all the crusading powers except Genoa, knew they were fighting for their lives, and buried old differences. The Muslims, however, were weakened by mistrust between Khalil and his Syrian vice-regent, who attempted to desert the siege.

Day after day the great mangonels showered the walls with jars of Greek fire, a highly combustible concoction whose exact components are unknown. As many as a thousand sappers tried to undermine the fortifications while the defenders poured

**Heedless of a ploughman toiling in the background, picnicking literati in a manuscript illustration find pleasure in debating points of grammar. The richness of the Arabic language encouraged cultured citizens to indulge in pastimes such as word games, riddles and versifying. At a more popular level, professional storytellers set up their pitches in markets and other public places, where they attracted audiences eager to hear tales of magic, romance and bawdy comedy.**

# CAIRO'S PALACE OF HEALING

Built under the patronage of Sultan Qalawun, the Mansuri Maristan in Cairo was the most sophisticated medical centre of its time. While suffering from a serious fever in the Nuri hospital at Damascus, Qalawun had vowed to construct an even better institution at Cairo. Once he had recovered, he did not forget his promise. Work on the new hospital was started in 1284, and with the aid of labour that was press-ganged off the streets Qalawun's great dream was realized in the short space of only 11 months.

Extravagantly funded, the hospital complex comprised a college mosque and a school for orphans besides incomparable medical facilities. In addition to the convalescent ward shown here, there were separate wards for the treatment of fevers, eye diseases, surgical cases, dysentery and insanity. The hospital was also equipped with its own laboratories, dispensaries, baths, kitchens, storerooms, and a lecture theatre where the chief of medical staff gave instruction. Fragrant herbs were strewn all over the floor in accordance with the doctors' belief that good air was essential to their patients' well-being, and a natural spring was canalized through the building to cool the atmosphere. All treatment was completely free of charge, and the patients' suffering was alleviated by professional musicians, who played instruments to entertain them, and 50 men who read the Koran day and night.

down retaliatory fire, and struck back with their own catapults at the Mamluks' siege weapons. A young Syrian prince, Ismail Abu al-Fida, wrote an account of the action: "They brought up a ship carrying a mangonel which fired on us and our tents from the direction of the sea. This caused us distress until one night there was a violent storm of wind, so that the vessel was tossed on the waves, and the mangonel it was carrying broke." For as long as possible the Franks kept the gates open and fought outside them; when they were forced to close them, they made sallies by night. In the words of Ismail, "The Franks . . . surprised the troops and put the sentries to flight. They got through to the tents and became entangled in the ropes. One of their knights fell into an emir's latrine and was killed there. The troops rallied against them and the Franks fell back routed to the town."

One by one the towers of the outer wall were undermined and abandoned. On May 16 the Mamluks forced their way through, driving the defenders back behind the inner wall. On May 18, 1291, the Sultan ordered a general assault on the city. "When the Muslims stormed it," reported Ismail, "some of its inhabitants took flight in ships. Inside the town were a number of towers holding out like citadels. A great mass of Franks entered them and fortified themselves. The Muslims slew and took an uncountable amount of booty from Acre. Then the Sultan demanded the surrender of all who were holding out in the towers, and not one held back. The Sultan gave the command and they were beheaded around Acre to the last man. Then at his command the city of Acre was demolished and razed to the ground."

Worried that the fall of Acre would provoke another Crusade, as its capture by Saladin had done more than a century earlier, Khalil ordered the destruction of all the remaining Frankish possessions that could provide a potential springboard for reprisal. Tyre, Sidon, Beirut and Haifa, together with the Templar castles of Athlit and Tortosa, were taken and the land round them laid waste. Thus ended nearly 200 years of Crusader rule in the Holy Land.

The fall of Acre and the destruction of the Crusader threat was the signal for a new round of Mamluk infighting to begin. The next 20 years saw a succession of six sultans, the political philosophy of whom was perhaps best summed up by the sultan Salar, whose stated aim was "Have him for dinner before he has you for breakfast". Salar's end was also symptomatic of the period; he was starved to death, ending up eating his own excrement.

Not until 1310 was there any respite. In that year al-Nasur Muhammad, a son of Qalawun, came to the throne. His 30-year reign was a period of relative stability, but after he died in 1340 violence resumed, with open warfare between Circassian and Turkish elements. As the Mamluks' factionalism increased, their quality as soldiers declined. Traditional fighting skills were neglected, and little attempt was made to introduce the new developments of firearms and gunpowder.

Meanwhile, the population of the Mamluk lands was reduced by a series of plagues that also devastated the economy. With villages deserted and agricultural land reverting to waste, the *iqta* revenue shrank in the late 15th century to a quarter of the level it had been at the beginning of the Mamluk regime. Government interference in commerce, native tribal revolts and, from 1500 on, fierce Portuguese competition for the Indian spice trade helped further impoverish the empire.

Yet for all the evidence of decline, the Mamluks hung grimly on to power until the second decade of the 16th century. They were finally overcome not by internal divisions but by a rival Muslim power: the Ottomans of Asia Minor.

# THE MAKING OF A MANUSCRIPT

Thirteenth-century Europe discovered an insatiable thirst for knowledge. Universities were founded across the continent, from Oxford and Cambridge in England to those in Paris and the Spanish city of Salamanca. Hordes of students – some as young as 14 years – flocked to the new academic centres to pursue scholastic careers that could span many years and several different countries. The widening audience for learning in turn created an increased demand for information in the form of the written word.

Manuscripts – literally, copies "written by hand" – of religious and classical texts had been produced by monks in Europe since before the fifth century for their own study and worship, but now there was a need for a much wider range of texts. Workshops were established in such cities as Paris, Oxford and Bologna in order to publish newly written treatises on logic, astronomy, law, mathematics and music; wealthy individuals could commission books to be made for them, such as grand Psalters and the increasingly popular volumes of personal devotions known as Books of Hours.

Improved production methods helped to meet the demand. Using fine quality parchment and new, angular Gothic lettering that replaced the larger, rounded Romanesque script, bookmakers produced single-volume editions of the Bible – such as the one shown below, measuring only 138 by 83 millimetres. Such volumes were small enough to be carried by mendicant Dominican and Franciscan friars on their travels. The flourishing booksellers of Paris made the recently discovered texts of Aristotle and the works of the prolific Dominican theologian, Thomas Aquinas, quickly available to the public.

Although speed and quantity were important factors in this developing industry, the medieval manuscript was not simply a utilitarian object. The skills of professional parchment-makers, scribes, artists and bookbinders took years to acquire, and were employed with justified pride. The manuscript was one of the main outlets for the creative talents of the time, and could be just as precious in its own right as the knowledge it transmitted.

# CONSTRUCTING A BOOK

An array of specialist skills were used in the production of a manuscript. First, the parchment (vellum) was made by soaking animal skins – cow or sheep for preference – in running water for several days, followed by lengthy immersion in lime and water. Hairs were scraped off, the soaking repeated, and the skins stretched on frames to dry in the sun. The parchment-maker finished by cleaning the skins with pumice and water.

The parchment was folded into leaves and trimmed to size before writing began. The leaves were then assembled into "gatherings" – standard units, usually eight, 12 or 16 pages – and stitched together by binders. These illustrations, from a mid-13th-century German Bible, show the stages involved in bringing a manuscript to readiness for binding.

A scribe would laboriously transcribe the text from a model manuscript, known as an exemplar, hired from public stationers. Poorer students were able to hire unbound exemplars, one gathering at a time, and make their own copies; the rich could commission entire manuscripts ready illuminated and bound. The accuracy of stationers' exemplars was regularly checked by university authorities to prevent the proliferation of mistakes, which could easily be made during copying.

A parchment-maker offers a sample of his wares to a monk, who examines it for holes and stains. During its preparation, the parchment was stretched across a wooden frame of the type shown in this picture. The curved knife at the foot of the frame was used to remove hairs from the skin.

Having folded the parchment into leaves of the required size and assembled these into sheaves or "gatherings", a scribe trims the edges with a ruler and knife. By the end of the 13th century, scribes were able to buy their parchment ready trimmed and conveniently packaged in boxes.

With his quill and knife poised above the parchment and an inkhorn at his side, a scribe prepares to write between the guidelines he has ruled. The knife was to sharpen the quill, to scratch out mistakes and to hold the page flat while writing. Gaps were left for the coloured chapter and page headings and the initials, which would be filled in at a later stage according to instructions written by the scribe in pale ink beside the text.

Guiding his right hand with his left, an artist paints the head of a man with colours selected from the palette beside his seat. The pigments were ground and then mixed with a binding medium of gelatin, gum or egg, which gave them a permanent lustre.

ORIGINAL TEXT

GLOSS

MINIATURE

RUBRICATED HEADING

ILLUMINATED INITIAL

ANNOTATION

DECORATED CAPITAL

The eye-catching variety and complexity which the format of a manuscript could accommodate is illustrated in this page from Pope Gregory IX's *Decretals*, official papal and episcopal letters with the status of Church Law. The original text – concerning marriage – is in black, surrounded by the paler script of the "gloss", or commentary, explaining and interpreting the main passage; annotations have been squeezed into available gaps. Probably written in Bologna, the chief source of legal textbooks, the decorative illumination was added later in France to appeal to the local market.

# DESIGNING A PAGE

The arrangement of the text and decorative effects on a manuscript page were carefully calculated both to enhance its visual appeal and to aid the reader's understanding. The columns and lettering of the text itself were aligned within a precisely measured grid of guidelines. Intricately worked initials marked the beginning of books or chapters, and headings – known as rubrics – were written or accentuated in red ink.

Many of the colours used by the rubricators and illustrators were expensive and difficult to obtain. Ultramarine – literally, "from across the sea" – was ground from semiprecious lapis lazuli imported from Persia and Afghanistan; kermes, a red pigment, was made from the dried bodies of certain female insects. Economy and careful integration with the overall design of the page were important; some artists were warned by the church authorities against indulging imagination too freely, lest readers were distracted from the text.

Sicut sagitte in manu potentis: ita filii
excussorum.
Beatus vir qui implevit desiderium
suum ex ipsis: non confundetur cum
loquetur inimicis suis in porta.
Beati omnes qui timent dominū:
qui ambulant in viis eius.
Labores manuum tuarum quia mā
ducabis: beatus es et bene tibi erit.
Uxor tua sicut vitis habundans: in
lateribus domus tue.
Ecce sic benedicetur homo: qui timet
dominum.
Benedicat tibi dominus ex syon: ut
videas bona ierusalem omnibus diebus
vite tue.
Et videas filios filiorum tuorum: pacem
super israel.
Sepe expugnaverunt me a iuventute
Filii tui sicut novelle olivarum: in circuitu mē
se tue.

The bottom line of this manuscript page from a 13th-century English Psalter and Book of Hours was accidentally left out of the main body of the text during copying. The error gave the illuminator an excuse for a playful diversion: the figure wearing a blue cloak and red cap – complementing the colours of the initials and the fancifully elongated men and foxes that end the shorter lines – points out where the omitted line, which he hauls after him on a rope, should be inserted.

# ILLUMINATING THE WORD

Shimmering with gold, this full-page miniature from the 13th-century Oscott Psalter combines regal majesty with vivid human detail. The two roundels depict the Adoration and the Dream of the Magi; the disproportionately large heads of the figures and the angular folds of their clothing show the influence of French style on the anonymous English artist.

Such miniatures, blazing forth from the text of medieval manuscripts, were primarily intended as an expression of religious faith. The term "illuminated" was used to describe a gold-decorated manuscript; it suggested a text both glorified and clarified by the light reflected from the gold, and echoed Saint John's description of the Word of God as "a light that shineth in darkness, by which all things were made, and that enlighteneth every man".

But they also expressed the skills of the professionals who created them. Following the stages depicted by a present-day illuminator on the opposite page, an artist might take four days to complete a miniature similar to the one shown here.

1 A detailed drawing is made in thinned ink or pencil; then size – a primer consisting of a mixture of sugar, plaster, lead and glue – is applied with a quill to those areas to be covered with gold leaf. When it has dried, the size is carefully scraped with a sharp knife to produce a smooth surface.

2 The illuminator moistens the size with his breath, then presses on to it small sections of gold leaf. Burnishing with a piece of polished agate or a shaped animal tooth set into a handle produces a brilliant shine.

3 The basic colours are blocked in, obscuring the detail of the original drawing. The colours which are used here include orange lead oxide, ultramarine, malachite, kermes, umber and raw sienna.

4 Darker shades of the colours already applied are then used to pattern the borders and to give shape and substance to the main forms of the illustration.

5 Strong black lines define the areas of colour and essential features of the illustration, adding vitality to the almost completed picture.

6 The illuminator applies the finishing touches: fine lines and shading that give character to the faces and hair; thin white bands as well as dots and circles to enliven the border patterns and drapery. The gold leaf is punched with a pointed tool to catch the light.

# THE WEST'S EMBATTLED EMPIRE

4

In the 1230s, strange stories were circulating about Europe's most powerful ruler, the Holy Roman Emperor. It was said that he was curious about the nature of the soul: he had had a condemned man sealed into a wine barrel and slowly drowned, while he and his learned courtiers watched carefully for any sign of an escaping emanation; finding none, they concluded the soul nonexistent. Again, the Emperor had decided to settle all argument concerning the original language of mankind: he had entrusted a group of infant orphans to the care of deaf-mute nurses on an uninhabited island, and visited them a few years later to discover the outcome. But alas, a lethal outbreak of plague had ruined the imperial experiment. Some people maintained that the Emperor was not even a believer; he had been heard to say that mankind had been deceived by three impostors: Moses, Christ and Muhammad. Almost as disturbingly for a century that regarded personal hygiene as an indulgence, it was rumoured that the Emperor took a weekly bath.

The man who so shocked and fascinated his contemporaries was Frederick II, grandson of the great emperor Frederick Barbarossa and the third successive member of the south German Hohenstaufen family to have held the imperial throne. Ruling a realm that stretched over much of central Europe, he boasted a title whose origins stretched back to the year 800, when the Frankish king Charlemagne had been crowned in Rome. It had been then and was still an attempt to re-create something of the glory of the original Roman Empire, whose ruins were everywhere and whose Latin tongue was still the preferred language of educated men. By Frederick's time, the emperor stood at the pinnacle of the pyramid of feudal obligations within his realm; without him the rest of the structure would have made little sense. But the empire's holiness was important, too, for it was seen as a Christian institution, directly endowed by God: legally speaking, the emperor was God's vicegerent, or deputy, and not easily subject to any lesser authority.

Yet he had a rival for the leadership of Christendom, one whose mandate was even more directly divine. The pope was Christ's vicar on earth and subject to no lesser authority whatsoever. The Church he directed stood at the heart of Western Christendom, and was the institution that gave meaning to all others. By tradition, each new emperor was crowned by the pope; zealous churchmen even claimed that it was thereby he who gave legitimacy to the secular monarch. This view was controversial; but most people agreed that at the very least cooperation between pope and emperor was essential to the wellbeing of Christendom as a whole.

In practice, though, cooperation was not always easy to attain. Since the 11th century, the pope and emperor had spent more time in conflict than they had in cooperation. The 13th century was to see the disagreements escalate to new levels of bitterness, culminating in internecine warfare. The struggle would cast a dark

**Braced for battle in helmet, chainmail and sleeveless tunic, this 13th-century German knight saw action only at medieval banquets, as a bronze *aquamanile*, or ewer. His real-life counterparts, armed with lance and lozenge-shaped shield, formed the backbone of an imperial task force, with which Frederick II was able to control the Holy Roman Empire and challenge the authority of the papacy.**

shadow over Frederick II's reign and would end, after his death, in an apparently absolute victory for the papacy and in the literal extermination of the ancient Hohenstaufen family line. Yet the triumph would in turn cost the Church dearly; it too was a long-term loser in both power and prestige.

Such a confrontation could hardly have been foreseen during the latter decades of the 12th century, when papal fears of the emperor's political domination seemed to be on the wane. Though the territories of the emperor were vast, incorporating Germany and its principalities, Bohemia, Burgundy, Provence and northern Italy, they were too disparate and loosely governed to give him as much power as a map would indicate. The pope, by contrast, ruled directly only the modest "Patrimony of Peter" – more or less the Latium region round the city of Rome – and even there his authority was often challenged by an unruly citizenry.

To the south of Latium, however, the independent Norman kingdom of Sicily provided an effective counterbalance to imperial power. Previously a Muslim emirate, the island of Sicily had been conquered in the 11th century by a brave and unscrupulous adventurer, Roger de Hauteville of Normandy. His son, Roger II, took the title of king – his father had ruled as count – and added territories in southern Italy to his domain. From Palermo, where he kept the most splendid court in Europe, Roger ruled a kingdom of "Sicily", the *Regno*, that in fact extended as far north as Naples and Abruzzi. And although it was under Norman-style feudal

**When Frederick II became Holy Roman Emperor in 1220, he controlled the largest feudal conglomeration in Europe: lands that spread from the Baltic in the north to the Mediterranean in the south, encompassing all Germany and most of the Italian peninsula. Only the Papal States, centred round Rome, denied his authority. Eschewing the imperial homelands in Germany, Frederick chose as his base the kingdom of Sicily, where he was born and raised, turning it into the richest and most cosmopolitan state of his age.**

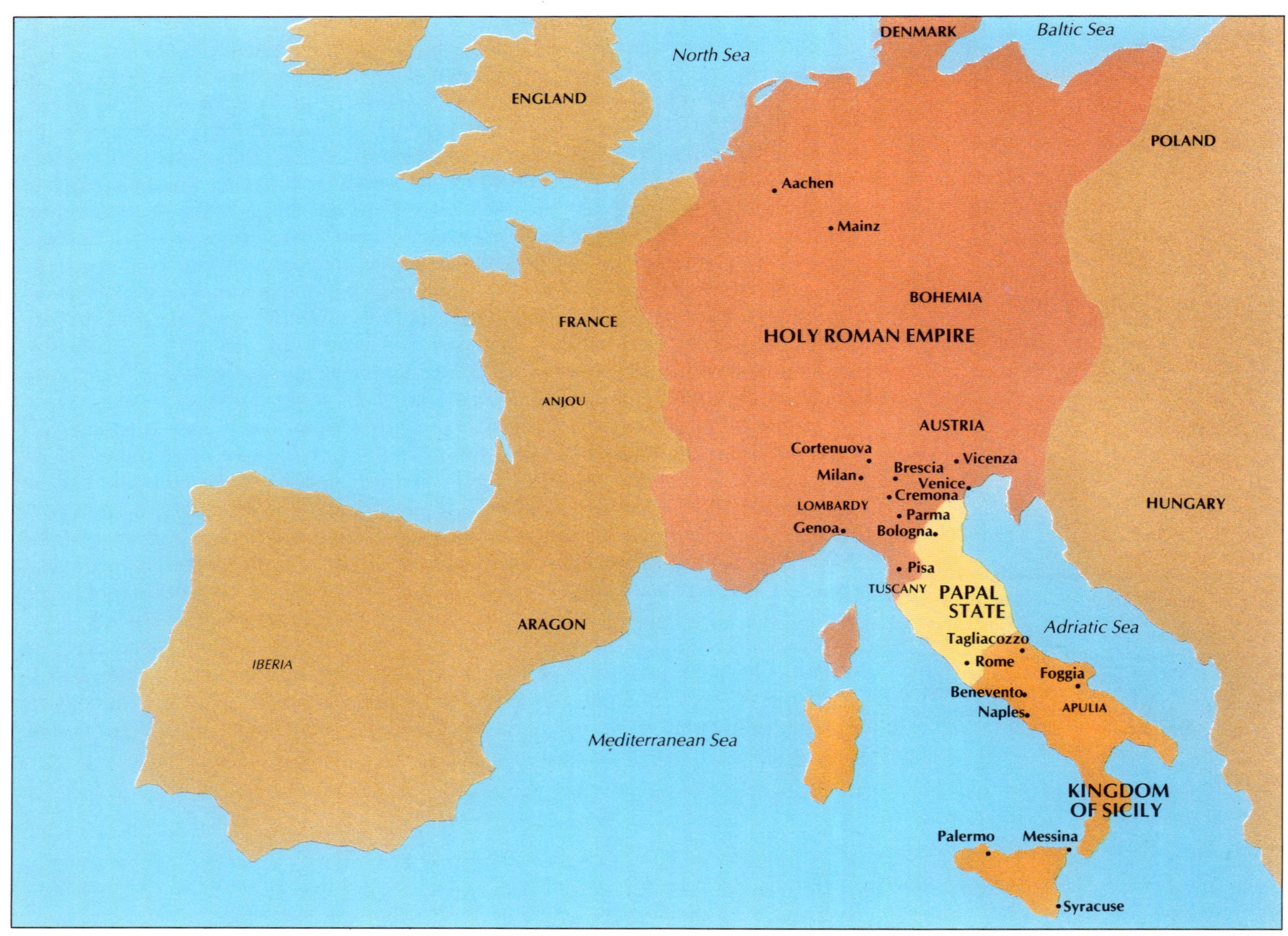

rule, this new realm embraced an open, cosmopolitan society, with an invigorating mixture of Muslim and Christian, Arab and Lombard and Greek.

From Rome's point of view, the Normans were clearly a significant improvement on their Muslim predecessors. Furthermore, they owed no allegiance to the emperor. And, after a few violent misunderstandings, the de Hauteville family came to enjoy excellent relations with the pope, who became their nominal suzerain and in turn guaranteed their possessions.

Unexpectedly, though, a fluke of dynastic succession brought a drastic change to the comfortable status quo. In 1186, Frederick Barbarossa's son, Henry, married Constance, a daughter of Roger II; four years later her nephew, the then king of Sicily, died heirless, leaving her as the principal claimant to the Sicilian throne. An illegitimate grandson of Roger disputed her title, however, and seized power. Meanwhile Barbarossa had died on crusade, and the 26-year-old Henry had been elected Holy Roman Emperor as Henry VI. At first he was too involved in German affairs to seize the opportunity presented by his wife's Sicilian claim; but in 1194 he swept into Sicily with his German knights, enforcing her title with a ruthlessness that earned him the name of Henry the Cruel. All possible rivals were put to death (one, who had died naturally shortly before, was hauled from his tomb so his corpse could be publicly beheaded) and at Christmas, 1194, Henry, in his capacity as Constance's husband, was crowned king in Palermo. With the exception of the small Papal States, the Emperor's power now embraced the entire Italian peninsula. The pope's political position was suddenly precarious.

Constance served her husband well. Not only had she presented him with a kingdom, but also, in the year of his Sicilian coronation, she gave him an heir. It was an occurrence so unexpected — Constance was 40 and had had no children in the first eight years of her marriage — that dark rumours spread of a demonic conception, but Henry was well pleased with his son, and named him Frederick after the boy's grandfather; the child may have been born in Italy (at Jesi, in the district of Ancona) but his father was determined to make a good German out of him. In 1196, he had Frederick proclaimed king of Germany at Frankfurt. The following year, he made arrangements to take the boy north for his formal coronation.

But the Emperor was not immune to the accidents of mortality that had granted him a new kingdom. On a hunting expedition on the slopes of Sicily's Mount Etna in 1197, he caught a fever, of which he died soon after. Plans for young Frederick's coronation were hastily abandoned: the bear-pit of imperial politics in Germany was no place for an infant king. The imperial succession was disputed, and the situation rapidly degenerated into a civil war that pitted Henry's brother, Philip of Swabia, against a claimant from a rival line, Otto of Brunswick, of the Welf family. The conflict between the Hohenstaufen and Welf houses was an old one. In Germany their respective battle cries had long been used to denote the opposing sides: "Welf!" denoted Otto's supporters, "Waiblingen!" — a family castle in Swabia — was the rallying cry of the Hohenstaufen loyalists. In the coming century, these war cries would move south; Italianized as "Guelph" and "Ghibelline", they would serve as party labels for years of struggle between pope and emperor.

At the time, however, it seemed to the papacy that the hand of God had saved it from imperial domination. Constance, too, was less than grief-stricken at the loss of her husband's northern possessions to civil war: she immediately ordered the expulsion of most of the German aristocrats and administrators whom Henry had brought with him to Italy, amid mass rejoicing that reached almost the level of a popular revolt. Frederick's future was now in his mother's hands: he would grow up as a prince of Norman Sicily, not of Germany.

Frederick had lost one chance of coronation. Now Constance made up for it with another, when she had him crowned king of Sicily in 1198. But the kingdom he inherited came with a heavy political debt: ailing and insecure, Constance had entered into an alliance with the papacy shortly after Henry's death. In return for protection and support, she pledged allegiance to Rome and conceded sweeping powers to the Church. She died a mere six months after Frederick's coronation, leaving her son under the guardianship of none other than the pope himself – the newly elected Innocent III. Meanwhile the *Regno* was to be run during Frederick's minority by men nominated by Innocent.

Henry would have been horrified, the more so since Innocent was a fervent exponent of the doctrine of papal supremacy. Moreover, he was well equipped with the industry, intelligence, political shrewdness and sheer force of personality needed to turn his ambitions into reality. In the course of his pontificate, he was to bring the Church to an unsurpassed level of temporal and spiritual power. He extended the Patrimony of Peter into a substantial territory that embraced most of central Italy. He intervened in the German civil war, affirming the papal right to confirm or depose an emperor. A great jurist, he became the recognized court of appeal for all Christendom. He even forced King John of England to surrender his kingdom and receive it back by papal grace as a fief of the Church.

For the *Regno* and its child-king, Innocent was a disaster. The prolonged regency inflicted years of intrigue and near-anarchy on the land and its people. Frederick received an unhappy upbringing at the hands of various magnates, mostly in the region of Apulia, the heel of the Italian peninsula. The experience left him with a lifelong love for Apulia's gentle landscapes, and a sense of injured personal dignity. Innocent himself admitted of his ward that "the need to expound his grievances granted him eloquence at an age when most children are only babbling". Nevertheless, the boy remained under the Pope's control. He came of age officially at 14 in 1208; the following year Innocent arranged his marriage to a Spanish princess.

Almost immediately, Frederick began to show dangerous signs of independence. Despite Innocent's objections, he dismissed the last papal regent and took over the rule of the impoverished *Regno* in his own right. Then, before the Pope could do more than remonstrate, events in the Holy Roman Empire forced Innocent to give his restive pawn a dramatic promotion.

The war in Germany had at last come to an end in 1208 with the assassination of Philip of Swabia, Frederick's uncle, and the following year Innocent had crowned his rival Otto in Rome as the new emperor. As an opponent of the Hohenstaufens, Otto was ostensibly the Pope's man; but first and foremost he was emperor, and he was determined to behave like one. Mindful of Henry VI's southern triumph, Otto turned his eyes towards Sicily. Only a few months after his coronation, he led an invading army into the *Regno*.

Innocent was outraged, and excommunicated the Emperor at once. This was a powerful sanction in an age of faith, not only placing Otto's immortal soul in peril but encouraging his followers to abandon the allegiance they had sworn to him. Even so, it was not enough to change Otto's plans. Innocent needed a political as well as a spiritual counterattack. The Pope's most effective weapon would be a rival emperor in whom he could invest authority. But there were few candidates who commanded enough respect to challenge Otto seriously.

In fact, there was only one – Frederick. Powerless to resist Otto's invasion, he had a ship prepared for flight to North Africa when he was invited by German princes, with papal consent, to go north to claim his inheritance. His wife and his counsellors advised against acceptance: the risk was too great, and the papal demand that Frederick should renounce the throne of the *Regno* in favour of his newborn son, Henry, was unacceptable. But Frederick had his own ideas. In 1212, accompanied by just a handful of companions, he travelled northwards to claim his inheritance, armed with little more than the Pope's blessing and his aristocratic name.

The combination was just enough. The journey itself was difficult and dangerous; several times Frederick came close to capture by Otto or his allies. But once he reached Germany, he received substantial support. He was, for the second time, elected German king at Frankfurt in 1212, and was crowned by the archbishop of Mainz a few days later. However, the position of the "Boy from Apulia" – as he was nicknamed by friend and enemy alike – was not yet secure. It took an alliance with France, engineered by Innocent's astute diplomacy, and two more years of fighting before Otto could be reckoned as defeated. In 1215 he was officially deposed, retiring to Saxony where he could still count on local support. Frederick was crowned once more, this time in Aachen as tradition demanded; the ceremony was universally accepted as a preliminary to receiving the imperial throne itself.

Frederick owed much to Innocent, but he had to pay a high price for the Pope's support: rights and privileges that his predecessors, notably Frederick Barbarossa, had enjoyed, passed into the hands of the Church. At the moment of his coronation in 1215, though, the new emperor seemed too exalted by the high honour he had received to care. In a mood of religious enthusiasm, he vowed to take the Cross and lead a Crusade to liberate the holy places in Palestine. Politics could wait.

For Innocent, Frederick's coronation was a political triumph. He set the seal upon it in 1215, when he called the greatest assembly of prelates in Church history, the fourth Lateran Council, named for the Roman palace in which its sessions were held. The Council reaffirmed the pope's supreme authority in ecclesiastical affairs. It also confirmed Frederick's election and Otto's deposition. The conflict between papacy and empire appeared to be over, and there was no doubt who had won.

Innocent died a few months later, in July 1216, but the proud legacy he left the Church seemed secure enough. For the next few years, relations between Frederick and Innocent's successor, Honorius III, were excellent, although the first signs of imperial backsliding on key promises were already apparent. Despite his oath to Innocent, Frederick remained king of Sicily. Far from replacing his father on the throne in Palermo, young Henry was taken north to be proclaimed duke of Swabia, an ancient Hohenstaufen title, then, at the age of eight, he was crowned in his father's place as German king; power was vested in successive regents during his minority. Honorius, a deeply religious man and no politician, let this pass. He was more concerned with another promise: Frederick's vow to lead a Crusade.

Instead of realizing this pledge, Frederick stayed in Germany until 1220, busily imposing some sort of imperial rule on a country grown dangerously undisciplined during years of warfare. For the most part, he bought peace, paying with concessions of authority to the ecclesiastical nobility – the great archbishops – and the rising towns. He actually had little choice, since his military strength was very limited. He could consolidate his authority only by diluting it, at least temporarily.

When Frederick returned to Italy in the autumn of 1220, however, it was as loyal son of the Church. He apologized for his delay in setting off on crusade: "You will not repent, O Blessed Father," he wrote to Honorius, "of having brought up and loved a son such as I. We are ready to set ourselves at Your Holiness' feet; and soon you will have the fruit you desire from the tree you have planted." The Pope allowed himself to be soothed with promises, and in April 1220 finally consented to crown Frederick as Holy Roman Emperor.

Negotiations were simplified by disorders in Rome itself. The city's politics were extremely complex and volatile; Honorius had been forced out of the city just six months before by fear of violence following a dispute among the leading Roman families. Only the presence of Frederick's escorting army allowed him to return safely to St. Peter's Cathedral for the ceremony.

Apart from renewing his crusading vows, Frederick swore to act with an iron hand against heretics of all sorts; Germany and Italy were then troubled by the Waldensians, advocates of an austere Christianity who were deeply hostile to the showier aspects of Church life, as well as by the Cathars, believers in the intrinsic evil of the material world. In addition, he reassured the Pope by declaring his German and Sicilian dominions to be constitutionally separate. For its part, the Church recognized Frederick's personal right to both the imperial and the Sicilian crowns. It was a subtlety that would make trouble later, but when Frederick left a subdued Rome to return to his long-abandoned *Regno*, he and Honorius parted amicably.

**The impassive features in this mosaic portrait of Pope Gregory IX belie the uncompromising determination that he brought to bear in his struggle against the Holy Roman Emperor. Believing that the spiritual authority of the Church would be undermined by the material wealth and political power of the empire, Gregory twice excommunicated Frederick II, and even made an alliance with the north Italian cities, whose notions of religious freedom he would normally have opposed.**

The kingdom of Sicily had had no real ruler since Henry VI died in 1197, and Frederick found waiting for him a land riddled with banditry, where even minor lordlings exercised arbitrary and near-absolute power over their petty dominions. He spent two years ruthlessly subduing his feudal vassals on the mainland. In 1222 it was the turn of the island of Sicily itself, where the Muslim population was in full rebellion. It took another two years of desperate warfare before the rebels were crushed and Frederick became king in fact as well as name.

He treated the vanquished Muslims with an unexpected leniency that had lasting consequences. Instead of massacre and slavery, their fate was a relatively humane deportation, in entire communities, to northern Apulia. There they were permitted to till the soil and carry on their traditional industries of carpet-weaving and arms manufacture. Even more extraordinarily, they were allowed to practise their Islamic faith unmolested. Frederick's policy turned the former rebels into passionate Hohenstaufen loyalists: from then until the end of the dynasty, the Muslims of Apulia provided the core of every imperial army, as well as the Emperor's personal bodyguard. Quite apart from their military prowess, the troops gave their master a valuable advantage in the conflicts that were to come: as Muslims, they were utterly unmoved by threats of excommunication from a Christian pope.

Even while pacifying the *Regno*, Frederick was creating a rigid framework of law and administration that would make it the most thoroughly governed state in Europe. There was nothing liberal about his developing constitution: virtually all powers – except those conceded, with reluctance, to the Church – were vested in the king himself. And these powers were to be absolute by law, not by whim.

Such a state could only function with the aid of a trained civil service, very much a novelty for the time. Frederick set out to create one to suit his purposes. In 1224 sick; an epidemic had struck his army. At once, he sent an apologetic explanation to the new pope. But Gregory IX was less accommodating than Honorius. An ascetic, something of a mystic and above all a profound believer in absolute papal supremacy, he was not disposed to listen to Frederick's excuses. In a towering rage, he ordered the immediate excommunication of the "so-called emperor".

Fredrick set off again, anyway, the following spring, an excommunicate with a Muslim bodyguard heading a Christian army on a mission of holy war. It was a paradoxical beginning to what turned out to be a very strange Crusade. Pausing at Crusader-ruled Cyprus to strengthen the island's imperial allegiance, Frederick landed in Palestine in September 1228. His army was small — probably no more than a thousand knights — and his chances of a military victory were slender.

He did not even attempt one. Instead, he entered into negotiations with Malik al-Kamil, sultan of Egypt, who controlled the Christian holy places. Al-Kamil was a highly cultured man, much interested in Arabic poetry and philosophy; so was the emperor Frederick II. Distracted by political problems of his own, al-Kamil had no taste for war with so congenial an adversary, and an accord was soon reached. The Sultan conceded Frederick Jerusalem, along with Bethlehem and a corridor from the Mediterranean coast; in return, Frederick undertook not to interfere with the mosques in his new domain. In due course, he crowned himself king of Jerusalem in the Church of the Holy Sepulchre. (He had no choice but to crown himself: mindful of his excommunication, the Catholic patriarch of Jerusalem refused any part in the ceremony, and excluded the Emperor from the triumphal Mass that celebrated his diplomatic victory.)

Predictably, the outcome infuriated Frederick's enemies. There was something unnatural about a Crusade that ended with neither bloodshed nor loot, not to mention the idea of a supposedly Christian emperor sipping sherbet and bandying Arabic politenesses with the heathen desolater of the holy places. Al-Kamil faced a

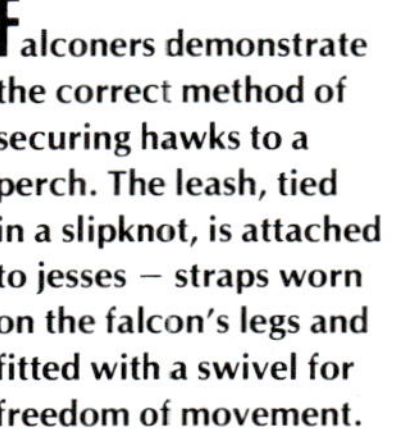

**Falconers demonstrate the correct method of securing hawks to a perch. The leash, tied in a slipknot, is attached to jesses — straps worn on the falcon's legs and fitted with a swivel for freedom of movement.**

similar reaction from his own Islamic fundamentalists. The agreement was doomed to failure: the Sultan's successors were less amenable to a Christian presence, and when Jerusalem fell to them in 1244 it was lost to Christendom forever.

By the time Frederick returned to Italy in 1229, he had no greater enemy than Gregory IX. During his absence, the Pope had launched a campaign of calumny against him — "reptile", "basilisk" and "patricide" were amongst some of the choicer epithets used — made formal alliance with the Lombard League and sought to elect a Welf "anti-king" in Germany. Finally, Gregory spread a false story that Frederick had died in Palestine and ordered troops into the *Regno*, where they met with little resistance from a bewildered population.

But the papal soldiers had no stomach for serious fighting. Frederick, very much alive, scraped up what loyal forces he could find and quickly cleared the *Regno* of the invaders. He called a halt at the border of the Papal States, in the hope of reaching a compromise with Gregory; but it took the diplomatic efforts of the grand master of the Teutonic Knights, a powerful crusading order, and most of the German princes as well as military defeat to force Gregory to agree to a reconciliation. At Ceprano in 1230 the bull of excommunication was at last rescinded, and the "reptile" was transformed, at least in public declaration, into Gregory's "dearest son". Few believed the transformation would endure.

For the time being, Frederick was content to set aside his ambitions for the Lombard cities and he returned again to the *Regno* and to his own thoughts about the nature of the emperor, the empire and its laws. The outcome was the Constitutions of Melfi. Named after the town in Apulia where they were first promulgated, they amounted to the first comprehensive legal code that Europe had witnessed since the time of the Byzantine emperor Justinian, 700 years before. Much of the drafting

**A sequence of pictures shows the correct stance for handling a falcon. The falconer kneels low to avoid frightening his bird when picking it up, and avoids looming over it when offering it a bath.**

This marble bust of an elegantly coiffed, bejewelled lady courtier, reflects the wealth and sophistication of Frederick's Sicilian court, while its classical style recalls the majesty of Ancient Rome which Frederick wished to emulate. Although the Emperor jealously kept his own wife hidden from sight, women were encouraged to display their skills in music and dancing, and enjoyed a prominent position at court. Courtiers of both sexes spent extravagant sums to keep up with the latest fashions in dress, and ladies of rank wore jewel-encrusted crowns in imitation of their queen.

Manfred managed to reclaim most of the old *Regno* and held it until 1266. By then, the papacy had enlisted the aid of the fiercely ambitious French warrior-prince, Charles of Anjou; Manfred was killed in a battle against him at Benevento, near Naples. Two years later, Conrad's 15-year-old son Conradin followed his father south in search of his dangerous inheritance. He was captured by French troops at Tagliacozzo in central Italy; a few months later, Charles of Anjou had the young "viper" publicly beheaded in Naples' marketplace.

Conradin was not quite the last of the Hohenstaufens. There was still Enzo, a prisoner in Bologna. He turned to poetry in his confinement. "Go, my song," he wrote, ". . . go to the plains of Apulia . . . Where my heart is, night and day." But he never saw Apulia again. He died in captivity in 1272, and with him went the last faint hope for a Hohenstaufen revival.

The destruction of the Hohenstaufens, however, served the papacy little. The sheer bitterness of the long quarrel had stripped it of much of the moral capital with which it began the century and, as Innocent IV's successors were to discover, such capital was far more easily spent than re-earned. The alliance with the French, which had brought Charles of Anjou and military victory in the south, proved no easier to manage than the Emperor had been. Quarrels soon broke out, and the Church became something of a pawn in the game of international conflicts. The way was prepared for the Great Schism of the 14th century, with rival popes blasting each other with invective and anathema while Mother Church wandered blindly towards the trauma of the Reformation.

Nor did Charles and his French entourage gain much from their Italian adventure. By 1282, they had made themselves so unpopular in Sicily that the population rose against them in the massacres known as the Sicilian Vespers. By the end of the century, the island and most of Frederick's *Regno* were in the possession of the Aragonese, who were building their own Spanish empire in the Mediterranean.

As for the Holy Roman Empire, it was never truly reconstituted. For 23 years after Frederick's death, there was an interregnum in Germany; when the imperial crown finally passed to an obscure family called Hapsburg, it retained only a shadow of its earlier authority — real power had passed to the dukes, counts, archbishops and bishops, who won virtual independence for their territorial states. It would be more than 600 years before a real national unity was created from the chaos.

Italy, too, passed through a period of prolonged civil war, a struggle between Guelphs and Ghibellines in which the names of the two great parties became so tangled with local politics that scarcely anyone could remember what they once had stood for. But although, in the wake of Frederick's great failure, national unity was to remain a hopeless dream, the rivalries and bickering of Italy's patchwork city-states had a vital, creative side from which, more than a century after the death of Frederick, would spring the Italian Renaissance.

What Frederick himself had sought was a return to the Roman Empire of the past. His career had demonstrated that such an ambition was impossible to fulfil. There were other ways forward. Even as Frederick lay on his deathbed, the rising new monarchies of England and France were demonstrating how a centralized state power could, in smaller and more homogenous societies, be reconciled with a vigorous commercial life. Frederick, in the not entirely approving words of the English chronicler, Matthew Paris, had "astonished the world". There were other ways to change it, as the French and English examples would show.

# THE BALTIC CRUSADES

5

In 1197, the Cistercian Abbot Berthold of Loccum, near Bremen, was invested as Bishop of Livonia (present-day Latvia), in the eastern Baltic. Far from the comforts of civilization, with a coast that was frequently wrapped in fog or cut off by ice, Livonia was the last place in which the venerable Berthold wished to wrestle for souls. His predecessor, the first bishop, had spent his last 17 years striving unsuccessfully to convert its pagan inhabitants, the Livs, and Berthold took up his new appointment with notable reluctance. At first, he tried to win over the population with gifts and banquets. The Livs were not impressed: on one occasion they tried to drown him; when this failed they set fire to a church in which he was preaching.

Having escaped the flames, he went back to Germany and there recruited a Crusader army with which to subdue the Livs. In a battle on July 24, 1198, the luckless Berthold was wounded by a Livonian lance, then torn to pieces by his recalcitrant flock. The Crusaders, enraged by the death of their leader, mounted a campaign of terror against the Livs, forcibly baptizing 150 of them in two days. However, once the Crusaders had embarked on the return voyage to Germany, the Livs renounced their new faith, plunging into the waters of the River Dvina to wash off their baptism and driving the remaining priests out of the country. Livonia, it seemed, was to remain impervious to the true religion.

It was to take less than a century, however, not only for Livonia, but for virtually the whole of the eastern Baltic, from Finland in the north to Prussia in the south, to fall under Christian rule. Fought in inhospitable terrain, with little of the glamour that surrounded the struggle for the Holy Land, the northern Crusades were conducted with a brutal efficiency that would ensure the survival of a Crusader state in the eastern Baltic long after the fall of that in Palestine.

When the 13th century began, the eastern boundary of Latin Christendom on the Baltic could be taken as a line running north from the Polish city of Danzig through the island of Gotland to the Swedish coast. Of the territories that lay beyond that line the Western world knew little, and what it did know it did not particularly care for. A 12th-century traveller who had journeyed through the woodlands east of the River Oder wrote that "it was very hard going, on account of the various snakes and huge wild beasts, and troublesome cranes that were nesting in the branches of the trees and troubled and tormented us with their croaking and flapping, and patches of bog which hindered our wagons and carts".

To the north and east, between the Vistula and Dvina rivers, the going was even harder. Here an intractable barrier of primeval forest, lakes and bogs stretched most of the way from the Baltic shore to the frontier with Russia. Comprising some 3,000 square kilometres, this was an area in which organized overland travel for large groups was impossible; the only certain routes were the rivers, which provided a

**Flanked by his queen and other members of the royal family, King Waldemar II of Denmark raises aloft a cross in this stone relief from Ribe Cathedral in Jutland. The Danish king was one of many Western Crusaders who travelled east during the 13th century to war against the pagan inhabitants of the southern Baltic coastlands. In the 1220s, Danish forces helped a Livonian religious order, the Sword Brothers, to subjugate the northern half of Estonia, which remained in Danish hands throughout the 13th century.**

passage for boats in summer and sledges in winter. At other times the rivers were often in flood as a result of autumn rain or spring thaws.

In this wilderness there lived a group of peoples who would later become known collectively as Balts, including Prussians, Lithuanians and Letts. Settled in tribes, each with its own defined territory, they lived scattered along the coast and in the valleys of the Vistula, Neman and Dvina rivers, farming, raising cattle and reaping a regular harvest of furs, honey and wax from the surrounding forest.

Farther north, between the Dvina and the Gulf of Finland, the country was more open and mountainous, with forests of oak, elm and ash gradually giving way to pine. This region was the home of three peoples – the Livs, concentrated along the Baltic coast as far as the River Au; the Estonians, occupying the southern coast of the Gulf itself and its offshore islands; and a second group of Letts, wedged in between the Livs and the Russians to the east.

Whatever their territorial divisions, Western Christendom saw these peoples as one in their devotion to paganism. They were animists, who worshipped such forces of nature as the sun, moon and stars, and whose festivals often involved human sacrifice. Building with stones and mortar was unknown to them, and their dwellings of earth and timber were decorated with animal skulls to ward off the evil eye. One German chronicler of the 1230s warned that Christians who fell into the hands of such "evil heathens" would soon "be robbed of life and property".

But if the eastern Baltic was dangerous, it was also enticing, with a vast supply of natural treasures – fur, fish, timber, honey, beeswax, amber – of which Western traders were anxious to obtain a share. Although the native tribes were willing to do business, exchanging their own wares for imported luxuries, such as wool, silver and iron weapons, relations between the two sides were far from harmonious. On

**Over the course of the 13th century, Christian forces brought virtually all the eastern and southern coastlands of the Baltic under their domination. In Finland, opposing armies from Sweden and the Russian principality of Novgorod struggled to be first to convert the native pagan population. From their base at Riga, the Sword Brothers conquered Livonia and Estonia, while to the west the Teutonic Knights struggled with the natives of Prussia. By 1300 the lands of the Sword Brothers had been subsumed in the territory of the Teutonic Knights, creating a formidable military state (shaded yellow) that stretched from Pomerelia in the west to the borders of Novgorod in the east. Only in Samogitia did native tribes still resist Christian rule, with the aid of neighbouring Lithuania, which remained pagan until the late 14th century.**

the one hand, the local peoples demanded a fairer exchange of goods and less interference in their affairs; on the other hand, the traders clamoured for a larger share of the local resources and better protection against marauding tribesmen.

Another source of concern to Western traders was competition from the Russians, primarily from Novgorod, who by the 12th century had several of the Baltic tribes under their control. The Catholic church was also alarmed: although Christians, the Russians' loyalty was to the Eastern Orthodox church, centred in Constantinople – a fact which, in the eyes of Rome, made them as much in need of salvation as the pagans themselves. Moreover, Russian missionaries were busy carrying out mass baptisms among the Baltic peoples, to the detriment of the Catholic cause.

It was amid the lakes and forests of southern Finland that the confrontation between Orthodox and Latin Christendom was to erupt into all-out warfare. To the southwest, the Catholic Swedes had colonized the region inhabited by the agricultural Suomi, while to the east the Russians had established virtual sovereignty over the fishing and fur-gathering Karelians. Only the Tavastians, hunters who lived along the central southern coast, remained largely untouched – a situation that both Swedes and Russians were determined to change.

The Russians moved first. In 1227, having taken the precautionary step of forcibly baptizing the Karelians, Prince Yaroslav of Novgorod led an expedition against the Tavastians. After causing much devastation, the raiders returned home with their plunder. The next year, the Tavastians counterattacked, crossing to the southern shore of Lake Ladoga by boat. However, they were routed and chased into the surrounding forest by the Russians' Karelian allies. The Karelians were traditional enemies of the Tavastians and gave them little chance of escaping to the northern shore of the lake. According to the *Novgorod Chronicle*, a 14th-century account of the principality's early years, "It is thought that 2,000 of them had come; God knows, and few of them escaped to their own country; all the rest perished."

Angered by Yaroslav's successes, the pope placed Finland under apostolic protection and, flexing his muscles as the spiritual leader of Western Christendom, invoked a trade embargo against Novgorod. The embargo, beginning in 1229, coincided with an autumn frost that destroyed the city's crops, with the result that thousands died of starvation. The chronicler described how "some of the common people killed the living and ate them; others cutting up dead flesh and corpses ate them; others ate horseflesh, dogs and cats . . . Some fed on moss, snails, pine-bark, lime-bark, lime and elm tree leaves, and whatever each could think of."

Fortunately for the Novgorodians, the wealthy trading communities along the western Baltic, such as Bremen, Lübeck and Visby, had no intention of sacrificing their lucrative eastern trade just to please the pope, and without their support the embargo soon collapsed. The next threat to Novgorod was more serious. It came during July 1240, when an army of Swedish Crusaders, with Suomi and Tavastian auxiliaries, sailed up the River Neva, intending, as the chronicler recounted, "to take possession of . . . Novgorod, and of the whole Novgorod province. But again the most kind and merciful God, lover of men, preserved and protected us from the foreigners since they laboured in vain without the command of God."

The Crusaders also laboured without the command of a general able to match the 21-year-old Novgorodian leader, Alexander, successor to Yaroslav. Rallying his outnumbered forces on the banks of the Neva, he inflicted a crushing defeat on the enemy, winning for himself the title of Alexander Nevsky – "of the Neva". Nine years later, the Swedes launched a second, more successful Crusade, occupying Tavastia and threatening the Russian position in Karelia. However, it was not until 1292, after more than 40 years of fierce but sporadic border fighting, that the Swedes, led by a nobleman, Tyrgils Knuttson, attempted to conquer Karelia itself.

Tyrgils failed in his main objective, but he did succeed in establishing a fortress at Vyborg, on the southern tip of Karelia, from which Swedish forces could harry the countryside round the lower Neva and Lake Ladoga. The war continued for a further 30 years, with neither side able to gain a decisive victory. They finally agreed to make peace in 1323, with each power receiving a part of the disputed territory.

A detail from the bronze doors of Poland's Gniezno Cathedral depicts the martyrdom of Saint Adelbert, an early Christian missionary, whose remains were subsequently purchased by the Poles from the pagan Prussians. Before the arrival of the Teutonic Knights, several attempts had been made to convert the Prussians by peaceful means, notably by a Cistercian monk consecrated by the pope as Bishop Christian of Prussia in 1215. Ultimately, however, his missions were failures and it was Christian himself who called for the first Crusade against the Prussians in 1223.

In fact, the treaty marked not the end of hostilities, but merely their suspension, and in less than a generation, the two would again be locked in conflict.

For the present, however, the Swedes were content to fold away their banners and await a more propitious time to strike against the heretics. In spite of copious blessings from the pope and the Swedish monarch, the struggle just concluded had not been universally popular. Not so much a Crusade as a series of ramshackle skirmishes, it had offered much discomfort, little profit and no glory. Few knights had been willing to serve on the dismal battlefields of Finland, and those who stayed to settle their new lands became known to the natives as "food Swedes", impressing less with their feats of arms than their prodigious appetites.

Such was not the case in Livonia, where crusading warriors established a rather different reputation. Following the debacle of 1198, a young German cleric, Albert of Buxtehude, had been invested as the new bishop. Unlike his predecessor, the martyred Berthold, Albert was rich, ambitious, and well connected — he was, indeed, the personal appointee of his uncle, the powerful archbishop Hartwig of Hamburg-Bremen — with ruthless arrogance that boded ill for opponents, whether pagan or Christian. In addition, he possessed remarkable energy and organizing ability — two qualities that he was to display to the full over the next 30 years.

In October 1199, within a few months of being appointed, he had secured a papal assurance that Crusaders, or pilgrims as they were called, who undertook to fight in Livonia would merit the same automatic remission of sins as those who fought in the Holy Land. Armed with this guarantee, Bishop Albert conducted a recruiting drive throughout northern Germany, and in the early spring of 1200, accompanied by priests, merchants, artisans and a force of Crusaders 500 strong, he sailed up the River Dvina to begin the conquest of his unruly diocese.

Fighting was no new experience to the Livs. Indeed, warfare was endemic, not only between the Livs and their traditionally hostile neighbours — the Letts, the Estonians and the Lithuanians — but also among the Livs themselves. So great was the danger of attack that each settlement had its own fortress. Normally this served as the residence of the local chief. But at the first sign of danger, it became a refuge for the surrounding population. Located on easily defensible sites, such as hill-tops or specially constructed earth ramparts, and consisting of thick timber walls, buttressed with towers and roofed with logs, bark and clay, these fortresses were usually strong enough to withstand the spears and arrows of tribal enemies.

They were no proof, however, against the onslaughts of the Crusaders. Into this wilderness the Western soldiers brought a war-machine well in advance of the Livs' rudimentary weaponry. Body armour, crossbows, catapults, siege towers and caltrops — spiked metal balls for laming horses — gave the Crusaders an advantage far outweighing the superior numbers of the native warriors. Even so, campaigning in Livonia was exhausting and dangerous, involving long marches through a wooded wilderness ideal for silent ambush and swift retreat. Simply getting there, across the pirate-infested Baltic, was a hazardous enterprise.

To compensate, the campaigning season was short, lasting only from June to September. With the approach of the paralysing winter the Crusaders would withdraw to Riga, Bishop Albert's new capital at the mouth of the Dvina, there to await the coming of spring and the arrival of a fresh batch of recruits.

The men who came across the Baltic were a ragbag of professional soldiers and amateur adventurers, but all were prepared to endure a year in Livonia in return for reasonable plunder and a papal guarantee of absolution. No doubt many recruits were swayed by Albert's decision to dedicate his primitive diocese to the Virgin Mary — a figure who excited almost as much veneration as the Saviour himself. Indeed, in 1215, Pope Innocent III was to declare that he felt the same solicitude for Livonia, "the Land of the Mother", as for Palestine, "the Land of the Son".

A Crusader's yearly expenses in Livonia, including the return passage, averaged 10 marks, only half the cost of crusading in the Holy Land. Even so, many recruits were poor and had to be subsidized by the merchants of Riga. Few merchants objected to this arrangement, since the Crusaders not only provided them with protection, but also sold them the booty captured in raids against the pagans.

Formidable though these summer warriors were, they lacked one vital quality: permanence. Because they served for such a short time, their task was only to conquer, never to occupy; yet, without occupation, it was impossible for Bishop Albert to maintain a continuing hold over the native population. He needed a force that could both spearhead the summer campaigns and garrison the newly won territories in winter. In 1202, therefore, he secured papal approval for the establishment

# PORT OF THE MERCHANT MAGNATES

Many of the towns dominated by the Teutonic Knights were members of the Hansa – a league of wealthy trading cities, centred in Germany but extending to neighbouring lands, that rose to prominence during the 13th century. Situated on the Baltic island of Gotland, the port of Visby *(right)*, with its towering limestone warehouses, was one such major entrepôt.

Using convoys of cogs – sturdy vessels that had hanging stern rudders and deep draughts – Hanseatic merchants plied a lucrative trade in goods from all over the known world. A major part of their profits came from the Baltic herring, salted in large quantities for the meatless fast days of European Christians.

By the 14th century the Hansa's power was such that it minted its own coinage, dealt directly with foreign rulers (taking royal regalia as pledges for loans), promulgated its own laws and was even capable of defeating nations in battle.

of a military order to be based in Livonia. Officially called the Brothers of Christ's Militia, its knights soon became better known as the Sword Brothers.

Bound by monastic vows of poverty, chastity and obedience, and clad in distinctive white mantles with red insignia — a cross and a sword — the members of the new order had only one purpose: to defend "Mary's Land" against the heathens. Like the Hospitallers, Templars and Teutonic Knights, crusading orders which had originated in Palestine in the last century, the Sword Brothers were divided into three classes: the knight-brothers, who formed the officer corps and from whom were elected the grand master and other senior dignitaries; the priest-brothers, who served as spiritual advisers to members of the order and who alone could hear confession and grant absolution; and the serving-brothers, including both foot soldiers and mounted men-at-arms, or sergeants, who were often equipped as knights.

The older crusading orders accepted only knightly Crusaders of noble birth, but the Sword Brothers, faced with competition from such prestigious rivals, were less selective. In the eyes of a hostile chronicler, their recruits "were rich merchants banned from Saxony for their crimes, who expected to live on their own without law or king". Certainly the Sword Brothers' conduct scandalized Christian opinion from Riga to Rome. When Bishop Albert persuaded some brethren to stage an instructive nativity play for his pagan flock, the knights inserted such terrifying fighting scenes that most of the audience fled. And as early as 1208, the first grand master, Wenno of Rhorbach, was axed to death by one of his own brethren.

A boldly delineated icon of Christ typifies the religious art of Novgorod, one of the principal players on the Baltic stage in the 13th century. Proudly styled by its citizens Lord Novgorod the Great, the city dominated the northern end of the river network linking the Baltic to the Black Sea, and controlled a vast fur-trading empire stretching east to the Ural Mountains and north as far as the Arctic Circle. Although it paid homage to the Mongol rulers of southern Russia, it nevertheless retained its independence and, under its able ruler Alexander Nevsky, expanded its territories into southern Finland and checked the eastward expansion of the Teutonic Knights.

Despite their dubious morals, the Sword Brothers proved to be outstanding warriors in the Christian cause. There were probably never more than 150 knights, yet it was largely due to their efforts that the resistance of the Livs and Letts was broken. Crucial to their success was the series of stone and brick fortresses they set up along the Dvina to control the surrounding countryside. Garrisoned throughout the year, these strongholds were impervious to every weapon in the enemy's arsenal, including fire. In addition, the order exploited old tribal rivalries. By offering to help the Livs and Letts against their traditional enemies, the Lithuanians and the Estonians, Bishop Albert and his men won much-needed local support.

By 1206 the Letts were firmly committed to the Christian cause — if only through the prospect of military advantage. However, many Livs still resented the foreign intruders. In that year, this resentment flared into bloody rebellion, and scores of Christians, both German and native, were brutally killed. Among the victims were two Liv converts — later proclaimed martyrs by the Church — who tried to negotiate with the rebels and had their arms and legs cut off and their livers torn out.

Aided by fresh troops from Germany and loyal Livonians, Albert's forces regained control, killing most of the rebels and repulsing a Russian army that tried to take advantage of the confusion. With their homeland safe, the Sword Brothers began to look north, towards Estonia. They had conquered Livonia on the basis that they keep one third of it for themselves — the other two thirds were retained by Bishop Albert — and they saw expansion to the Gulf of Finland as a way of securing greater holdings. To that end, in 1208, the Brothers, together with German Crusaders and levies of baptized Livs and Letts, embarked on a series of savage campaigns that reduced the southern half of Estonia to a starving and disease-ridden wasteland.

Their first objective was the frontier province of Saccalia, through which they cut a bloody swathe. In 1211 they laid siege to Fellin, the stronghold of the province, where they paraded the prisoners taken en route before the fortifications, offering to spare their lives if the garrison would surrender and accept the true God. The Estonians refused, jeering at and mocking their attackers, and showing off captured German armour. The prisoners were duly killed and thrown into the moat. The siege continued for six days, with heavy casualties on both sides. Finally, with every surviving defender wounded and their supplies of water almost exhausted, the Estonians surrendered, begging, according to one of Bishop Albert's mission priests, Henry of Livonia, "that you spare us and mercifully impose the yoke of Christianity upon us as you have upon the Livonians and the Letts". The survivors were then sprinkled with holy water and catechized as a prelude to baptism.

Such campaigns continued in regular relays so that, over the course of a single summer, nine separate armies rampaged through southern Estonia, burning, torturing, killing and looting, and so devastating the land that "neither men nor food were found there". As Henry explained, the aim of these forays "was to fight long enough so that either those who were left would come to seek peace and baptism or they would be completely wiped from the earth".

By 1219 Bishop Albert had gained tenuous control over the southern half of Estonia, defeating not only the unruly Estonians, but also Russian armies from Pskov and Novgorod, who were equally keen to gain control of the land. And in 1220, with the help of an army of Danes which arrived under the leadership of the Danish king Waldemar II, the Crusaders succeeded in subjugating the northern half of the country. "It was now the Bishop's twenty-second year," wrote his faithful chronicler-priest, "and the land of the Livonians rested a bit."

The rest was cut short in 1223, when the Estonians rose up in savage fury against both Danes and Germans. At Fellin, Odenpah and Dorpat they attacked the Sword Brothers, reducing their ranks by a third; at Jerwa they disembowelled every soldier of the Danish garrison and ate the governor's heart. By now the Estonians were skilled in the use of war machines, and used captured German weapons to break the enemy's fortifications. They were supported by a Russian army, which marched in from Novgorod and Pskov to besiege the main Danish stronghold of Reval.

It took a year for the Crusaders to regain control. In 1224, they stormed Dorpat, killing all but one of its defenders, a Russian, who was given a horse and sent back to Novgorod to report on the triumph of the Latins. The victory was a clear demonstration of the Crusaders' prowess, and both the Russians and Estonians sued for peace. In the aftermath, the victors divided the country according to an agreement made two years earlier; the Danes received northern Estonia, and the Brothers retained their southern conquests. But arguments between the two soon broke out, with the land-hungry order seizing Danish territory. In 1225, in an attempt to end the dispute, the pope placed the whole country under the control of a papal legate.

This arrangement, too, soon led to conflict. In 1229, a new legate, Baldwin of Alna, arrived in Riga. Bishop Albert had died earlier that year, and Baldwin's brief was to look into the controversy that had arisen over the election of a successor. Unfortunately, Baldwin of Alna was ambitious, intemperate and meddlesome, and his relations with the Sword Brothers rapidly deteriorated. Matters came to a head in 1233, when the order refused to relinquish the castle of Reval, which they had seized from the Danes. Baldwin tried to take the castle by force and, in the ensuing battle, the papal troops were defeated and Baldwin himself was captured.

Although quickly released, the outraged prelate was in no mood to forgive his enemies. Instead, he brought an ecclesiastical lawsuit, charging the Brothers with disobedience, rebellion and heresy. Specific offences included killing converts, assaulting monks and preventing would-be Christians from receiving baptism. The verdict went against the Sword Brothers and they were censured by Pope Gregory IX, who directed them to return to King Waldemar the Danish provinces of Estonia seized in 1224 and pay compensation to the victims of their misdeeds. In the event, the order did not survive long enough to carry out either of these directives.

In the summer of 1236, Grand Master Folkwin was persuaded by his crusading reinforcements to launch an invasion into Lithuania. Proceeding as far south as the River Saule, the Christian forces, in the words of a contemporary chronicler, "robbed and burnt wonderfully in many bands, and ravaged up and down the land freely". However, when the Lithuanian warriors appeared and opposed them, Folkwin's Crusader allies lost their nerve and the entire host was "cut down like women". More than 2,000 of the Crusaders perished, including the Grand Master himself and some 50 of his comrades. It was a disaster from which the Sword Brothers never recovered. Condemned by the Pope, opposed by the Danes and now defeated by the Lithuanians, the surviving brethren began negotiations to be absorbed into another crusading order, the Teutonic Knights.

The Teutonic Knights, also known as the Cross Bearers, from the black cross on their white mantles, had been founded in 1198 by German Crusaders to the Holy Land. With their headquarters at Acre, the order had enjoyed a rapid growth in wealth, power and prestige, due in no small measure to the veteran Crusader, Herman of Salza, who was elected grand master in 1210. Born around 1170 in Thuringia, Fra Herman was described by an admiring contemporary as "eloquent, affable, wise, careful and far-seeing, and glorious in all his actions". Certainly, he

## The Holy Beggars

**A new element in Christendom during the 13th century were the mendicant friars — wandering monks dedicated to preaching, poverty and scholarship, who relied on begging as their only means of sustenance. The first order to be founded was the Dominican, established by a Castilian cleric in 1216 to evangelize the Cathars of southern France. At about the same time the young Saint Francis, the son of a rich Italian cloth merchant, was converted to the cause of voluntary poverty and gathered together a band of followers that formed the basis of the Franciscan order. In a time of growing ecclesiastical wealth, the asceticism of the mendicants won widespread admiration from clergy and laity alike.**

**Though novel to Christendom, the mendicants' way of life was paralleled in other religions. The Islamic countries harboured mystics belonging to the Sufi order, who wandered the roads seeking ecstatic union with God. In India the adherents of Jainism vowed to renounce all worldly goods, to injure no creature, and to remain chaste in order to reach a state of freedom from all mental and bodily encumbrances. And all over Asia and the Far East, roving Buddhist monks sought enlightenment through a life of contemplation and self-denial.**

Part of a series depicting Saint Dominic — founder of the Dominican order — at prayer, a miniature shows two images of the saint continuing his devotions even while travelling.

knew how to impress the influential, winning the favour both of the Pope and of the Holy Roman Emperor. From the former the Teutonic order received papal privileges, and from the latter, land — in Italy, Greece, Germany and Palestine.

The order's involvement in eastern Europe began in 1211, when King Andrew II of Hungary invited it to defend part of his frontier against the warlike Cumans of central Asia. In fact, the Cumans proved to be less of a menace than the Teutonic Knights who, having defeated the nomads, proceeded to set up an independent state of their own, even bringing in German farmers to colonize the land. By 1224, King Andrew was determined to rid himself of the danger. Describing them as "fire under the shirt, mouse in the bag, viper in the bosom", he told the Knights to leave; when they refused, his army descended on them and expelled them by force.

Almost immediately they received another invitation — this time from the Polish duke Conrad of Mazovia, who wanted them to tame his heathen and warlike neighbours, the Prussians. All previous attempts had attained only limited success. Various missions seeking to win converts through persuasion rather than force had

**Carved in wood, a row of tiny Buddhas emerging from the mouth of a Japanese saint reveals his adherence to the Pure Land Sect, which preached that the path to enlightenment lay in constant repetition of the phrase, "Homage to the Amida Buddha".**

**Sculpted in white marble, a naked Jain monk sits deep in meditation. Called "ford-makers", such monks were believed to help the Jain faithful cross the stream of existence to reach their spiritual goal.**

made modest inroads, but the vast majority of the Prussians remained implacably hostile. In 1220, inspired by the example of the Sword Brothers, the Poles had founded a military order, the Knights of Dobrzyn, to provide some protection against pagan attacks. But the new order — little more than a dozen knights — was scarcely able to defend its own castle. A Crusade had even been launched, in 1223, but Prussian reprisal raids had been so savage that the borders of Mazovia and the other adjoining Polish duchies were in greater jeopardy than ever before.

Now, in return for their help, Conrad offered the Teutonic Knights the province of Kulmerland, including the fort of Kulm, together with any other territory they might conquer. However, Grand Master Salza wanted no repetition of the Hungarian debacle, and it was not until Emperor Frederick II himself had guaranteed the order's right to retain all conquered territory — a guarantee later confirmed by Pope Gregory IX — that the Teutonic Knights were given the signal to march north.

The main contingent, consisting of 20 knights and 200 sergeants under the command of one of the order's greatest heroes, Herman Balke, arrived at Kulm in 1230. Like the Sword Brothers in Livonia, they used the rivers as invasion routes, marking their advance with a string of forts from which to strike into the surrounding forest. As each new district was conquered, it was settled with a community of German knights and burghers, who not only helped to colonize the land, but also provided the order with a ready source of income and military service.

One advantage that the Teutonic Knights had over the Sword Brothers was independence. The Brothers had been created as the instrument of Bishop Albert, with a duty, not always undertaken with zeal, to obey and protect him. The Knights, on the other hand, were an autonomous order, free from episcopal restraints. In addition, the Teutonic Knights had a plentiful supply of crusading allies. Whereas the Sword Brothers had to rely on the reinforcements that Bishop Albert could scrape together on his annual preaching tours of North Germany, the Teutonic Knights had a vast network of convents, castles and commanderies to serve as recruiting centres. Moreover, many German Crusaders who had quailed at sailing through the dangerous waters of Livonia were prepared to make the overland journey to Prussia. The Teutonic Knights also had close ties with many powerful noblemen, Polish now, as well as German, and these sent a steady stream of men and supplies.

Despite such advantages, campaigning against the Prussians was far from easy. Although their wicker shields and wooden forts were no match for the crossbows and siege engines of the Crusaders, the native tribes fought back with the ferocity of desperation. Accompanying the Crusader armies were Dominican priests who offered peace in return for conversion, but it was rare for their offer to be accepted. The Prussians asked for no quarter and gave none. The chronicles of the Teutonic order, for instance, described the fate of two knights captured by the Prussians. One was placed in a cleft tree trunk held apart by ropes. The ropes were then released, so that the knight was crushed, and the tree was set ablaze. The other captive was tied to his horse, then both he and his luckless mount were hoisted to the top of an oak, beneath which a great fire was lit. The Crusaders acted in the same summary manner, usually hanging or beheading their prisoners.

The dominant motive of the Teutonic Knights was desire for redemption through battle. "Who fights us," proclaimed the order, "fights Jesus Christ." But in the case of the warrior-monks, the enemy was not just the unrepentant pagan — it was also the Satan within themselves. In an effort to vanquish this unseen but deadly foe, the

## Spoils of the Spanish Crusade

**In Spain as in the Baltic, Christian knights fought a continuous Crusade throughout the 13th century. There, the enemy were the Islamic forces who had held much of the country since the eighth century. The victory of Las Navas de Tolosa, 100 kilometres north of Granada, in 1212 — when the caliph's banner shown here was won as a battle spoil — was a turning point in the long struggle between the two religions. For the first time since the original invasions, Christian forces now controlled most of the Iberian Peninsula.**

**The Muslim strongholds that remained offered stern resistance, however. It took the armies of Ferdinand II of Leon and Castile and James I of Aragon another 35 years to retake the island of Majorca and the towns of Cordoba, Valencia, Murcia and Seville. Control of the Strait of Gibraltar was not achieved until 1344, while the Muslims held Granada until 1492.**

knight-brother submitted to a Draconian regime of prayer, discipline and self-denial. He owned no property, but was issued with a sword and armour, as well as a pair of breeches, two shirts, two pairs of boots, one surcoat, one sleeping bag, one blanket, one breviary and one knife. He could have two or four mounts, as required, but these, like his clothing and equipment, belonged to the order. He was forbidden to consort with laymen, and had to be silent at meals, in the dormitory, on the march and in the latrines. He was not permitted to joust. He could hunt solely those animals that attacked the crops and livestock of the settlers – the wolf, lynx and bear, for example – and only if he forfeited the assistance of hounds. His one lawful amusement was woodcarving.

All forms of vanity, such as displaying personal coats-of-arms, were forbidden. Hair had to be short, though beards were permitted. The knight-brother slept in his shirt, breeches and boots, sword at hand, and was required to rise four times a night to recite the offices. On Fridays he took the discipline, flagellating his own body until blood was drawn. Derelictions, spiritual or military, were dealt with by a senior officer, the marshal, using his rod in camp and his club on the battlefield.

Besides the usual Lent abstinence, the knight-brother was not allowed to eat meat during most of November and December, or on any of 20 specified fast days, or on a Monday, Wednesday, Friday or Saturday at any time of the year. For the most part his diet consisted of eggs, milk, porridge and water. In addition, he was expected to resist all temptations of the flesh: one postulant trained himself to curb his carnal desires by choosing the prettiest girl he could find, and sleeping beside her for a year without touching her. Others suppressed their longings through pain, wearing their chain mail under their shirts until the raw skin rusted the metal.

Despite such privations, the knights made an awesomely effective fighting force. In 1235, their order swallowed up the remnants of the Knights of Dobrzyn. By 1236, after six years of warfare, they had penetrated as far as the Vistula delta and were ready to start advancing eastwards along the Baltic shore towards the River Neman. However, the union with the Sword Brothers in May, 1237, following their defeat at Saule, brought the Teutonic Knights a Baltic dominion that stretched far beyond the borders of Prussia. A few weeks later the master of Prussia, Herman Balke, arrived in Riga to take charge of the Crusade in Livonia.

His first priority was to pacify the Danish ruler, King Waldemar, who was still demanding the return of his Estonian territories. In 1238 both sides agreed to return to the original partition scheme of 16 years earlier, with the Danes receiving the northern provinces and the order retaining the Sword Brothers' conquests in the south. However, Estonia still remained under the protection of the Holy See, and the price for papal approval was a promise by the Danes and the Teutonic Knights to join in a grand Crusade against the Russians of Novgorod. Accordingly, in 1240 a combined German and Danish force marched out of Livonia and, having captured the cities of Izborsk and Pskov, prepared to overrun Novgorod itself. This was a time of mortal peril for the principality, which faced an invasion threat not only from the Crusaders but also from the Mongols, under Batu Khan, who had spent the previous three years devastating southern and central Russia.

But Batu, instead of attacking Novgorod, headed west into Poland and Hungary, and the Crusade against the Russians was temporarily superseded by the Crusade against the Mongols. On April 9, 1241, an army of Poles and Germans, including a strong detachment of the Teutonic Knights under the Prussian master Poppo of

The castle of Lochstedt, near the port of Königsberg, was just one of many that the Teutonic Order placed strategically along the Baltic coast and up river valleys to subjugate Prussia. Built of brick, the fortress featured a chapel, a dining hall, an armoury, a chapter-house for meetings, a kitchen and a dormitory for the knights, as well as a latrine tower; the tower drained directly into the sea and was separated from the main body of the castle by a covered passageway. An adjoining complex contained estate offices for the steward who administered the surrounding farmland, barns, workshops, stables, a hostelry for visitors and quarters for the other ranks. The castle would have held a total garrison of about 60 men, including priests, sergeants and some 10 to 20 knights.

Osterna, clashed with the Mongols at Liegnitz, in Silesia. Disdaining to wait for reinforcements, the knights made a valiant charge at the densely packed ranks of the enemy, only to be cut down with a hail of arrows. Poppo managed to escape, but others were not so fortunate. The severed head of the Christian commander, Duke Henry of Silesia, was born aloft on a lance, while the ears of his dead comrades were cut off, gathered up into nine sacks and presented to Batu.

Fortunately for Catholic Europe, the great khan Ogedei died in late 1241 – an event that sent Batu hurrying back to Mongolia for the succession dispute. The Novgorodians meanwhile, relieved of any immediate danger from the Mongols, took the opportunity to settle accounts with the Crusaders. Early in 1242, only two years after his victory over the Swedes on the Neva, the young prince of Novgorod, Alexander Nevsky, recaptured the Russian territory occupied by the Danes and Germans. In a doleful account of the fall of Pskov to the Russians, a German chronicler claimed that only two knight-brothers had been left to defend the town. "If Pskov had been held, it would have benefited Christianity to the end of the world. It was a mistake to have taken the land and not have occupied it properly. He cries most about the pain who could have avoided it easily."

Worse pain was to follow. On April 5, 1242 – almost exactly one year after the disaster at Liegnitz – the two Christian armies clashed beside Lake Peipus. At first the heavily armoured cavalry of the Crusaders had the best of it, breaking through the Russian ranks. But they were overwhelmed by Nevsky's superior numbers and, according to one chronicle, were driven on to the ice of the frozen lake, where the majority were either killed or captured.

The Crusaders barely had time to recover from this latest defeat when they were confronted with an even more serious crisis – a rebellion by the Prussians. The insurgent tribesmen destroyed all but three of the order's forts and settlements, and it took the brethren a full seven years to suppress the uprising.

Anxious to avoid trouble in future, the papacy persuaded the Teutonic Knights to deal generously with the vanquished tribes. Under the Treaty of Christburg, in 1249, Prussians who renounced their paganism and accepted the Christian faith were guaranteed the same rights as Germans and Poles. They could buy, sell, litigate and worship on a basis of full equality with the immigrant burghers, and they were entitled to become priests and knights.

It was around this time that the Lithuanian chieftain, Mindaugas, whose powerful and well-organized state was under attack from Poles, Russians, Mongols and Crusaders, decided to neutralize at least one of his enemies by accepting the embrace of Rome. So delighted was Pope Innocent IV that he gave the new convert a royal crown. Mindaugas, for his part, invited German merchants and settlers to enter Lithuania, and even arranged for the Teutonic order to take over his lands, should he die without leaving an heir – a not altogether unlikely event, given the murderous inclinations of the Lithuanian nobility. More importantly, he offered to turn over to the brethren the coastal territory of Samogitia, which would complete the land link between Prussia and Livonia.

However, the Samogitians refused to accept Christian rule, and in July 1260 they routed a Crusader army at Durben, in western Curonia. It was the worst defeat that the Teutonic Knights had suffered since coming to the Baltic – 150 of the knight-brothers were killed, including the master of Livonia and the marshal of Prussia – and it sparked off another general uprising by the Prussians. The revolt spread to other tribes, and even Mindaugas, seeing an opportunity for further self-aggrandizement, decided to resume his war against the Christians. Although he was murdered by his brother-in-law in 1263, this had little effect on the military situation, since many Lithuanians still continued to support the rebels. Indeed, so desperate was the plight of the Teutonic Knights that Pope Urban IV, who had been planning a Crusade against the Mongols, urged all those who had taken the cross to go to the assistance of the order, promising full remission of sins for any length of service, no matter how short.

By now, the pagan warriors had learnt the techniques of modern war from the Christians themselves, and they were well armed, well led and well organized, with the ability both to attack the enemy's fortresses and to engage them in open battle. Nevertheless, although the Crusaders met with some heavy defeats, they usually inflicted more casualties than they received. In 1290, after 30 years of war, they finally brought their rebellious subjects to heel, although the Samogitians and Lithuanians remained defiantly belligerent.

With the Teutonic Knights firmly in control, the trickle of settlers into their territory became a flood. Livonia was largely ignored by the newcomers because of its forbidding location, but it was a different story in Prussia. Attracted by the prospect of large land-holdings for low rents, peasant colonists from North Germany arrived in such great numbers that, within half a century, they had founded some 1,500 towns and villages, with an estimated population of 150,000. (The indigenous population, which had been decimated by the many years of slaughter and starvation, was scarcely larger.)

**Presented to the cathedral of Plock by Duke Conrad, ruler of the Polish province of Mazovia, this gold paten, used to hold the bread for the service of Mass, bears on its upper right quadrant the image of its donor offering a chalice. Disturbed by Prussian border raids, Conrad invited the Teutonic Order to subdue his pagan neighbours in 1225. The order's knights arrived in 1230 and in the ensuing 50 years made Prussia an independent state under their direct control. Their success eventually jeopardized Poland's own position, and bitter enmity grew up between the two powers. Not until the 15th century was the matter settled, after a combined Polish and Lithuanian army defeated the Teutonic Knights at the Battle of Tannenberg.**

To ensure efficient cultivation of the Prussian wilderness, the Knights employed *locators*, or colonizing agents, whose job it was to recruit peasants, allocate plots and organize the villages. For this service, a *locator* received his own plot of village land – usually one-tenth of the whole – the position of village judge and headman, and often ownership of the mill or inn. A village was made up of about 20 families, each holding 40 to 60 hectares. In Germany, the peasant was bound by his duty to the lord of the manor, whereas in Prussia he was largely free to come and go as he pleased. His only obligations were to pay his annual rent on time and to perform military service as required.

The local merchants, based mainly in Riga, were also left alone to pursue their own affairs. As a result, they built up prosperous trade links stretching from the wealthy ports of North Germany to the land-locked cities of Hungary, Lithuania and Russia. (Trade continued between the Lithuanians and Russians irrespective of wars and religious

# BATTLE ON THE ICE

The campaigns of the Baltic Crusades were fought in difficult terrain and often in intemperate weather conditions that could hardly have been more different from the blazing heat of the Holy Land. A typical encounter took place on April 5, 1242, when a group of Teutonic Knights with native allies clashed with the Russians at Lake Peipus, in eastern Estonia. Returning from a raid into the principality of Novgorod, some 30 mounted knights, with the same number of mounted sergeants and about 250 Estonian foot soldiers, met a force of 300 Russians under the leadership of Alexander Nevsky.

Clad in distinctive white mantles emblazoned with a black cross, the knights were well equipped with helmets, mail coats, swords and spears. Confident of their superior armour and weaponry, they charged in a wedge formation into the Russian ranks, only to be encircled and driven back. According to one chronicle they were forced on to the frozen lake, where most of them were slaughtered.

differences.) Although required to pay customs duties, merchants could transport their goods without charge in Prussia and Livonia, using the well-kept roads or the rivers, which were policed by patrolling brethren.

The Teutonic order itself carried on a large and lucrative trade, maintaining a merchant fleet to take its goods across the Baltic. Its main exports were grain and Prussian amber — the latter, a monopoly of the order, being much prized for rosaries. The order also minted its own coinage, set up an internal postal service and enforced a uniform system of weights and measures. Matters of policy were decided by the master of Prussia and his senior officials, but day-to-day running of the country — the collection of taxes, the administration of justice, the organization of defence — was left to local commanders, each supported by a convent of at least 12 brothers. Many of these were skilled book-keepers, who made sure that the financial affairs of the convent were in order. They submitted weekly accounts to the local commander and he, in turn, submitted monthly accounts to a senior administrator. The commander also compiled a personal dossier on each of the brothers, sending the information to the main archives at Marienburg Castle.

Whatever the demands of their role as scribes and clerks, however, the Teutonic Knights never lost sight of their main priority: the defence of the realm against heathens and unbelievers. The benefits of Christian rule were meant only for Christian subjects; accordingly, no Jew or necromancer was allowed to settle in the order's domains. In addition, the native Prussians continued to be regarded with fierce suspicion. The small minority who had remained loyal during the great rebellion were treated no differently from the German settlers themselves, receiving lands and liberties appropriate to their rank. But Prussians who had reverted to paganism, or were suspected of being less than wholeheartedly Catholic — and this constituted the vast majority — were recruited as menial labourers on German estates and denied the right even to open a shop or an inn. Indeed, so deep-rooted was the distrust of the natives that, whenever Prussians and Germans were drinking together, the Prussians were required to drink first, to reduce the risk of poisoning.

As the 13th century entered its final decade, the Teutonic Knights had never appeared more secure, with greater wealth, power and prestige than most secular monarchs. But appearances were deceptive. In 1291, the Muslims stormed Acre, overrunning the order's ancient headquarters, and forcing it to establish a new base in Venice. This melancholy event was followed by more trouble in the Baltic — not from the resentful pagans of Prussia, but from the Christian burghers of Riga.

The Rigans and the Teutonic Knights had been set on a collision course for some time, with the former demanding more independence, and the latter refusing to give up their sovereignty over the city. The issue came to a head in 1297, when the knight-brothers demolished a bridge the Rigans had built over the Dvina River. In the ensuing violence, blood flowed on both sides, and houses were burnt, merchants arrested and goods impounded. Angry citizens stormed the local convent of the order, destroying it and throwing six captured brethren into prison. In response the knight-brothers devastated the surrounding farmlands, burnt manors and barns, cut down fruit trees, drove off livestock and killed the burghers who tried to intervene. On Christmas Eve, they routed a force from the city, and then mocked the terrified inhabitants by shouting, "Where is your pope?" In desperation, the Rigans turned for help to the knight-brothers' most implacable foes, the Lithuanians, who immediately invaded Livonia, defeating and killing the Livonian master, together with 60 of his knights. Even though the Lithuanians soon returned to their home country, the conflict between the Rigans and the knight-brothers continued.

Appalled at this turn of events in the Baltic, Pope Boniface VIII demanded an explanation, and in July 1299 representatives of both sides pleaded their cases before him. According to the Rigans, the Teutonic Knights were mere ruffians, more interested in making money than in fighting the heathens. Archbishop John III of Riga, whose estates had been seized by the brethren and who had been held by them for 30 days, was especially vehement in his denunciation. The order was given Livonia, he claimed, to assist in the work of converting the natives and to defend the country from attack; instead of which it had hindered the task of conversion and refused to fight the pagans. It was the Teutonic Knights, he insisted, who had driven King Mindaugas into the wilderness, and who, by their "savagery, cruelty and tyranny" had deterred natives from accepting the Christian faith.

The order indignantly denied the accusations, arguing that the knight-brothers had paid with blood to achieve the conversion of Livonia. Such was their success, they claimed, that if a native was asked, "Do you believe in God?" he would reply, "I believe in God and the Holy Roman Church, and in the catechism, like other true and good Christians". Pope Boniface tried to arrange a compromise between the two sides, persuading the Archbishop and the Rigans not to pursue charges in return for a promise by the order to give back what it had taken.

However, in 1306 the quarrel was revived by Archbishop John's successor, who added witchcraft, sodomy and genocide to the original charges against the order. Previously, the Teutonic Knights had been able to rely on good standing with the curia to help them through difficulties with awkward prelates. But the new pope, Clement V, elected in 1305, was a close ally of Philip IV of France – and Philip's declared aim was to abolish the existing military orders and set up a new one with himself at its head. In October 1307, he arrested all members of the Templar order then resident in his realm and had them tried for heresy. A year later, he prevailed on Pope Clement to authorize the arrest and trial of Templars throughout Europe. Although the charges were groundless, confessions were obtained under torture, and many knights who had fought against the infidel were burnt alive at the stake.

The lesson was not lost on the Teutonic order which, in 1309, hastily transferred its headquarters from Venice to Marienburg castle in Prussia, beyond the reach of either pontiff or monarch. The move came just in time. The following year, Clement appointed a commission to investigate all outstanding charges against the Teutonic Knights, who "shaming all the faithful, and damaging the faith, have become . . . familiars of the enemy, not fighting in the name of Christ against the enemies of the faith, but rather, astounding to hear, waging war on behalf of such people against Christ, with various cunning ruses".

In the event, there was little the Pope could do. Without signed confessions, there were insufficient grounds for proscribing the order, and its enemies had to be satisfied with a papal directive banning the knight-brothers from Riga – a directive that was rescinded only a few months later.

The brethren's problems with the papacy did not prevent them from pursuing their expansionist ambitions in the Baltic. In 1308, they had occupied the Polish province of Pomerelia, including the coastal city of Danzig, thus sparking off a prolonged, if intermittent, conflict with Poland. They also pressed on with the war against the Lithuanians, who were now united under the powerful Liutaras dynasty.

With the loss of Acre, it was no longer possible to take the cross to Palestine, so adventure-seeking nobles from all over Europe flocked to join the Baltic Crusade.

The Teutonic Knights, though themselves abstemious, gave lavish hospitality to such guests, providing sumptuous banquets and entertainments, with music, juggling and jousting. The main event of the programme — the *reysen*, or raids, against the Lithuanians — depended on the season. The *winter-reysa*, involving 200 to 2,000 Crusaders, was a rapid foray, aimed at clearing and plundering an area as quickly as possible. There were usually two *winter-reysen* — one in December, the other in January or February, with an interval for the Christmas feast.

The *sommer-reysa*, held in August or September, was larger and more elaborate, the object of the undertaking being to conquer new territory, either by destroying an existing stronghold or by building a new one. One of the French knights who took part in a *reysa* saw it as "a grand affair, and very honourable and beautiful", what with the "great assemblage of knights and squires and noblemen, both from the kingdom of France and elsewhere".

Despite their theatrical trappings, *reysen* were not for the faint-hearted or the physically unfit. Whatever the season, the Crusaders had to spend several weeks hauling armour and supplies through dense forest in order to reach their objective. Although they usually had Prussian guides, Crusader armies sometimes lost their way never to be seen again. And always there was the risk of the unexpected — a sudden flood in summer or a thawing of the ice in winter, an attack by wild beasts, an ambush by Lithuanians. But such rigours seem to have had little effect on the warlike ardour of the Crusaders, who fought with their usual remorseless savagery.

Although captured Lithuanians were often ransomed by the Crusaders, as were captured Crusaders by the Lithuanians — the Teutonic order promised to pay for the release of any Christian knight who fell into enemy hands — this courtesy was extended only to the rich and highborn. The common soldier and hapless peasant could expect less tender treatment. Such was the reputation of the Crusaders that the inhabitants of one Lithuanian village decapitated one another rather than be captured by besieging Christians. One old woman killed over 100 warriors in this way and, when the Crusaders finally broke in, used the axe to split her own head.

Throughout the early and mid-14th century, the Teutonic Knights enjoyed a high summer of unprecedented power and prestige. But by 1386 their downfall was in sight. In that year, the Lithuanian leader, Grand Duke Jogaila, became a Catholic, married the Polish queen Jadwiga and was crowned King Vladislav IV of Poland. Not only was it now difficult for the Teutonic Knights to justify the continuation of a Crusade against a Christian ruler, but also the dynastic union of Poland and Lithuania posed a serious military threat to the order.

A day of reckoning was inevitable, and it came on July 15, 1410, at Tannenberg (Grunwald), near the Prussian border with Poland. In a bloody, 10-hour encounter, a Polish and Lithuanian army decimated the forces of the Teutonic order. Among the fallen were the grand master, the chief officials and some 400 of the brethren. However, the triumphant allies failed to take Marienburg itself, and after a 57-day siege, the Poles and Lithuanians withdrew leaving the order with most of its territories intact. It would, indeed, be another century and a half before the order, overwhelmed by enemies both from within and without, was forced to cede the last of its lands to Poland. But Tannenberg was the turning point, marking the start of the order's decline and effectively ending the Baltic Crusade.

# THE GOTHIC ZENITH

As men sought to provide an ideal setting for the worship of God, 13th-century Europe witnessed a proliferation of both art and architecture in a dramatic new manner. The pioneers of the style known today as Gothic – a name bestowed on it by hostile writers of the Renaissance who identified it with medieval barbarism – aimed to create no less than an earthly prefiguration of paradise.

Churches became thronged with images of saints, prophets and martyrs. Artists adopted an arresting realism, abandoning the stylized Romanesque figures of the 11th and 12th centuries. Both painters and sculptors showed a fresh interest in the humanity of Christ, and invested his actions – as in crowning his mother, the Virgin Mary *(right)* – with new tenderness.

At the same time, architects aspired to create buildings whose soaring spaces would emphasize the mystery and the immensity of God. They were inspired above all by the symbolism of light, the element they believed resembled most closely the power of God, illuminating the darkness of creation.

Conceived at the abbey of St.-Denis outside Paris in the years after 1137, the mode attained an aesthetic peak in a series of great cathedrals built in northern France under the personal patronage of the French kings. With pronounced local variations, the style spread to England, Germany and other neighbouring lands.

Previously churches had been buildings full of gloom and shadow. To support the immense weight of the masonry and roof, Romanesque builders had had to rely upon the rounded arch, sustained with the aid of massive walls and very thick internal pillars. The Gothic style introduced such technical innovations as the flying buttress – an external stone brace supporting the walls – and the pointed arch, which reduced lateral thrust and could sustain a skeleton of stone ribs to bear the weight of the roof.

Relieved of part of their load-bearing function, the outer walls of churches could be transformed into delicate shells encompassing wide expanses of stained glass. Soaring to unprecedented heights, the windows created an architecture of light, drenching the interiors of churches in a multicoloured radiance.

# THE UPWARD URGE

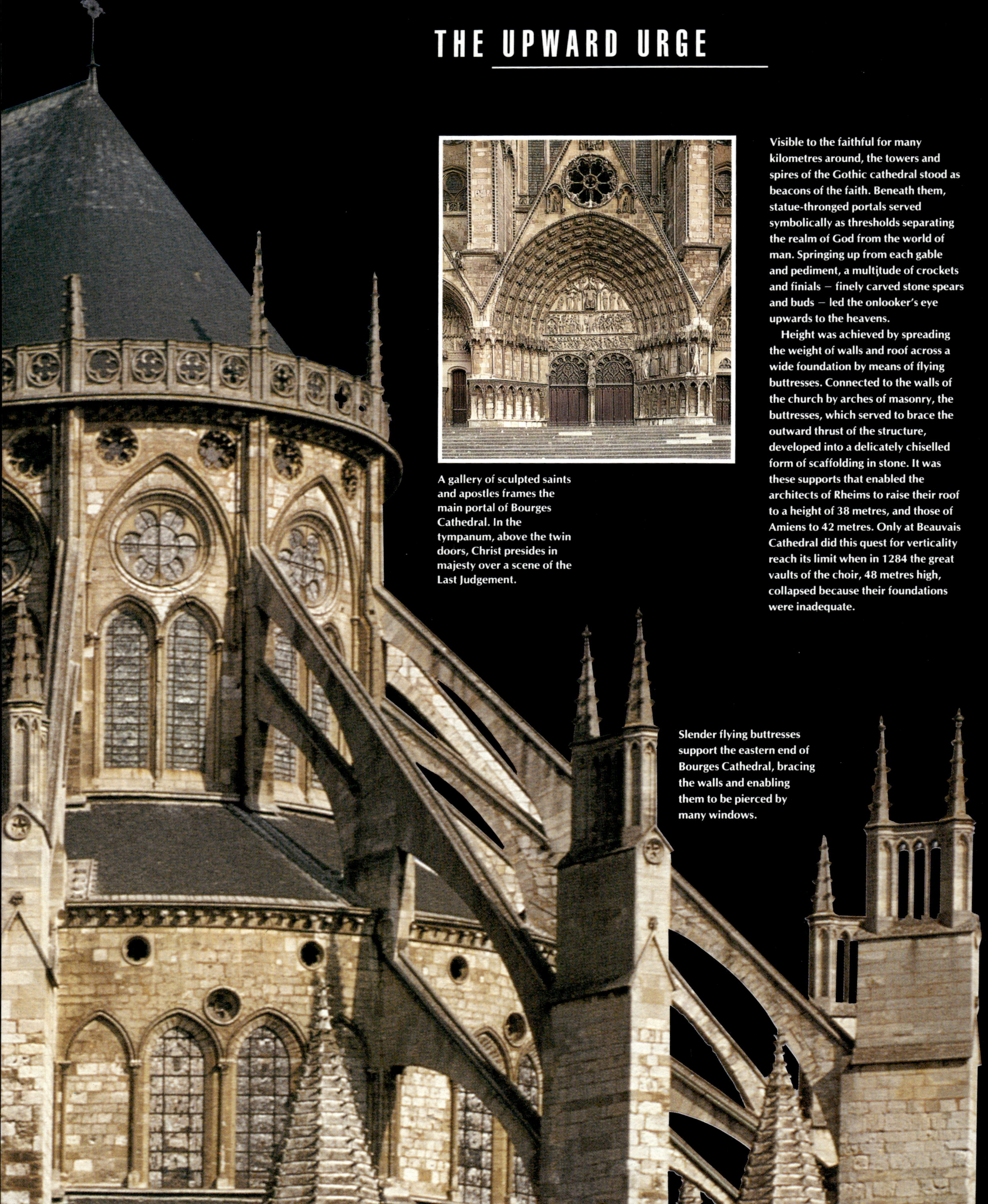

A gallery of sculpted saints and apostles frames the main portal of Bourges Cathedral. In the tympanum, above the twin doors, Christ presides in majesty over a scene of the Last Judgement.

Visible to the faithful for many kilometres around, the towers and spires of the Gothic cathedral stood as beacons of the faith. Beneath them, statue-thronged portals served symbolically as thresholds separating the realm of God from the world of man. Springing up from each gable and pediment, a multitude of crockets and finials – finely carved stone spears and buds – led the onlooker's eye upwards to the heavens.

Height was achieved by spreading the weight of walls and roof across a wide foundation by means of flying buttresses. Connected to the walls of the church by arches of masonry, the buttresses, which served to brace the outward thrust of the structure, developed into a delicately chiselled form of scaffolding in stone. It was these supports that enabled the architects of Rheims to raise their roof to a height of 38 metres, and those of Amiens to 42 metres. Only at Beauvais Cathedral did this quest for verticality reach its limit when in 1284 the great vaults of the choir, 48 metres high, collapsed because their foundations were inadequate.

Slender flying buttresses support the eastern end of Bourges Cathedral, bracing the walls and enabling them to be pierced by many windows.

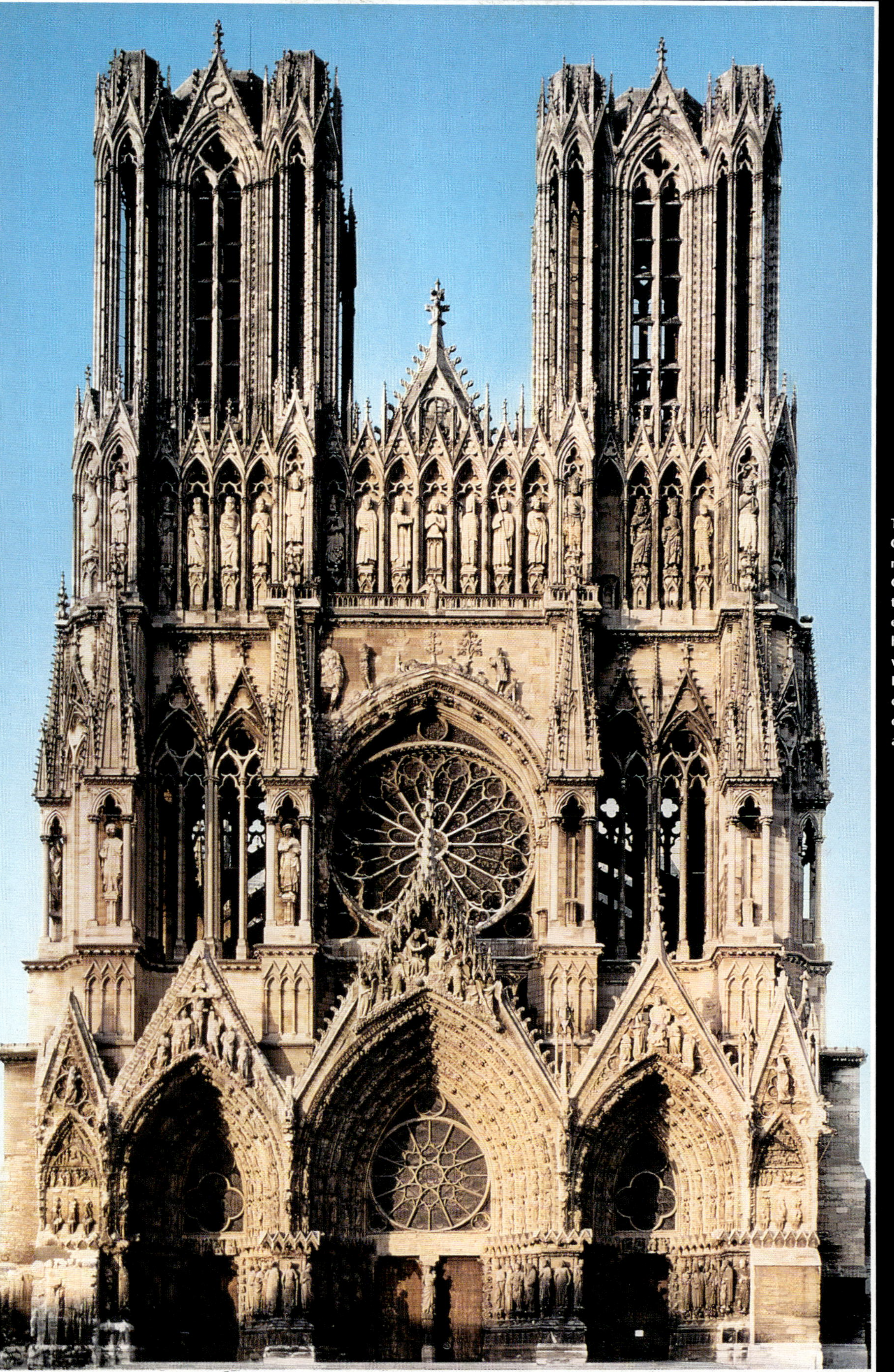

The west façade of Rheims Cathedral is an enduring monument to the vision of Gothic architects seeking to make their churches earthly counterparts of the heavenly kingdom. Visitors were reminded that Rheims was the coronation church of France by a row of Old Testament kings set above the west window.

Its arches aimed like arrows to the heavens, a side aisle parallel to the nave of Rheims Cathedral draws the eye inexorably to the glow of stained glass at its eastern end.

# THEATRES OF LIGHT AND SHADE

Bathed in a richly hued glow, the interior of the Gothic cathedral was intended as a theatre for the performance of the Christian liturgy. Builders achieved the effect typically by the insertion of at least two rows of windows – one to illuminate the nave and aisles near ground level, the other immediately below the roof – separated by a pillared gallery. The columns that bore the weight of the roof were carved into clusters of delicate shafts, surmounted by stone ribs which sprang out to meet in pointed arches at the centre of the vault. The angle of the arch could be widened or narrowed to support roof areas of differing width at the same height – a feat impossible with the earlier system of rounded arches and barrel vaults.

Buttercups adorn a capital in Southwell Minster.

Borne on slender, shafted pillars, the nave of Bourges Cathedral soars to a height of 40 metres in three tiers – an arcade at ground level, a pillared gallery or triforium, and an upper range of windows known as the clerestory.

# A NEW HUMANITY IN STONE

Carrying a chalice and a pennanted cross, a statue from Strasbourg Cathedral symbolizes the role of the Church in dispensing the sacraments.

A realistic statue adorns Naumburg Cathedral.

Statues, placed inside the cathedral or arranged in rows on its outer walls, functioned as sermons in stone, reminding the faithful of a biblical character or a benefactor, or illustrating theological messages, for example by juxtaposing Old Testament prophets with the gospel writers to emphasize the continuous transmission of the word of God. In this way stone carving served not only to provide a visual reference work for congregations who were for the most part illiterate, but also to convey religious ideas by means of sculpted parables and allegories.

A pair of statues from the west façade of Strasbourg Cathedral show a foolish virgin preparing to accept an apple proffered by a handsome tempter.

Juxtaposed with the figure representing the Church shown opposite, this symbolic statue of the Synagogue, shown with eyes blindfolded, was intended to emphasize the superiority of the New Testament faith over that of the Old.

# PAINTING IN LIGHT

A roundel, or small circular window, from the north choir of England's Canterbury Cathedral depicts an incident during the siege of the city by the Danes in 1011.

The crowning glory of Gothic architecture was the stained glass that turned church windows into lustrous visions of a better world. Enclosed within a tracery of lead, the windows were held in place by supporting spokes of iron driven into the surrounding masonry. Various pigments were added to the glass to create its rich colours, the most popular being a brilliant sapphire blue made from cobalt oxide sand imported from Bohemia. A brown resin was used to sketch in details such as faces and drapery. The characteristic ruby red was produced from copper oxide, so deep in hue that sheets of clear glass had to be laminated on to layers of the red to make it transparent. The end product was a gemlike radiance that transformed light – in the words of a contemporary English scholar, Robert Grosseteste – into "the mediator between bodiless and bodily substance, at the same time spiritual body and embodied spirit".

Circled by apostles, angels, saints and martyrs, Christ is portrayed in glory at the centre of the southern rose window of Notre Dame, the great cathedral church of Paris, completed in the year 1230.

The greatest monument to the Gothic passion for stained glass, the Sainte-Chapelle in Paris, was built by King Louis IX to house one of Christendom's most holy relics, Christ's crown of thorns. The King purchased the crown in 1239 for 135,000 livres, more than thrice the cost of building the chapel.

# EUROPE'S NEW MONARCHIES

6

At first glance, Louis IX of France and Henry III of England would seem to have been remarkably similar. They were closely related by blood, both being descendants of Henry II of England and Eleanor of Aquitaine. Both commanded territories in France for the better part of the 13th century, and because of this, their fates were inextricably entwined. Each acceded to his throne when he was only a boy, and each had redoubtable regents during his minority: chief among Henry's was William Marshall, earl of Pembroke, the most famous knight in Christendom; Louis' regent was his mother, the masterful Blanche of Castile. Both kings – and their brothers – married sisters, daughters of Raymond of Provence. Both were pious men who sponsored the construction of soaring churches that were the flower of the Gothic style – Westminster Abbey in London, the Sainte-Chapelle in Paris. Both men had to deal with an unruly feudal nobility and with a powerful clergy. Both presided over the beginnings of true nationhood for their countries.

But the differences between the fates of the monarchs – and those of their kingdoms – were profound. Henry Plantagenet died bereft of authority, reviled by the chroniclers. Louis Capet died in the fullness of his power, so revered that he was canonized shortly thereafter. Henry left territories vastly shrunken from what they had been in his grandfather's day, and a monarchy held in check by England's baronage: the parliamentary system had been born. The French royal domain, by contrast, grew from a relatively small area surrounded by often hostile feudal dependencies to a huge state, united under monarchs whose absolute authority only increased as the century waned.

Some reasons for the differences may be found in the natures of the countries: France was large and diffuse, an advantage for a strong king. England was compact and more homogenous. Thanks to their diversity, the French never established a tradition of communal resistance to the king; thanks to their similarity, the English did. Just as important were the characters of the kings who reigned in the age of change. The successes and failures of Henry and Louis depended in large part on their own personalities – and on those of their fathers and grandfathers.

**In this detail from an illuminated bible commissioned by King Louis VIII of France, a king is depicted holding the orb and sceptre that symbolized his office. Reigning for only three years before his death in 1226, Louis was one of five monarchs to ascend the French throne in the course of the 13th century – a period that saw a consolidation of royal authority not only in France but also in the realm of its old rival, England.**

Few in France could have foreseen the developments of the 13th century as the 12th drew to its close. When Philip II, Louis' grandfather, came to the throne as a 14-year-old in 1180, the French monarchy was weak. Europe was a continent still in the process of settling down after centuries of disorganization and terror. When the migrations and invasions that had shattered the structures of the ancient world at last slowed down and stopped, in about 1000 AD, they left behind a fragmented continent in which a contractual, or "feudal", relationship of mutual support between local warlords and their dependent vassals was the best guarantee of security. The relationship of the king to his lords had the same character: support and protection in return for allegiance and service.

But the degree of allegiance could vary widely. When Philip became king, he acquired two quite separate degrees of authority over different parts of his realm. In territories forming the so-called royal domain – those lands which answered directly to him as their lord – royal power was indeed a reality; but the territory concerned was small. Centred on the île de France and the city of Paris, it stretched barely 150 kilometres at its greatest extent from the capital.

Beyond the royal domain, the king reigned in little more than name. In theory he was feudal overlord of all the various counties, duchies and other territories that made up the land of France. In practice, however, the lords who controlled these regions ruled virtually as independent monarchs, and resisted the encroachment of royal power whenever they could. They acknowledged a formal allegiance to the king as their overlord, but did all they could to maintain their independence.

One such vassal lord was particularly well placed to challenge the French king, and that was the king of England, who had sizable land-holdings on the French mainland. Since the Norman conquest of 1066, the English throne had had links with the duchy of Normandy. The French connection had become greater after 1154, when the throne passed to Henry II, son of the count of Anjou, a leading French magnate. With him had come a disparate empire including – apart from

**In the early 13th century, France was a tangled web of duchies and counties governed by local magnates who recognized a largely theoretical bond to their feudal overlord, the king. Only in the lands of the royal domain – the landlocked île de France around Paris – did the ruler exert unchallenged authority. Controlling Normandy, Anjou and Aquitaine, the greatest of his vassals was the king of England, whose possessions on either side of the English Channel formed the powerful Angevin empire. By the end of the century, however, the situation was very different. Under a series of strong kings, France had wrested from the Angevins almost all of their continental possessions except for that of Gascony (shaded orange on the map), leaving an English realm that – although it now incorporated Wales – was considerably shorn of power.**

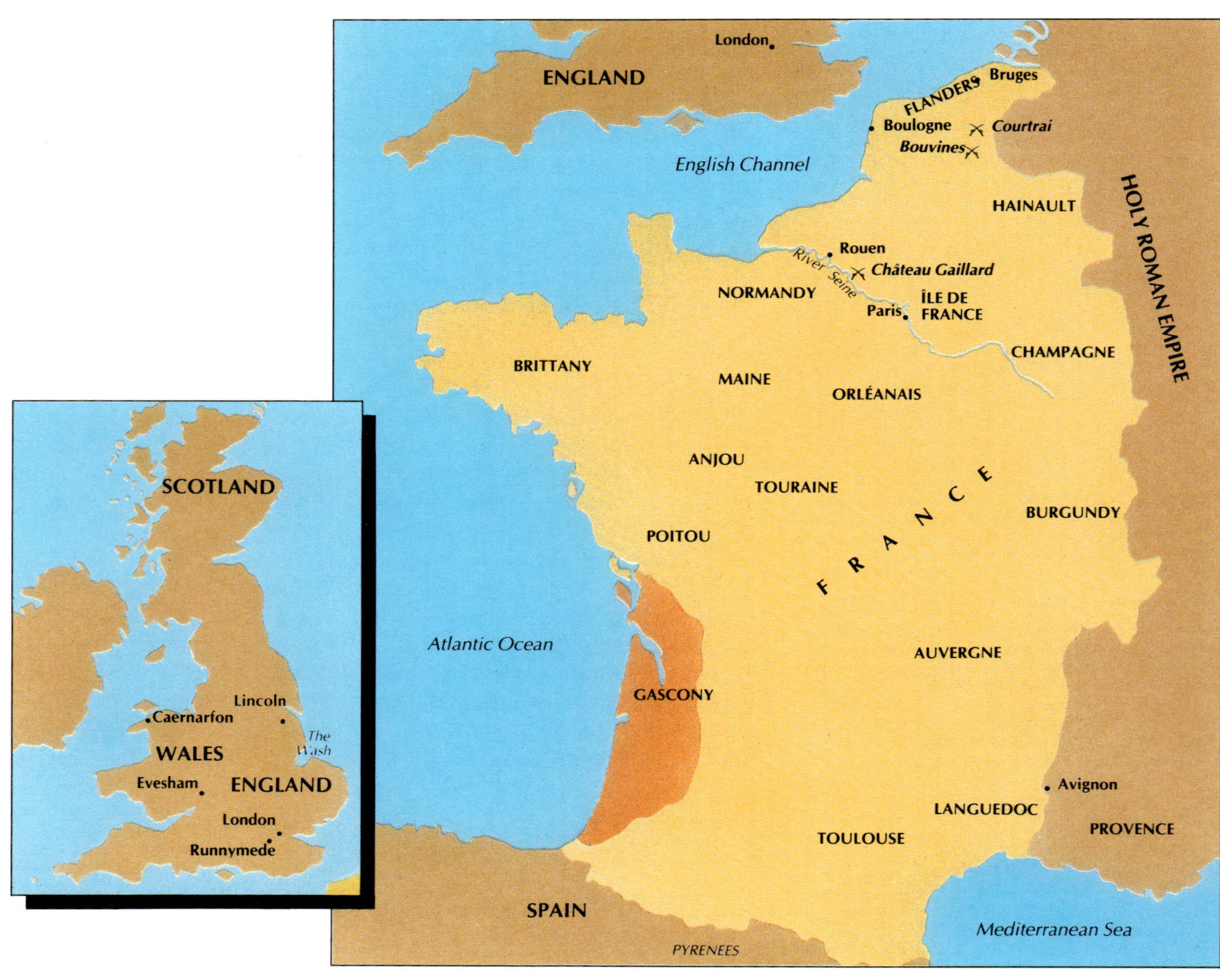

Anjou – Maine, the Touraine, Aquitaine (incorporating Gascony and Poitou) and, from the 1160s, Brittany: in practice the entire western seaboard of France, with its hinterland as far as the Massif Central. Together with England, Normandy, and parts of Ireland these lands made up the so-called Angevin empire.

The Angevin territories in France, held for the most part in vassalage to the French king, were actually far more extensive than Philip's own domain. Henry's heir, Richard Lionheart, had underlined the fact by building a showpiece fortress, Château Gaillard, on the River Seine at Les Andelys, a mere day's march from Paris. Employing the most advanced military architecture of its day, the castle posed a direct challenge to Philip's authority; "I could hold Château Gaillard," boasted Richard, "if it was made of butter".

Philip could make little impression on the Angevin stranglehold while the warrior Richard held the throne. His chance came in 1199, when Richard died and was succeeded by his brother John. The new king's ill-understood character, more complex than that of the ruthlessly effective Richard, led him into diplomatic blunders from which Philip profited. John soon alienated a lord of Poitou by snatching the lord's betrothed bride for his own wife. The noble appealed to Philip, his suzerain, for satisfaction, and in 1202 Philip arraigned John as his vassal to answer the charges against him. John refused, giving Philip an excuse to appropriate his lands and initiate the process of uniting France under a French king.

Philip began by invading Normandy. Château Gaillard fell after a seven-month siege in 1204, and with his strongest defensive position gone, John could no longer control his fiefs. Philip's triumph, aided by well-placed concessions to the English king's former vassals, was soon complete. By 1205, all of John's territories north of the River Loire had fallen, and the richest and most advanced parts of the Angevin empire belonged to Philip. John's overriding purpose was now to regain his lands in France, and it was this determination that led him into a disastrous campaign. Joining with other of Philip's enemies, he set out to conquer the French king.

The decisive battle took place on Sunday July 27, 1214, near the tiny Flemish village of Bouvines, where the boundaries of France, Germany and Flanders converged. The harvest had already begun on the broad sloping fields of the monastery of Cysoing, a small foundation dating from the ninth century, but no one was at work among the sheaves. Glinting across the empty cornfields, two armies confronted each other, committed to battle after days of manoeuvring.

With the sun burning their backs stood the feudal host of France – some 1,300 knights, with the same number of mounted sergeants and several thousand foot soldiers, under the command of the experienced king Philip himself. The oriflamme, the sacred banner of France, had been brought from its usual home in the abbey of St.-Denis near Paris to the King's side in the centre of the front rank.

Opposite the French ranks stood France's enemies. At their centre was the Holy Roman Emperor, Otto, with the standard of his authority: an eagle perched on a dragon, raised on top of a pole. On the right wing, the earl of Salisbury – illegitimate brother and right-hand man of King John – commanded a body of English troops and a horde of Flemish mercenaries paid for with English silver. At Salisbury's side was the energetic count of Boulogne, Renaud de Dammartin. Count Ferrand of Flanders took the left wing with many skilled Flemish knights.

John himself was not present. He was 500 kilometres away to the southwest in Poitou. He had planned to trap the French king with a pincer movement between

# A KEY FORTRESS FALLS

In February 1204, the army of King Philip II of France finally breached the outer walls of Château Gaillard, situated some 80 kilometres northwest of Paris.

The castle had been built in the 1190s by King Richard of England, as part of a chain of forts guarding the duchy of Normandy, then ruled by the English monarch. Modelled on crusader castles in the Holy Land, it featured the most up-to-date military architecture, with two wards or courtyards, a citadel and a keep, all with walls of up to four metres thick. Set on a rocky spur 100 metres above the Seine and flanked on two sides by steep cliffs, it was considered impregnable.

In 1199, the English throne passed to Richard's brother John, and Philip saw the chance to invade Normandy. In August 1203, he laid siege to the stronghold, placing a barrier of boats across the Seine to deny the garrison river-borne relief. While French crossbowmen on a high wooden tower fired at the English garrison, sappers tunnelled beneath the walls, weakening their foundations by setting fires in the passages. In February 1204, the outermost tower fell, and Philip's troops poured into the outer ward, as shown here. An open latrine window gave access to the second ward, and using catapults and mines they took the citadel. On March 6, the remaining 186 defenders surrendered. The duchy's fate was now sealed; within just over three months it was in the control of the French king.

two forces — his own and his allies'. However, Philip's son Louis had him pinned down, and his army had made little headway.

On the sweltering battlefield the commanders were at the ready, each one surrounded by a bodyguard of specially picked knights of skill and rank. But even before the trumpets sounded for the onset of battle, fighting began. King Philip's most active and resourceful adviser, the bishop of Senlis, dispatched a force of mounted sergeants to harry Ferrand's Flemish knights in preparation for a French cavalry charge. The Flemings, indignant at confronting common soldiers instead of their knightly equals, refused to ride out to meet them. Instead they waited for them to charge before driving them back contemptuously.

A vast dust cloud, stirred up by the charging horses, soon obscured the fighting, so that it was impossible for an observer to gain a general impression of the fray. Under the masking dust, individual knights picked out worthy opponents to challenge in combat, while foot soldiers dashed in to strike at a knight's horse or pin down a fallen warrior until a knight came to take his submission. From time to time, tired by bouts of combat, the knights retreated to regain their breath before rejoining the ranks. Well protected by their armour, and by the battlefield convention that captured opponents of noble stock should when possible be taken alive for ransom, they could afford a sporting attitude towards warfare, secure in the knowledge that, barring accidents, they would live to fight again. Typically, most of the casualties of Bouvines were foot soldiers; even the mounted sergeants sent to harass the Flemish ranks suffered only two fatalities when their attack was repulsed.

The tide of battle swept back and forth. At one point John's allies came close to victory, when Otto's German knights made a determined push to reach the French king. Philip's bodyguard held them off, but as they fought German foot soldiers slipped through to surround Philip and kill his horse. The standard-bearer swung the oriflamme wildly to summon aid, and Philip's assailants were put to flight.

Taking a fresh mount, the King urged his men on to attack the German emperor. Otto was less fortunate than Philip. Wounded in the fighting, his horse bolted; his retainers followed their master, leaving the imperial standard behind them. Leaderless, the German knights continued to fight bravely until sundown, but the Emperor's departure was a heavy blow for their cause.

On the allies' left wing, the 28-year-old count of Flanders was also wounded, and was subsequently captured by the French. On the right, the count of Boulogne fought on, gathering his knights within a protective circle of closely packed and heavily armed foot soldiers, tough and battle-hardened mercenaries from the Netherlands; the circle opened to allow sorties against the enemy and to receive knights returning to safety when sorely pressed. But by now the odds were telling against the allies. As evening drew on their ranks became thinner, until eventually the brave count was left with only half a dozen men to continue the struggle. The end came when a French foot soldier succeeded in lifting the section of mail that protected the Count's horse and driving his sword up into its belly. The beast fell, trapping its master under it. After an unseemly squabble among several French knights as to who should take him prisoner, the Count was able to yield to the bishop of Senlis himself, and was led off to join Count Ferrand in captivity. The earl of Salisbury was also taken, and by nightfall the alliance was vanquished.

Back in the French camp, the prisoners taken in the battle were brought before the King. They included five counts and 25 lords of sufficient rank to fight under their own banners. Magnanimous in victory, the King granted them their lives, and dispersed them in bonds to strongholds throughout the country, to await ransom.

Confronted with the collapse of all of his plans, King John had no choice but to conclude a truce with his victorious enemy and return to England. His defeat was the death knell of his hopes. Although no further land was lost, the English monarch's territories on the French mainland were now decisively restricted to the lands that lay south of the River Loire — territories in which an unruly local nobility made overlordship a comparatively profitless business.

Philip, by contrast, won for himself a security on which he could build. In Paris, a storm of rejoicing broke out; it was not stilled for a week. Reorganization of the administration followed, and Paris was developed as the Capetian capital. The name Bouvines became the cornerstone of a royal propaganda edifice. The great day was celebrated again and again in literary works, of which the *Philipide* of William the Breton, Philip's chaplain and an onlooker at the battle, was the earliest. It was William who gave his master the sobriquet of Augustus, "the majestic" — and as Philip Augustus this effective ruler was to be remembered by his people.

The chronicle was completed in Latin by 1224, a year after Philip's death. The monarch was succeeded by his son, Louis VIII, whose brief reign was almost seamlessly continuous with his own. Louis had been actively associated for many years with his father's policies. It was his successful southern campaign that had pinned King John's forces down in 1214; he had subsequently followed up John's retreat to England by crossing the Channel at the invitation of a faction of rebel English barons. The invasion of England was short-lived, however, and Louis devoted his own three years' rule to solving problems in France.

In 1224, at the end of the 10-year truce following the Battle of Bouvines, Louis overran Poitou and started the process of binding that traditionally anti-Capetian region to the throne by awarding grants of money and privileges to nobles, Church and towns. Next he concentrated on the project of extending Capetian dominance into the south of France — a region that was more foreign to the northerners even than England in climate, culture and mentality.

The pretext for the annexation of the south was a war against heresy. In the Languedoc, the doctrine of Catharism — a dualistic religion — was a serious threat to the Catholic church. Its doctrine, which preached that God ruled only the spiritual realm of heaven while Satan held power in the physical world on earth, was incompatible with orthodox beliefs. The pope, after failing to limit the spread of Catharism by political and diplomatic pressure, had made an open offer of his endorsement to whoever would take up arms against its adherents, and northern French barons had been fighting in Languedoc since 1208. By the time Louis joined them after returning from his abortive invasion of England, progress had been made in destroying the ruling families of the south and transferring their lands to their northern attackers; but the French monarchy had not yet gained a real foothold. In 1226, Louis mounted a massive expedition to the Languedoc. Battered by nearly 20 years of savagery and war, the south collapsed. Louis died that year, while his army was still in the field, but the independence of the Languedoc province — though it remained unruly — was already a thing of the past.

Louis IX now succeeded to a royal domain that, thanks to both his father and grandfather, extended from the English Channel to the Mediterranean. The glories of his reign could hardly have been predicted at the time, for Louis was a child

# AN ARCHITECT'S ALBUM

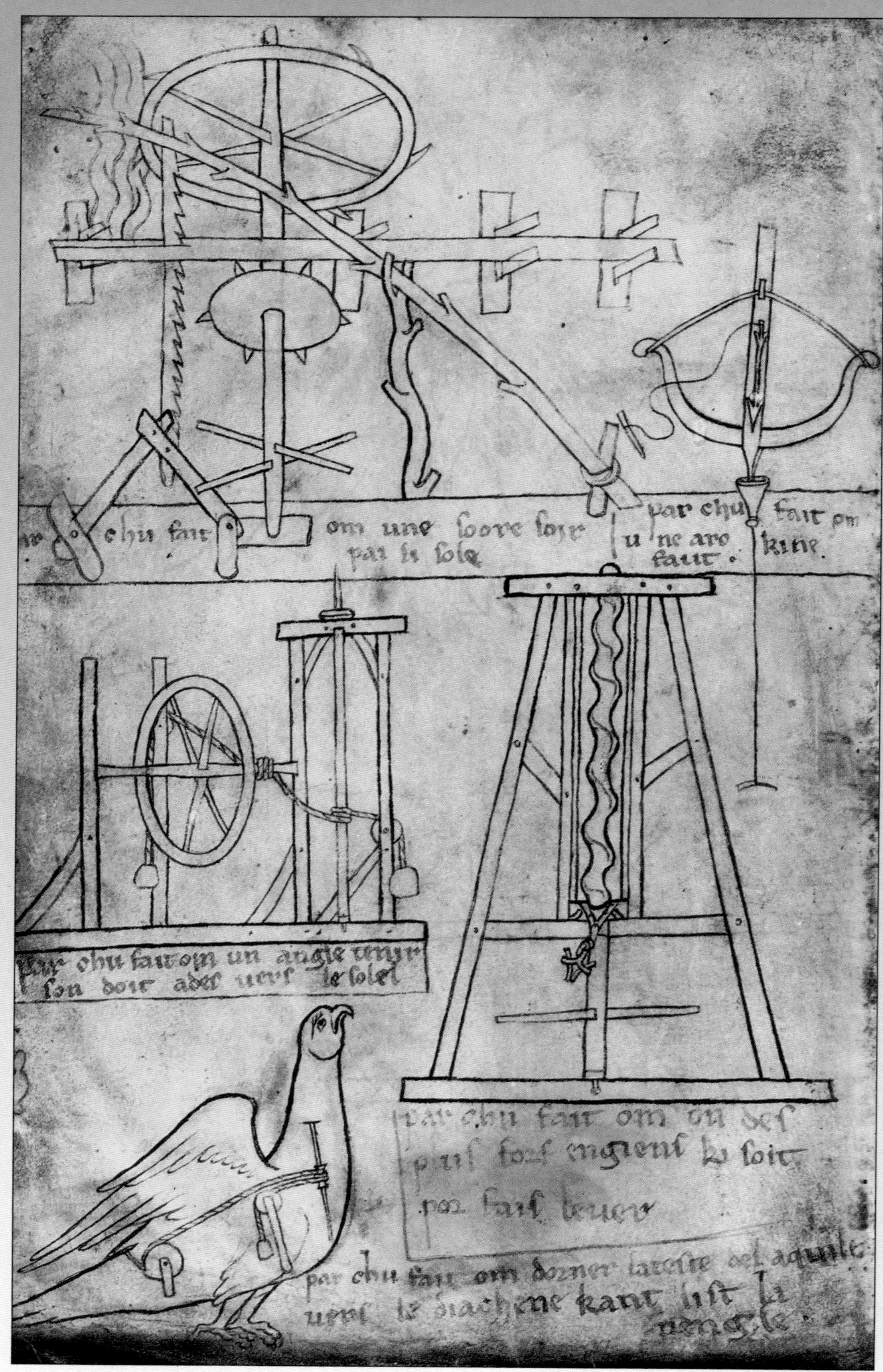

Honnecourt's mechanical drawings ranged from designs for a saw powered by water and a perfectly accurate crossbow *(top)*, to a lectern-mounted eagle which would face the deacon whenever he read the gospels *(bottom, left)*.

Compiled between 1220 and 1235, the sketchbook of the French architect Villard de Honnecourt provides a fascinating insight into the mind of a medieval artist. Combining the roles of designer, sculptor and engineer, a master mason of the calibre of Honnecourt directed, and often personally performed, every stage in the erection of a building, from drafting the plans, to laying foundations, to making scaffolding and machines for transporting stone, to the final decorating. Grouped in "lodges" – exclusive professional bodies, with secret archives containing formulae and methods – such craftsmen enjoyed a particularly high social status.

Like many of his colleagues, Honnecourt was constantly on the move, executing commissions as far afield as Switzerland and Hungary, searching for new materials, examining new designs, and consulting with fellow architects. In an age when copyright was nonexistent, designs were frequently imitated in distant lands. Honnecourt's sketchbook – intended as an exemplar for his apprentices, or possibly for his lodge – contained a wealth of knowledge on proportion, measurement, ground plans, elevations, and architectural learning gleaned from Byzantine and Arab as well as from European sources, in addition to his own pictorial musings on the nature of mechanics and anatomy.

Expressive of utter exhaustion, a figure of Christ lies prostrate. Honnecourt's notebook contained many such drawings, intended as models for sculptural decoration.

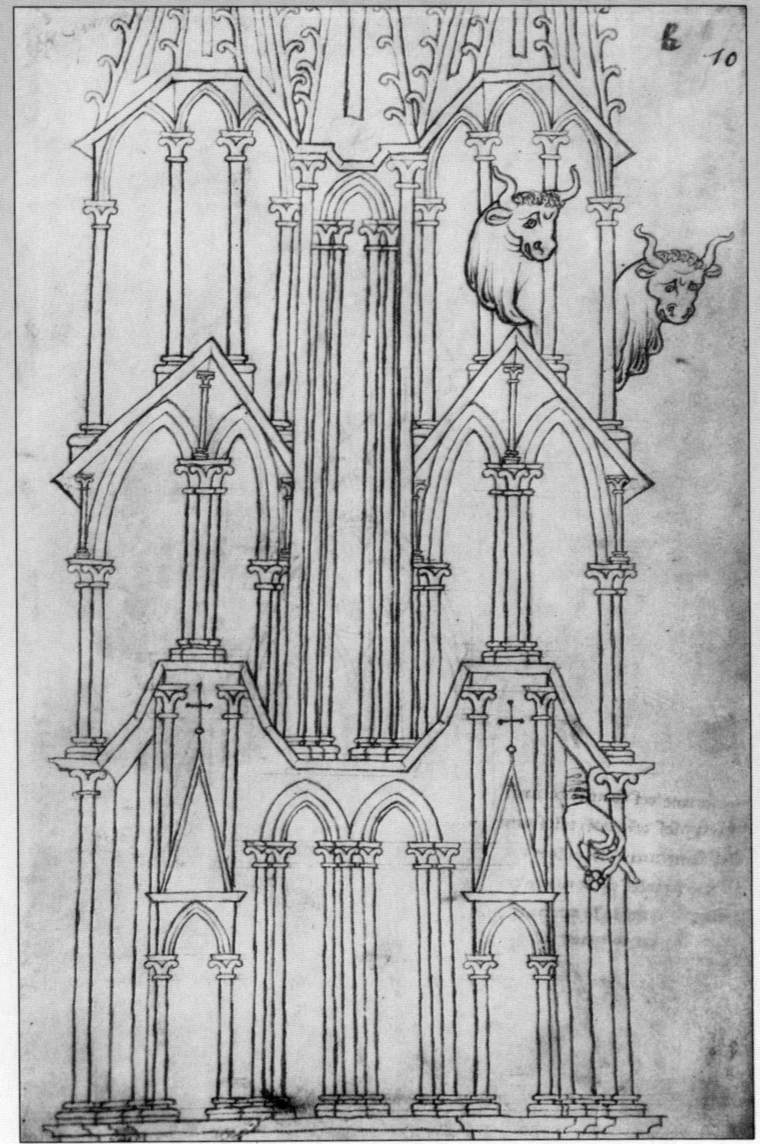


This sketch of Laon Cathedral's towers depicts two statues of oxen, possibly a reminder of the beasts used in the construction. But the hand featured on the right is Honnecourt's own whim.

Depicted revolving round a central axis, four masons chisel each other's feet in this design for a bell-striking machine.

of 12 when his father died, and the barons and princes who had seen their position compromised by the growing power of the throne recognized a chance to regain some of the ground they had lost. So did King John's son, the young Henry III of England, who responded to overtures from the rebel French barons by attempting unsuccessfully to fight his way back into Poitou. But Louis' mother, Blanche of Castile – herself a granddaughter of Henry II of England – emerged as a resolute and able stateswoman; the barons could not agree among themselves long enough to make lasting gains, and Blanche's masterful actions saw the monarchy safely through Louis' minority. So fiercely resolute was Blanche that street songs called her a she-wolf. And even after Louis came of age and married Margaret of Provence, Blanche remained Louis' most valued advisor until her death in 1252.

Blanche's own piety was the formative influence in Louis' upbringing. Louis impressed his contemporaries with his good humour and wit, but above all with his devoutness and his generosity in almsgiving. Although he had strong convictions as to the overriding prerogatives and duties of royalty, and lived amid much magnificence, his personal style was austere and simple. It was said that his clothes, once he had finished wearing them, were not worth handing on to anyone else.

An impressively moral, responsible and religious monarch, Louis made an early start on a series of magnificent endowments and building projects, which enhanced the splendour of the monarchy along with the glory of God. Perhaps the most notable was the Sainte-Chapelle in Paris, designed to house one of Christendom's most sacred relics, the crown of thorns supposedly worn by Jesus.

Louis also embarked on an extensive programme to unite France under royal administration. Relations with Henry of England were made more stable, and the disruptive lords who had caused trouble in his minority were soon brought to heel. In 1247, to aid public justice, he sent commissioners, more often than not friars, known as *enquêteurs* – inquirers – round his territories to deal with complaints against the bailiffs and provosts who processed provincial administration.

Louis showed a concern for just dealing that few of his contemporaries could demonstrate. His friend and chronicler, Joinville, described his way of giving audience to his subjects: "In summer, after hearing mass the king went often to the wood of Vincennes, where he would sit with his back against an oak; . . . those who had any suit to present could come to speak to him without hindrance from any man." Personal probity was to emerge as Louis' dominant characteristic.

Unlike many other kings of the period, Louis answered the papal call to liberate the Holy Land. When Blanche heard that her son had taken the cross, she mourned (in the words of Joinville) "as if she had seen him lying dead". He did return alive – although she did not live to see him – but only after suffering disastrous reverses that left an ineradicable mark.

Louis' Crusade, the best prepared and most expensive expedition ever mounted to the Middle East, set out in August 1248. His forces landed in Egypt, where they soon captured the delta port of Damietta, but from then the expedition found itself in trouble. Disabled by an epidemic of dysentery and scurvy, much of the army – including the ailing king himself – was captured by the Muslim forces while attempting to retreat from an ill-judged advance inland. Louis' queen, Margaret, who had been left at Damietta in an advanced state of pregnancy, saved the venture from complete disaster by promising large sums of money to the captains of the Italian ships that had brought them, thereby preventing their desertion. A vast

Medieval bestiaries — manuscripts describing animals and their behaviour — combined text and pictures to produce "pocket zoos" that often drew parallels between animal conduct and the correct moral deportment of mankind. Based on an early Greek prototype, the *Physiologus*, such books relied more upon popular mythology than accurate observation, describing real animals alongside such creatures as the unicorn and the phoenix. Hedgehogs *(below)* were presented as models of parenthood, feeding their hungry infants with grapes shaken from vines and then impaled on their prickles. Barnacle geese *(right)*, which had no apparent moral significance, were believed, according to Aristotle, to ripen in an underwater nursery, sprouting like fruit from the arms of the barnacle.

ransom secured Louis' freedom, but he had lost a great many of his men. He spent the next four years fruitlessly engaged in Middle Eastern warfare and diplomacy before finally returning home in 1254, having received news of his mother's death the year before.

Louis had been away for a full six years. He could not forgive himself for his failure to free the holy places, and for the loss of Christian lives that the attempt had incurred. For the rest of his reign he devoted himself to living out the role of a Christian king, practising and preaching the ideals of justice and charity and living an increasingly ascetic personal life. The King's concern with just government was everywhere apparent. A reforming edict that was issued in 1254 not only bound the administrators of the royal lands by oath to behave honestly, but also more practically instituted a machinery of appeal should they fail to do so. At the same time, the mission of his peripatetic *enquêteurs* was put on a regular annual footing. The 1254 ordinance was proclaimed throughout the realm of France, the first such to be so. Louis by now intended to rule as a king of the whole nation. The barons were less than happy, particularly when Louis insisted on making them, too, subject to royal justice. He made persistent efforts to forbid the practice of judicial duels, by means of which disputes between nobles were settled by force of arms; in their stead, he encouraged disputants to submit their cases to the Crown.

By now the royal court was the undisputed seat of authority in France. With his officers, Louis devised a variety of means of tapping the wealth of the growing towns, whose rich professional guilds increasingly stood outside the rigid structures

of feudal society. To the traditional royal sources of income — proceeds from the royal domain, now greatly increased in extent, and feudal services in the form of money — were added subventions for specific purposes cajoled out of the towns, special levies, and the proceeds from judicial processes, including fines and the revenues of confiscated properties. In addition, the Church was subjected to heavy taxation. Louis' piety was no bar to the exercise of his prerogatives.

Louis' foreign affairs, however, were less successful. Relations with the English king, who had launched two fruitless expeditions to Poitou, in 1230 and 1242, continued to provide a sour note. Not until the Treaty of Paris, made in 1259 between Louis and John's successor, Henry III, was the reality of French domination given a formal accord. But even then, the terms contained in the treaty pleased the supporters of neither king, and the discord between the two sovereign powers muttered on. And six years later, Louis involved France in the troubled affairs of the Italian peninsula, when he allowed his ambitious brother, Charles of Anjou, to accept a papal offer of the crown of Sicily, contested between the supporters of the papacy and the German imperial house of Hohenstaufen.

Louis was by then growing old. In 1270, ill and failing, he set off again on crusade, but got no further than Tunis before he died. His bones were brought back and buried in the abbey of St.-Denis, to become the object of intense veneration.

After his death, the French monarchy was in a state of such spiritual and political dominance that it looked unchallengeable, not only in France but in Europe. Under the two kings whose reigns saw out the century, the move towards territorial enlargement and centralization of power swept on with a new ruthlessness.

During the 15-year tenure of Louis' son, Philip III, the royal lands were swelled by important acquisitions, most notably the county of Champagne. Long one of the richest and most independent of the great principalities, and geographically central to the consolidation of royal territories, the county was united to the domain by the betrothal of its three-year-old heiress to the King's son and successor. By the time of Philip's death, in 1285, the royal domain far outweighed in size and wealth the remaining duchies of Brittany, Burgundy, Gascony and the county of Flanders.

The new king, Philip's 17-year-old son, Philip IV, continued the trend. Under the ruthlessly efficient influence of a new breed of university-trained lawyer-politicians, guided by Roman civil law rather than the clerical tenets of Louis IX's time, a naked determination to extend direct royal control into all corners and all levels of France emerged as the chief preoccupation of the government.

One of the major targets was the power of the papacy in France. King and pope were soon at odds about the right of the monarch to exact levies from the Church without papal permission. The argument escalated into a conflict over the basic issue of papal authority. Not until 1303 was the issue settled, when Philip took the drastic measure of capturing the pope. When a Frenchman was elected pope in 1305, the papacy was transferred to Avignon, only just outside French territory.

To combat the papal threat to his sovereignty, Philip and his advisers sought to recruit the sympathies of the three estates of the realm: clergy, townspeople and nobles. Representatives of all three were several times summoned to meetings with the King. The expedient provided an invaluable two-way channel of communication: the King was able to explain his case and to receive the endorsement of the people for his policies. The meetings, however, had no legal power to bind the French king; amongst his own people Philip's sovereignty was untrammelled.

**In a detail from the façade of Rheims Cathedral, a Crusader receives bread and wine from the hands of a priest. The crusading movement, originally launched in 1095, still drew thousands of Christian warriors throughout the 13th century. Of many European notables who took the cross, the most ardent was King Louis IX of France — canonized a mere 27 years after his death — who even built a special port at Aigues-Mortes on the Rhone delta, from which his crusading armies could depart. However, his two Crusades were failures: in 1250 Louis was captured in a fruitless assault on Egypt, and in 1270 he died while besieging the North African port of Tunis. By the end of the 13th century, the last Christian territories in Palestine had fallen to the Mamluk rulers of Egypt, and the movement was virtually at an end.**

Philip's mastery of his remaining feudal vassals was much less certain. The two most powerful were the duke of Gascony, alias the king of England (by this time Edward I, Henry III's son) and the count of Flanders. In 1297, goaded by Philip's interference, the two joined together in an alliance reminiscent of the Bouvines campaign. Edward and the Count were at first outmanoeuvred by Philip. But the Flemings so resented the way the French wielded their resulting control that in 1302 they massacred occupying Frenchmen and collaborators in Bruges. An open revolt followed, bringing down on them in vengeance a host of French knights.

But times were changing. When the two forces met at the Battle of Courtrai in 1302, the overweening French cavalry, careless in their knightly superiority, foundered on the bristling pikes of ranks of Flemish foot soldiers. Philip was forced to settle with Edward and failed in renewed efforts to subdue Flanders.

The financial costs of Philip's campaigns were crippling. They led him ever further into new exactions which alienated and alarmed important groups. Mounting provincial resentment greeted the continuing encroachments of his central control. Trouble was brewing that would break out in the dark century to come.

England in Henry III's grandfather's time seemed to have a much more promising future than France – and a much stronger throne. For one thing, England had been conquered in the 11th century by William, duke of Normandy, who had replaced

## A Pagan Survival

**A popular subject for sculptors working in the new Gothic style during the 13th century was the foliate head, or Green Man, whose face, shrouded with leaves, appeared in the stonework and woodwork of churches throughout Europe.**

**A leftover from pagan days, probably descended from either Celtic or Roman gods, the Green Man originally presented a demonic countenance, to inspire fear in the hearts of early churchgoers who associated the natural world with lust and sin. The Gothic sculptors, however, transformed the leafy head into a benign image to symbolize renewal and resurrection. The elevation of the Green Man's character enabled him to be portrayed in central positions within churches, and even in association with Christianity's most sacred figures, Christ and the Virgin Mary.**

**A profusion of carved acanthus leaves forms a foliate head in Germany's Bamberg Cathedral. This Green Man adorned the console of an equestrian statue, dubbed "The Bamberg Horseman".**

its Anglo-Saxon landholding nobility with his own Norman vassals. These lords, having received their lands by direct royal grant, were beholden to the monarchy. As a result, the feudal system had a clearer shape than in France.

The situation grew more complicated in the mid-12th century, when young Henry Plantagenet, count of Anjou, added the throne of England to his existing French possessions. The task of administering lands that stretched from the Scottish border to the Pyrenees conditioned the nature and development of Angevin rule. Outlying regions such as Ireland and Brittany or the Welsh and Scottish marches were left under the control of virtually independent lords. In the Angevin heartlands of England, Normandy, Anjou, Maine and Touraine, however, the king governed through local officials – in England a justiciar, on the continent, seneschals – who answered directly to him. Written instructions were sent to these local officials, travelling commissioners monitored the workings of the organization, and the king himself was ceaselessly on the move. With his itinerant court he migrated from one province to another to review the whole process, try cases and answer complaints, halting to see the queen through another confinement, or even perhaps to gather the scattered family together for a brief Christmas reunion before moving on again.

Organizing the administration of England was only one of an Angevin king's preoccupations, albeit an important one. The English vassals now part of this empire greatly resented the expansion of the Angevin administration, the demands

**A Green Man takes a rare aggressive attitude.**

**Foliage adorns a Poitiers choir stall.**

**A foliate head in Winchester exudes benign calm.**

for money, the interference in local and personal affairs; but at least the king was not always present to irritate them. Richard Lionheart, Henry's heir, was only in England for about one year throughout the whole of his 11-year reign, and John, Richard's brother and successor, stayed away for the first four years of his rule, apart from a three-week visit for his coronation in 1199.

All this changed after the loss of the French provinces to Philip II and the defeat at Bouvines in 1214. Deprived of his favourite continental lands, John was now forced to reside more or less permanently in his English realm. Equally, many of the King's vassals who had held lands spread widely through the Angevin territories now found themselves confined to their English possessions.

John never gained the affection of his vassals, though some of his advisors were conspicuously loyal. His enemies pictured him as a villain of cruelty, lechery, avarice and cowardice, perhaps because his continual conflicts with the Church – he was excommunicated in 1208 and only regained favour in 1213 by making his kingdom a papal fief – alienated the monasteries where the chronicles detailing his crimes were composed. More objective documentary evidence of John's reign shows him to have been, at his best, an energetic and meticulous administrator. He was an educated man who always had books by him – often historical chronicles – but he had also inherited the ungovernable temper typical of the Angevin family. Minor vexations had been known to send his father, Henry II, into tantrums in which he would tear off his clothes and chew the straw covering the floor beneath his feet. John was no more stable, alternating between bouts of energetic decisiveness and an inexplicable, disabling lethargy.

It was not just John's personality, though, that caused problems for him on his return to England in 1214. Lacking the enormous resources of the Capetians, he had completely exhausted his exchequer by the export of huge quantities of silver to pay for the French expedition. In addition, many of the lords and barons whom he had summoned to do feudal service had failed to campaign personally and had sent none of the knights that they owed. During John's absence the kingdom had been left in the hands of administrators – some of them not English – who were unaccountable to anyone but the monarch himself.

The result was a sharp increase in friction between the King and the powerful magnates of the land. John resorted to ever more savage fiscal measures in order to remain solvent. During his reign, succession dues, payable by a baron on his accession, rose from 100 marks to as much as 10,000 marks. The fines exacted by the King's justices for even minor misdemeanours spiralled upwards alarmingly. And John was quite capable of stooping to outright blackmail to raise funds; a record from his exchequer reveals that one northern baron had to offer the King five first-class palfreys in 1210 "that he would keep quiet about the wife of Henry Pinel", paying in addition, a large sum to regain the King's "goodwill". John was also prepared to use the nobles' own wives in his dealings; another record reveals that "The wife of Hugh Neville promises the lord king two hundred chickens that she might lie one night with her husband". The King's harsh exactions raised a growing chorus of discontent that peaked following the defeat at Bouvines.

During the winter that followed John's return from France, he attempted to collect payments in lieu of service from those who had refused to campaign. The barons resisted openly, demanding that the despotic innovations of the Angevin regime be thrown out, and that the customs of Anglo-Norman days be restored.

An ardent advocate of experimentation, the English scientist Roger Bacon carried out systematic studies to draw this diagram explaining how light is refracted when it enters the human eye. Realizing the potential of artificial lenses, he noted that convex lenses could be helpful for reading, a suggestion that heralded the first use of spectacles in Europe. He even suggested that huge refractive mirrors might be built to enable nations to spy on their enemies. A mathematician, alchemist and practitioner of the occult sciences, Bacon was born around 1214 and lived at a time of intense scientific enquiry, during which the works of Aristotle and other Greek philosophers, newly translated into Latin, were being rediscovered by Western thinkers.

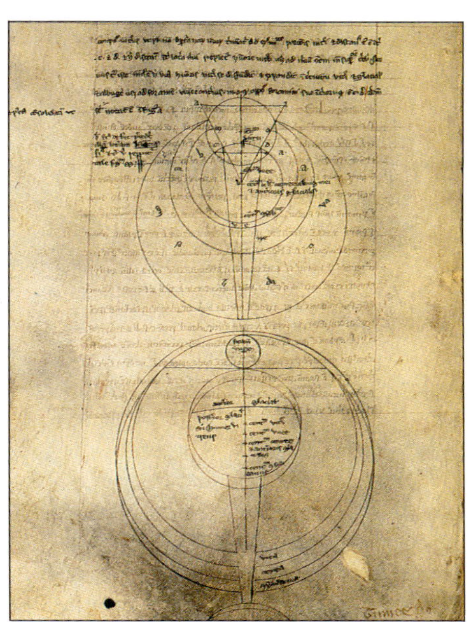

John played for time, going so far as to take crusading vows, thus putting himself and his property under the Church's protection. Meanwhile he sent to Aquitaine and Flanders for mercenaries to crush the rebels. Before they could arrive in force, the barons repudiated their oaths of fealty and took up arms. They failed to capture the important town of Northampton, but Bedford opened its gates to them and they were also able to occupy London, never a stronghold of loyalty to the Angevins. Under pressure from moderate advisers in his court, John asked for a truce.

In June of 1215, the two sides conducted detailed negotiations at the meadow of Runnymede, 30 kilometres up the River Thames from London. By the terms of the agreement they finally reached, the barons renewed their loyalty to the King in return for the issue of the document that came to be known as Magna Carta, the Great Charter. Its 63 clauses consisted of specific promises that were extracted from the King to redress the barons' complaints.

The force of the charter's most important provisions was to assert the supremacy of the rule of law over the arbitrary power of the king. So, in clause 39, the king proclaimed that "No free man shall be taken or imprisoned, or stripped of his rights or possessions, or outlawed or exiled, or in any way ruined, nor will we go or send against him, except by the lawful judgement of his peers or by the law of the land". There was no abstract attempt to define the law; ancient customs such as trial by ordeal or judicial duel were not dead, yet objective inquiries and the taking of evidence were well established too. What the opponents of the King forced him to acknowledge was that he could not proceed against free men on his own whim.

Another central provision was the stipulation that no extraordinary payments to the Crown, whether in lieu of military service or for special needs as they arose, should be made except with the consent of "the common counsel of our realm" — an advisory body comprising, in theory, all who held land directly from the king. Many clauses were devoted to attempts to make the justice of the royal courts more promptly and effectively available; others limited the numerous devices that the Angevins had developed for transferring money from their subjects' pockets to their own. Some paragraphs were no more than restatements of time-honoured customs that the autocratic Angevins had come to ignore; some simply named certain hated royal agents and announced that their careers were henceforth at an end. The merchant community of London was rewarded for supporting the barons with guarantees of freedom of movement for goods and an attempt at standardizing currency and weights and measures. Perhaps the most limiting feature of the agreement from the royal point of view was that 25 of the barons were nominated as a tribunal, to which complaints could be addressed concerning breaches of the charter. As such, it had the power to restrain the king, if necessary by force.

In retrospect, the Magna Carta can be seen as a milestone on the path away from autocracy. In the short term, however, the momentous charter could not prevent England from collapsing into chaos. It was impossible for John's government to cope with the volume of work called for, and some of the more ambitious barons, still hoping to overthrow John, actively sought to renew the conflict. Despite the intervention of Prince Louis' invading troops, who temporarily occupied London, the barons failed to make much headway. John had by now had time to put an effective mercenary force in the field, and the French invasion bogged down.

But John was by now ill with dysentery and weakening fast. Disaster struck on October 12, 1216. Returning with his army from breaking a rebel siege at Lincoln,

John became separated from his baggage train in the fenlands of Cambridgeshire, near the coast of the great bay called the Wash. While attempting to take a short cut across the tidal estuary of the River Wellstream, the packhorses and their drivers came to grief. In the words of a contemporary chronicler, "many members of his household were submerged in the waters of the sea, and sucked into the quicksand there, because they had set out incautiously and hastily before the tide had receded". In the accident King John lost a great deal of his harshly exacted wealth, as well as many of his household effects. He did not long survive the disaster; within the week, in the castle of Newark, he was dead.

His nine-year-old son was speedily crowned king as Henry III; a victory over the invaders and their allies in May 1217, and the destruction of a fleet of reinforcements in August, sent Louis back to France with a face-saving truce; and Magna Carta was reissued (though without the committee of 25 barons) to confirm that the gains of the civil war were not to be reversed. The party of the rebels melted away.

During Henry's minority, a degree of order was restored to England under the regency of William Marshall. After the regent's death in 1219, the young king began increasingly to assume power. England was still under the theoretical protection of the pope, however, and it was 1223 before the young king was granted papal approval to govern the country "principally by the counsel of his own servants". The fact that Henry derived his authority from the pope rather than his own people was greeted with suspicion by the great lords, as was the fact that they now found themselves excluded from the King's confidence by an inner circle of royal advisers – skilled, ambitious men who were often not even English, though they might be rewarded with English lands and titles. In 1225 a further reissue of the Great Charter in return for a general grant of money reassured the barons; nevertheless, the gulf between King and magnates continued to widen.

At 20, with the approval of the pope, Henry came of age. For almost all his long reign – he died in 1272 – he faced his near-contemporary Louis IX across the Channel, and the rivalry he felt for the French king was a lasting theme of his life. He did not profit by the comparison, for Louis outdid him in piety and prestige, as well as political achievements. Yet Henry was a generous and perceptive patron of the arts, and although his reign saw a renewed episode of civil war, he left the kingdom at his death more united and prosperous than it had been at his accession.

The young king was soon alienating the barons by his high-handed actions. He dispensed with his moderate, trusted justiciar, Hubert de Burgh, and deprived that office of its former power; new appointees performed a thorough reform of the administration, both local and central. The chief organ of government became the king's council, a restricted group whose members took a formal oath of office. It included magnates and ministers, but the full-time administrators held the greater influence, thanks to their professional expertise and their closeness to the king.

Henry also infuriated his subjects by his apparent love of foreigners. In 1236 he married Eleanor of Provence, a sister of the French queen, who brought a number of her relatives from Savoy with her to England. Two years later the King's own sister, also called Eleanor, took a French husband, Simon de Montfort. Increasingly the English barons found that they were pushed to one side, as Henry appointed his new French relatives to earldoms and bishoprics.

To the barons it appeared as if all the gains of 1215 were being rapidly eroded. Not only was the King acting in an increasingly autocratic manner, but the foreign administrators that had been a hated hallmark of John's reign seemed once more to be getting the upper hand. Furthermore, King Henry seemed to be uncomfortably dominated by the pope. He was reported to have said, "I neither wish nor dare to oppose the lord pope in anything". By 1238, Henry's unpopularity had reached such proportions that, to safeguard his life against assassins, he thought it would be prudent to have bars fitted not only to the windows of all his chambers but also to the outflow of the royal lavatory at Westminster.

Figures of an apostle and a saint, adorning the sumptuous ecclesiastical cloak known as the Syon Cope, exemplify the style of embroidery known as *Opus Anglicanum*, "English work". Richly decorated with gold and silver thread and studded with precious stones, such garments were prized by popes and emperors and were considered sufficiently valuable to be accepted as security for loans. Merchants made special arrangements for their export, concealing them within bundles of ordinary cloth before risking them upon the pirate-infested seas of Europe.

The nationalistic emotions that Henry aroused among his barons were not in the least assuaged by his attempts to regain the Angevin territories in France. In 1242 Henry became involved in a campaign in Poitou, on the instigation of his mother, who had married a French lord with claims to the province. The campaign ended disastrously, leading ultimately to the Treaty of Paris in 1259, with Henry doing homage to his brother-in-law Louis for Gascony, and formally renouncing all claim to the remaining Angevin lands.

All the barons were strongly opposed to Henry's French adventures, and to other extravagant foreign undertakings in which he dabbled – particularly his acceptance of Pope Innocent IV's offer of the crown of Sicily for his son Edmund (prior to its acceptance by Charles of Anjou). This somewhat ill-judged project involved Henry in an expensive and embarrassing failure that served to further increase the barons' resentment of the Pope's political influence over the King. Henry had similarly disturbed the English bishops by his willingness to allow the Pope to bestow offices and raise money from the Church in England without reference to their wishes. When one papal legate had arrived in 1245, to impose levies on the clergy, the English magnates had told him that he would be torn to pieces if he did not depart.

In 1258 a crisis arose. Resentful of the growing number of foreigners at the court, dissatisfied with the way the country was being ruled, and stung by their distancing from the monarch, the magnates refused to grant Henry the money he needed to finance his rash undertakings abroad. Specifically, they took exception to a demand for a tax to subsidize his Sicilian ambitions, and to the activities of Henry's fortune-seeking half-brothers, who had arrived from Poitou in 1247. Exerting pressure that stopped only just short of armed coercion, the barons forced the King to promise to obey their advice in all matters, placing him under the direction of 15 baronial councillors. They went on to make detailed and very significant proposals for reform. Regular meetings of the council of magnates, now coming to be known as parliaments, were to be held three times a year for baronial representatives to discuss the affairs of the realm. The chief officials of the kingdom were to be responsible to the council. At a local level, knights were to hear complaints and present them to a justiciar appointed by the barons. Knights representing shire communities – the lesser gentry who had long played a part in local administration – were summoned to some parliaments. A regular forum was developing for consultation on affairs of the realm, and the practice of selecting representatives of large groups was gaining currency.

But Henry's resentment at the controls imposed on him led inevitably to renewed conflict. After skirting civil war for several years, the barons and the King agreed in 1263 to refer their dispute to independent arbitration. Their choice of mediator was Louis IX of France, whose reputation for moral rectitude had by now become such that even his old rivals accorded him their grudging admiration. Louis' own belief in royal sovereignty brought him down against the barons, and his judgement released Henry from the restrictions that they had laid on him. The barons – now led by Simon de Montfort, who had emerged as a man of stature whose idealism had separated him progressively from the self-interest and the incompetence of the King – could not accept the negation of their whole achievement implied by Louis' judgement, and there was no escape from war.

Initially the baronial party was successful, capturing the King in battle at Lewes in 1264. But the provisional government set up by Simon in the King's name lacked popular support, and the next year further hostilities resulted in a final defeat for the King's opponents at Evesham, where de Montfort was slain and brutally mutilated.

Among the heroes of the day at Evesham was Henry's son and heir Edward. Unlike his father, Edward was a courageous and effective military leader, who loved war and tournaments and cherished the traditions of chivalry. Tall and curly-haired, the young prince's imposing presence was marred only by a slight lisp and a drooping left eyelid. A true Angevin, Edward had an extremely volatile temper – on one occasion he chased a hunting companion with drawn sword for failing to control a falcon properly – but this was tempered by a deep sense of piety and a keen intelligence that he honed with games of chess.

Following the victory at Evesham, Edward emerged as an influential force in the governing of the land, and he duly ascended the throne as King Edward I on his father's death in 1272. Despite the defeat of the reformers, Edward had in the intervening years shown an awareness of the need for change, and throughout his reign he continued and extended the practice of summoning parliaments. As the highest court in the land, parliament became the arena in which Edward enacted a great series of statutes, aimed at providing remedies for specific grievances, from measures that were intended to prevent subinfeudation – a process by which lands were split up through inheritance into ever smaller circles of feudal obligation – to provisions for the care and maintenance of the roads.

Each parliament was summoned for a range of purposes: to hear petitions and judicial appeals, to grant taxes and to assent to acts of the king. Magnates and bishops were individually summoned; knights of the shire and burgesses from the

## Vignettes of a Prosperous Era

**In England and France, the 13th century was a time of burgeoning populations and widening horizons. Forests were felled and marshlands drained to provide new land for cultivation. In addition, relative political stability encouraged the spread of agricultural technology: windmills, introduced into Europe in the 12th century, now became widespread, and increased use was made of such fertilizers as the mineral-rich sediment, marl.**

**Towns expanded, fed by agricultural surpluses and enriched by profits from fairs and markets. Many larger cities purchased charters for self-government, thus freeing themselves from exploitation by feudal overlords or the Church.**

**This prosperous world, embellished with the glories of Gothic architecture and enriched by a growing number of schools and universities, is reflected in the pages of the Luttrell Psalter. Vignettes of English life crowd the margins of this book of psalms produced for an English noble in the early 14th century.**

**Sheltered from the elements and from prying eyes, the ladies of a royal court travel in a carriage large enough to accommodate many servants and lap dogs.**

boroughs were sometimes called to act as representatives of their communities; and later in the century, members of the lesser clergy were also given a voice.

Edward's reign saw many investigations into the way the country was governed. The first of these, initiated in 1274, sent out royal commissioners to establish who was wielding what powers throughout the realm. Although designed to see whether the rights of the Crown were being usurped, the investigation produced numerous examples of the abuse of power; a prior of Spalding in Lincolnshire, for instance, was discovered to have unjustifiably detained a man in such terrible conditions that his feet had rotted away. These scandals were subsequently dealt with by parliamentary legislation. More important still were the quo warranto inquiries, initiated in 1278, which aimed to establish the principle that all jurisdictional rights were delegated by the Crown. As in France, regional authority was steadily being transmuted into that of the realm.

The main task for which the borough and shire representatives were required was to grant the King money for wars that could no longer be waged solely with the resources provided by traditional feudal obligations of military service. Succeeding English kings had tried to extend their dominion into the unassimilated corners of the British Isles, but both Wales and Scotland had resisted effective intrusion into their Celtic hinterlands – though this was at the price of formally acknowledging the overlordship of the English king. The Welsh chieftains, in particular, had taken advantage of the chaos of the later years of Henry III's reign to renounce this allegiance, and had risen in revolt. Their leader was Llywelyn ap Gruffudd, recognized by a treaty with the English in 1267 as Prince of Wales, the first time such a title had been used. When Llywelyn refused homage to Edward, the scene was set for a showdown that was to prove disastrous to the Welsh cause.

Edward launched a crushingly effective invasion in 1277 that deprived Llywelyn of all but a portion of his lands. Leniently treated after his first defeat, the Prince revolted again in 1282, in resentment at the spread of English influence in the principality. This time Edward resolved to show no mercy, revealing a newly aggressive and expansionist aspect to the power of the English state. By 1284 he had destroyed for ever the ability of the Welsh to resist and integrated the land – held down by a chain of newly built towns and castles – into the English administration.

His army reinforced by large bodies of Welsh archers, Edward next looked to Scotland, which, traditionally linked with France, was a potentially dangerous

**Servants prepare a banquet for their masters, whose rich diet was often enhanced by the addition of oriental spices.**

neighbour. For most of the 13th century, English interference there had been small; successive Scottish kings, married to English princesses, were considered as allies. But the death of Alexander III in 1286, followed by that of his only heir, a little girl of six, left the way open for Edward to make a move. Between 1296 and 1306 he sent eight armies of invasion to Scotland, but the harshness of the English commanders he left in charge led to grim and savage revolts. The final uprising, in 1306, under the able Scottish baron Robert Bruce, proved to be Edward's undoing. Sixty-seven and already terminally ill, the King dragged himself northwards to deal with it. He died on the way in July 1307, and his son and successor, Edward II, lacked the character to combat Bruce's resourceful leadership. His faltering efforts were disastrously repulsed at the Battle of Bannockburn in 1314, leaving Bruce to dominate England's northern boundary as king of a still independent Scotland.

The repeated and sustained campaigns required to subdue Celtic resistance to the King's territorial ambitions, as well as excursions into France to protect Edward's rights in Gascony, damaged the King's generally harmonious relationship with his subjects. The fact was that such wars could no longer be represented to the feudal vassals as shared necessities that required their loyal support, nor could they be concluded within the 40 days of service that feudal custom sanctioned. Payment for military service was unavoidable, whether it was given to barons and knights to keep them in the field after their customary service had expired, or to foreign mercenaries. The need to raise revenues for such purposes led to a confrontation in the year 1297, when Edward was forced to mollify an angry nation by reissuing Magna Carta yet again, this time with the added provision that no taxes, over and above the traditional feudal levies, would be raised without the "common assent of all the realm, and for the common profit thereof". The King later reneged on the agreement, winning a papal dispensation to cancel his promise, but nonetheless a precedent had been set for future generations to pursue.

The century during which the monarchies of England and France thus began to move into a post-feudal world was a century of continuing economic vigour and expansion. The population of both countries was growing, marginal land was being brought into cultivation to support the extra mouths, and growing agricultural surpluses encouraged the development of urban centres. New towns came into being, and existing ones spread out into cities. And money now circulated in ever increasing quantities, with far-reaching effects on every side of life.

**A group of English villagers take turns at archery practice.**

In the century to come, the growing population of Europe would contribute to food shortages, urban unrest and declining living standards, but for the moment it was against a background of relative prosperity that France and England led the way in the development of national spirit.

The implications of the national monarchy were many and various. Each country sought to assert its rights over the Church within its boundaries, occasioning conflicts with the papacy. There was a tremendous increase in the scale of government activity on both sides of the Channel; not only were there many more officials at work, but there were also now attempts — in France via the *enquêteurs*, in England through Edward's administrative investigations — to keep some sort of check on their activities. The study of Roman law, which emphasized civic responsibility and the good of the state, was spreading in both lands, and its concepts slowly started to oust older, feudal views of personal obligation.

Both nations managed to consolidate the lands over which they had control into more practical geographical entities. Indeed, Henry's failure to regain England's French territories ultimately produced a more manageable and coherent realm. In addition, both the English conquest of Wales and the French annexation of the Languedoc helped to create states approximating far more closely to the nations that now bear the names of France and England than the oddly shaped feudal conglomerates of the year 1200. Gascony, however, remained in the hands of the English king. Its retention was to prove a running sore constantly troubling relations between the two lands; in the course of the next century it would plunge them into the horrors of the Hundred Years' War.

Yet there were also significant differences between the two emergent nations, most notably the nature of their rulers. In France, an autocratic monarch ruled through a large body of royal administrators, his actions little hindered by the need to consult with local assemblies. In England, however, the king was held in check by his own subjects, and a tradition of opposition, growing out of Magna Carta, resurfaced regularly during the century to demand a more general consultation. By the year 1300 the seeds of future constitutional development in the two lands had been sown and were already beginning to germinate.

**Soldiers brave the waves in a turreted warship that resembles a seaborne fortress.**

# CASTLES OF A CONQUEROR

The 13th century was a great age for castle-building in Europe, especially in contested lands, where the strongholds – and the soldiers that were housed inside them – could be used to impose a ruler's will on recalcitrant subjects for many kilometres around. This strategy of conquest was never more thoroughly employed than in the subjugation of Wales by England's king Edward I.

Long after Norman invaders had imposed their rule on southern Wales in the 11th and 12th centuries, the northern lords of Gwynedd remained defiantly independent, isolated from their English neighbours by language, culture and the formidable mountain barrier of Snowdonia. Unable to subdue them by military means, King Henry III of England had recognized the most powerful, Llywelyn ap Gruffudd, as prince of Wales in return for an oath of fealty to the English crown. But Llywelyn consistently refused to pay homage, and Henry's successor, Edward, determined to crush his unruly vassal and impose his supremacy over all of Wales.

In 1277, Edward I mounted a great campaign of conquest, cutting through Llywelyn's territory to seize the island of Anglesey in the northwest, whose vital grain fields had enabled the rebels to sit out previous sieges in their mountain fastness. A truce was arranged, but in 1282 rebellion erupted once more, resulting in a crushing defeat for Llywelyn, who was himself slain; with him died the last hope of Welsh independence.

The previously independent parts of Wales were reduced to the status of a colony, governed from London. English law was introduced, English taxes were levied, and Welsh troops were recruited into English armies. A rebellion in 1294 failed, and seven years later Edward sealed his conquest by making his own son and heir prince of Wales.

By 1300, Edward had secured the wild hinterland of Snowdonia with a ring of great castles on or near the coast, indicated on the map opposite: Hope, Flint, Rhuddlan, Conwy, Beaumaris, Caernarfon, Criccieth, Harlech, and Aberystwyth to the south. Beneath the walls of each he created new towns in which English immigrants were encouraged to settle by grants of land and other privileges. Edward already had experience of creating fortified towns in Gascony, and the castle-town complexes he erected in Wales were imposing statements of military, economic and social domination. Linked to the castles by strong walls, the towns provided secure havens from which their inhabitants could trade in deliberately favoured competition with the native peoples.

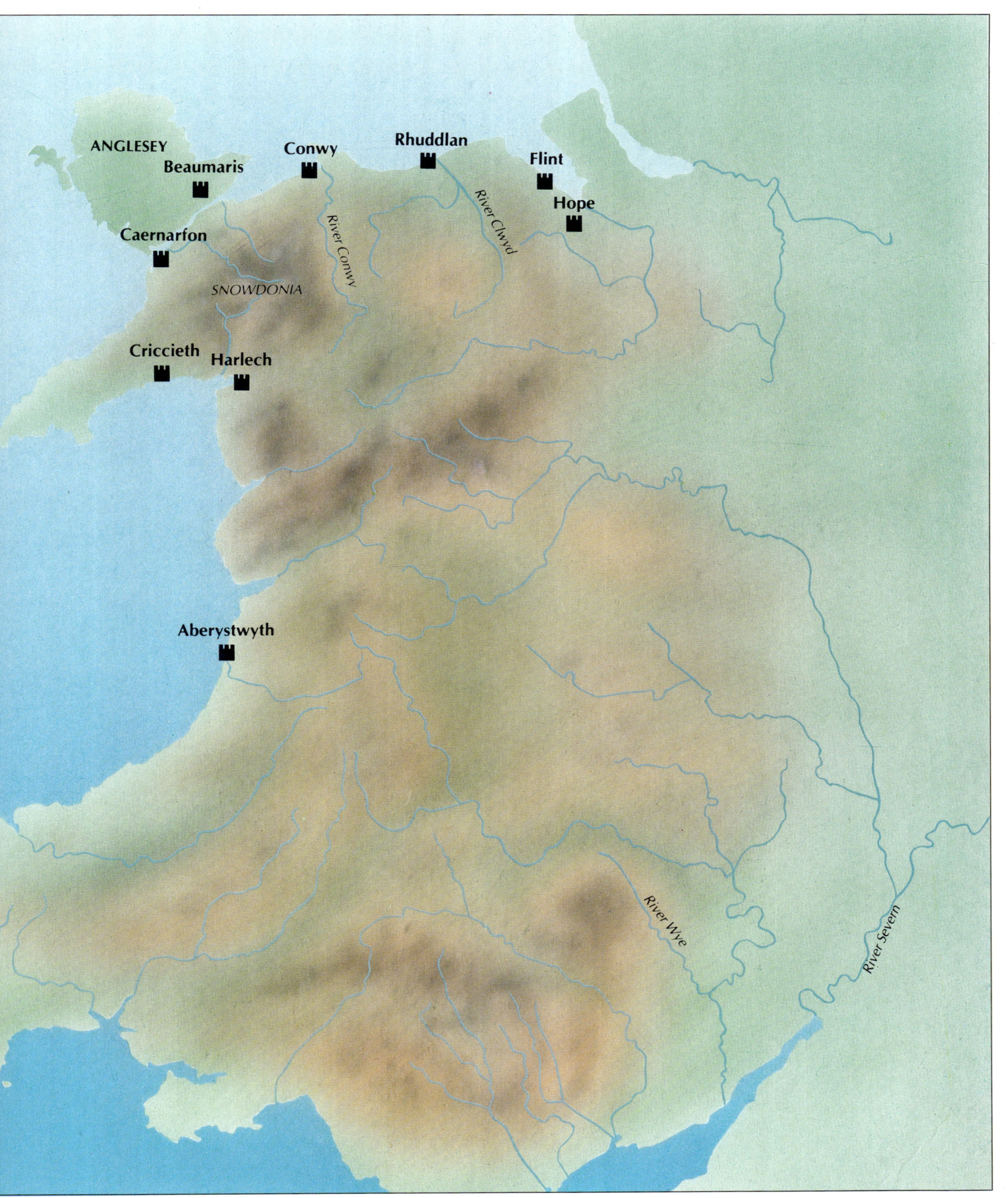

ANGLESEY
Beaumaris
Conwy
Rhuddlan
Flint
Hope
Caernarfon
River Conwy
River Clwyd
SNOWDONIA
Criccieth
Harlech
Aberystwyth
River Wye
River Severn

# CAERNARFON: OUTPOST OF THE ENGLISH

Massively fortified, and strategically situated on the Menai Strait, Caernarfon was the mightiest link in Edward's chain of castles, designed to resist any attack. Its sandstone-banded walls and multiangular towers were modelled on those of Constantinople, which was built in the fifth century and was still reputed to be the strongest fortification in the world.

The town at its base was also protected by a sturdy wall, 734 metres long, behind which lay a grid of cobbled streets dividing the land into equal plots of 18 by 24 metres. These burgages, as they were known, were granted to English settlers, who were encouraged to construct houses, to cultivate the surrounding countryside and to rent stalls in the newly built market and round the harbour. The town had its own civic buildings and law court, under whose partisan jurisdiction the trade of immigrant leather workers, tanners and wool merchants flourished.

# STRUCTURES DESIGNED FOR DEFENCE

Using the latest military designs, Edward's Savoyard architect, James of St. George, linked Caernarfon's seven towers and two gates with galleried curtain walls, giving defenders great freedom of movement. Arrow slits commanded every approach, some allowing a single archer to shoot in many directions, others focusing the aim of several bowmen on to a single target. All entrances were heavily protected; the King's Gate was equipped with a drawbridge, five sets of massive doors, six portcullises, arrow slits in the walls, and "murder holes" in the ceiling through which projectiles could be hurled.

Caernarfon, however, was more than just a defensive structure. As the seat of royal government in north Wales, and the site of the exchequer and judiciary, it contained capacious living quarters, administrative offices, and no fewer than six chapels.

A view of the western bailey in 1300 shows the Queen's Tower and the triple-turreted Eagle Tower, the highest in the castle. A cutaway of the castle wall, against which the Great Hall would later be built, reveals two tiers of passages from which archers could pour fire at the enemy.

A first floor cross section of the Eagle Tower reveals both the bastion's main chamber and the complicated construction of its 4.5-metre-thick walls, honeycombed with small chambers and passages. The stairwell serving the tower was accommodated within the thickness of the walls; so was a private chapel.

| | 1200-1210 | 1210-1220 | 1220-1230 | 1230-1240 | 1240-1250 |
|---|---|---|---|---|---|
| **WESTERN EUROPE** | King John of England loses Château Gaillard to the French (1204); within a year the French take all English territory on mainland France north of the River Loire.<br>Pope Innocent III calls the Albigensian Crusade against the Cathars of Languedoc in southern France (1208). | At Bouvines Philip II of France decisively defeats a coalition of his enemies brought together by King John of England (1214).<br>English barons force King John to sign a charter of rights, the Magna Carta (1215). | Frederick II is crowned Holy Roman Emperor (1220).<br>Louis IX ascends the throne of France (1226). | Frederick II defeats the Lombard League – a coalition of north Italian cities – at Cortenuova (1237). | Pope Innocent IV formally deposes Frederick II as Holy Roman Emperor (1245). |
| **THE BALTIC** | Bishop Albert of Riga establishes the military order of Sword Brothers (1202).<br>Bishop Albert's forces subdue the Livs and the Letts, and march on Estonia (1208). | Christian forces destroy the Estonian stronghold of Fellin (1211). | The Sword Brothers, reinforced by Danish forces, finally conquer Estonia (1224).<br>The pope places Finland under apostolic protection, and invokes a trade embargo against Novgorod (1229). | A military religious order, the Teutonic Knights, arrives to subjugate the pagan Prussians (1230).<br>The Sword Brothers are all but annihilated by the Lithuanians at Saule (1236).<br>The Teutonic Order absorbs the territory of the Sword Brothers (1237). | Alexander Nevsky of Novgorod defeats the Swedes on the banks of the Neva (1240).<br>The Mongols defeat a Christian army at Liegnitz in Poland; they proceed to invade Hungary but withdraw on the death of their Great Khan (1241).<br>Alexander Nevsky defeats the Teutonic Order on Lake Peipus (1242). |
| **CENTRAL ASIA AND THE FAR EAST** | The Hōjō family gains control of the military government effectively ruling Japan from Kamakura (1203).<br>Temujin unites Mongolia and takes the title Chingis Khan (1206).<br>The Mongols invade North China (1207). | The Mongols take the Jin capital Zhongdu (1215).<br>Power in Japan passes from the shōguns, or military leaders, to their regents (1219). | In the Jokyu War, the Kamakura military government defeats an uprising of the imperial forces based in Kyōto, who resent their control (1221).<br>Chingis Khan dies on a campaign against the Tanguts (1227), and is succeeded by his son Ogedei (1229). | The military rulers of Japan draw up the Jōei Formulary, a new legal code (1232).<br>The Mongols extinguish the Jin Kingdom in North China (1234). | |
| **AFRICA AND THE MIDDLE EAST** | | | The Mongols overwhelm the Iranian empire of Khwarizm (1221).<br>Frederick II gains Jerusalem by diplomacy in the Sixth Crusade (1229). | | The Mongols defeat the Seljuks of Rum (1242).<br>On the Seventh Crusade, Louis IX of France takes Damietta in Egypt, but is later captured (1249). |

# A Chronology of Major Events: AD 1200-1300

| 1250-1260 | 1260-1270 | 1270-1280 | 1280-1290 | 1290-1300 |
|---|---|---|---|---|
| rederick II dies (1250).<br>3y the Provisions of Oxford, Henry III of England agrees to he establishment of a baronial council with the power of veto over his actions (1258).<br>The Treaty of Paris gives formal accord to Louis' domination of northern France (1259). | Prince Edward defeats rebellious English barons at Evesham (1265).<br>Charles of Anjou takes the throne of Sicily (1268). | Edward I ascends the throne of England, and initiates a series of administrative reforms (1272). | The "Sicilian Vespers" rebellion ousts Charles of Anjou, and gives Peter III of Aragon the crown of Sicily (1282).<br>Edward I of England completes the conquest of Wales (1284). | Edward I invades Scotland (1296).<br>Louis IX of France is canonized (1297). |
| | The Samogitians defeat the Teutonic Knights at Durben, sparking off a native uprising against their Christian rulers in the southern Baltic (1260). | | | The south Baltic tribes are finally subjugated by the Teutonic Order (1290).<br>The Swedes establish the strategic fort of Vyborg in the region of Karelia, disputed with the Russians (1292). |
| The Mongols campaign against he Song of southern China 1253). | Chingis' grandson Kublai defeats his brother to become Great Khan (1264). | In China, Kublai Khan declares himself first emperor of the Yuan dynasty (1271).<br>The first Mongol invasion of Japan ends in the withdrawal of the attacking forces (1274).<br>The Mongols complete the conquest of Song China (1279). | A second Mongol invasion of Japan fails due to a typhoon that became known as the *kamikaze*, or Divine Wind (1281). | Kublai Khan dies (1294). |
| The Mamluks seize power in Egypt from the Ayyubids (1250).<br>The Mongols capture Alamut and defeat the Assassins (1257).<br>The Mongols sack Baghdad and destroy the Abbasid caliphate 1258). | Following the death of Mongke Khan, Mamluk forces defeat the Mongols at Ayn Jalut (1260).<br>The Mamluk sultan, Baybars, re-establishes the caliphate in Cairo (1261).<br>The Mamluks take Antioch from the Crusaders (1268). | Louis IX dies at Tunis in the course of the Eighth (and final) Crusade (1270).<br>The Mamluks defeat the Mongols in Asia Minor and temporarily occupy Caesarea (1277).<br>The Mamluk sultan Qalawun comes to power (1279). | Qalawun defeats the Mongols at Homs (1281). | The Mamluks take Acre, the last crusader outpost in Palestine (1291). |

# BIBLIOGRAPHY


**BALTIC**

**Brundage**, James A., transl., *The Chronicle of Henry of Livonia.* Madison: University of Wisconsin Press, 1961.

**Christiansen**, Eric, *The Northern Crusades: The Baltic and the Catholic Frontier 1100-1525.* London: Macmillan, 1980.

**Evans,** Geoffrey, *Tannenburg 1410-1914.* London: Hamish Hamilton, 1970.

**Michell,** Robert, and Nevill Forbes, transl., *The Chronicle of Novgorod 1016-1471.* London: Camden Society, 1914.

**Probst**, Christian, *Der Deutsche Orden und seine Medizinalwesen in Preussen.* Bad Godesberg: Verlag Wissenschaftliches Archive, 1969.

**Riley-Smith**, Jonathan, *The Crusades: A Short History.* London: Athlone Press, 1987.

**Setton,** Kenneth M., ed., *A History of the Crusades, Vol II.* Madison: University of Wisconsin Press, 1975.

**Seward,** Desmond, *The Monks of War: The Military Religious Orders.* London: Eyre Methuen, 1972.

**Steinbrecht**, Konrad, *Schloss Lochstedt und seine Malereien. Ein Denkmal aus des Deutschen Ritterordens Blütezeit.* Berlin: Königliche Technische Hochschule zu Berlin, 1910.

**Urban,** William, *The Baltic Crusade.* De Kalb, Illinois: Northern Illinois University Press, 1975.

**Vernadsky,** George, *Kievan Russia.* New Haven: Yale University Press, 1959.

**Zamoyski,** Adam, *The Polish Way.* London: John Murray, 1987

**WESTERN EUROPE**

**Anderson,** William:
*Castles of Europe.* London: Paul Elek Productions, 1970.
*The Rise of the Gothic.* London: Hutchinson, 1985.

**Barlow,** Frank, *The Feudal Kingdom of England 1042-1216.* Harlow: Longman, 1972.

**Barraclough,** G., *The Origins of Modern Germany.* Oxford: Blackwell, 1946.

**Branner,** Robert, *Manuscript Painting in Paris During the Reign of Saint Louis.* Berkeley: University of California Press, 1977.

**Brunskill,** R.W., *Illustrated Handbook of Vernacular Architecture.* London: Faber and Faber, 1971.

**De Hamel,** Christopher, *A History of Illuminated Manuscripts.* Oxford: Phaidon, 1986.

**Duby,** G., *Le Dimanche de Bouvines.* Paris: Gallimard, 1973.

**Götze,** Heinz, *Castel Del Monte.* Munich: Prestel-Verlag, 1984.

**Hallam,** Elizabeth, *Capetian France 987-1328.* Harlow: Longman 1980.

**Hampe,** K., *Germany under the Salian and Hohenstaufen Emperors.* Oxford: Blackwell, 1973.

**Harvey,** John, *The Master Builders: Architecture in the Middle Ages.* London: Thames and Hudson, 1971.

**Jackson,** Donald, *The Story of Writing.* London: Barrie & Jenkins, 1981.

**Kantorowicz,** E., *Frederick the Second.* New York: R.R. Smith, 1931.

**Lassus,** M.J.B.A., *Facsimile of the Sketch-Book of Wilars de Honecort.* London: John Henry and James Parker, 1859.

**Leuschner,** J., *Germany in the Later Middle Ages.* Amsterdam: North-Holland, 1980.

**Lobel,** M.D. ed., *Historic Towns, I.* London: Lovell Johns Ltd., 1969.

**MacDermott,** M., *Military Architecture.* Transl. from the French of E. Viollet-Le-Duc. Oxford: James Parker, 1879.

**Masson,** Georgina, *Frederick II of Hohenstaufen: A Life.* London: Secker & Warburg, 1957.

**Morris,** J., *The Matter of Wales.* Oxford: Oxford University Press, 1984.

**Norgate,** Kate, *England under The Angevin Kings.* London: Macmillan, 1887.

**Previt-Orton,** C.W., *The Shorter Cambridge Medieval History.* Cambridge: Cambridge University Press, 1952.

**Robb,** David M., *The Art of the Illuminated Manuscript.* London: Thomas Yoseloff, 1973.

**Roderick,** A., ed., *Wales: A History.* London: Michael Joseph, 1986.

*Royal Commission on Ancient and Historic Monuments in Wales and Monmouthshire: Caernarvonshire Vol. II: Central.* London: HMSO, 1960.

**Simpson,** W.D.:
*Exploring Castles.* London: Routledge and Kegan Paul, 1957.
*Castles in England and Wales.* London: Batsford, 1969.

**Swaan,** Wim, *The Gothic Cathedral.* London: Paul Elek Productions, 1969.

**Toy,** S., *Castles of Great Britain.* London: Heinemann, 1953.

**Van Cleve,** T.C., *The Emperor Frederick II of Hohenstaufen.* Oxford: Clarendon Press, 1972.

**Vaughan-Thomas,** W., *Wales Through the Ages.* Llandybie: Christopher Davies, 1959.

**Warner,** Philip, *Sieges of the Middle Ages.* London: G. Bell and Sons, 1968.

**Warren,** W.L., *King John.* London: Eyre Methuen, 1978.

**Wilkinson,** B., *The Later Middle Ages in England.* Harlow: Longman, 1969.

**Wood,** Casey, and Marjorie Fyfe, transl., *The Art of Falconry.* Boston: Charles T. Branford, 1955.

**CENTRAL ASIA AND THE FAR EAST**

**Bloom,** Alfred, *Shinrans's gospel of pure grace.* Tucson: University of Arizona Press, 1965.

**Brent,** Peter, *The Mongol Empire.* London: Weidenfeld and Nicolson, 1976.

**Cameron,** Nigel, and Brian Brake, *Peking: Tale of Three Cities.* New York: Harper and Row, 1965.

**Chambers,** James, *The Devil's Horsemen.* London: Weidenfeld and Nicolson, 1979.

*China* (Life World Library series). New York: Time Inc., 1963.

**Dumoulin,** Heinrich, S.J., *A History of Zen Buddhism.* New York: Pantheon Books, 1963.

**Duus,** Peter, *Feudalism in Japan.* New York: Alfred A. Knopf, 1969.

**Frederic,** L., *Daily Life in Japan at the time of the Samurai.* Transl. by Eileen M. Lane. London: Allen & Unwin, 1972.

**Gabriel,** Ronay, *The Tartar Khan's Englishman.* London: Cassel, 1978.

**Galt,** T., transl./ed. *The Little Treasury of One Hundred People, One Poem Each* as compiled by Fujiwara No Sadaie. Princeton: Princeton University Press, 1982.

**Gascoigne,** Bamber and Christina, *The Treasures and Dynasties of China.* London: Jonathan Cape, 1973.

**Gibson,** Michael, *Genghis Khan and the Mongols.* London: Wayland, 1973.

**Hall,** J.W., and J.P. Mass, eds., *Medieval Japan: Essays in Institutional History.* New Haven: Yale University Press, 1974.

**Humble,** Richard, *Marco Polo.* London: Weidenfeld and Nicolson, 1975.

**Hurst,** G.C., *Insei: Abdicated Sovereigns in the Politics of late Heian Japan 1086-1185.* New York: Columbia University Press, 1976

**Ipsiroglu,** M.S.:
*Painting and Culture of the Mongols.* Transl. from the German by E.D. Phillips. London: Thames and Hudson, 1967.
*Saray-Alben, Diez'sche Klebebände aus den Berliner Sammlungen.* Wiesbaden: Franz Steiner Verlag Gmbh, 1964.

**Ishii,** Ryosuke, *A history of political institutions in Japan.* Tokyo: University of Tokyo Press, 1980.

**Jien,** *The Future and the Past.* Berkeley: University of California Press, 1979.

**Kidder,** Jr., J. Edward, *The Art of Japan.* Tokyo: Shogakukan, 1981.

**Kitagawa,** H., and B. Tsuchida, transl., *The Tale of the Heike.* Tokyo: Tokyo University Press 1975.

**Kitagawa,** Joseph M., *Religion in Japanese History.* New York: Columbia University Press, 1966.

**Kodansha,** *Encyclopedia of Japan.* Tokyo: Kodansha, 1983.

**Kyōtarō,** Nishikawa, and Emily J. Sano, *The Great Age of Japanese Buddhist Sculpture AD600-1300.* Fort Worth: Kimbell Art Museum/Japan Society, 1982.

**Latham,** Ronald, transl., *Marco Polo: The Travels.* London: Penguin, 1958.

**Lewis,** Suzanne, *The Art of Matthew Paris in the Chronica Majora.* Cambridge: Scolar Press, 1987.

**Lu,** David John, *Sources of Japanese history, Vol. 1.* New York: McGraw-Hill, 1974.

**Mass,** J.P., *Warrior Government in Early Medieval Japan.* New Haven: Yale University Press, 1974.

**Mass,** J.P. ed., *Court and Bakufu in Japan.* New Haven: Yale University Press, 1982.

**Mills,** Douglas E., transl., *A collection of tales from Uji: a study and translation of Uji shui monogatari.* Cambridge: Cambridge University Press, 1970.

**Miner,** Earl, *An introduction to Japanese court poetry.* Stanford: Stanford University Press, 1968.

**Mori,** Hisashi, *Sculpture of the Kamakura Period.* Tokyo: Weatherhill/Heibonsha, 1964.

**Okudaira,** Hideo, *Narrative Picture Scrolls.* New York: Weatherhill, 1973.

*Peking* (The Great Cities series). Amsterdam: Time-Life Books, 1978.

**Phillips,** E.D., *The Mongols.* London: Thames and Hudson, 1969.

**Rockhill,** William Woodville, ed., *The Journey of William of Rubruck to The Eastern Parts of The World 1253-55.* London: Hakluyt Society, 1900.

**Sadler,** A.L., transl., *The Ten Foot Square Hut and Tales of the Heike.* Sydney: Angus and Robertson, 1928.

**Sansom,** G.,
*A history of Japan to 1334.* Stanford: Stanford University Press, 1958.
*A Short Cultural History.* London: Cresset Press, 1946.

**Satō,** Kanzan, *The Japanese Sword.* Tokyo: Kodansha International and Shibundo, 1983.

**Saunders,** J.J., *The History of the Mongol Conquests.* London: Routledge and Kegan Paul, 1971.

**Shinoda,** Minoru, *The founding of the Kamakura shogunate.* New York: Columbia University Press, 1960.
**Smith,** Bradley, and Wan-go Weng, *China: A History in Art.* London: Studio Vista, 1973
**Swann,** Peter C., *An introduction to the arts of Japan.* Oxford: Bruno Cassirer, 1958.
**Totman,** Conrad, *Japan before Perry: a short history.* Berkeley: University of California Press, 1981.
*The Travels of Marco Polo.* London: Sidgwick and Jackson, 1984.
**Turnbull,** Stephen:
*The Book of the Samurai.* London: Arms & Armour Press, 1982.
*The Samurai: A Military History.* London: George Philip, 1988.
*Samurai Warriors.* London: Blandford Press, 1987.
**Yule,** Sir Henry, *The Book of Ser Marco Polo the Venetian concerning the kingdoms and marvels of the east.* London: John Murray, 1921.

**AFRICA AND THE MIDDLE EAST**
**Ashtor,** E. Liyahn, *A Social and Economic History of the Near East in The Middle Ages.* London: Collins, 1976.
**Atil,** Esin:
*Art of the Arab World.* Washington D.C.: Smithsonian Institution Press, 1975.
*Renaissance of Islam: Art of the Mamluks.* Washington D.C.: Smithsonian Institution Press, 1981.
**Coste,** Pascal, *Architecture Arabe Ou Monuments Du Kaire* 1818-1826. Paris: Didiot Freres, 1837.
**Creswell,** K.A.C., *The Muslim Architecture of Egypt, Vol. 2.* Oxford: The Clarendon Press, 1959.
**Ettinghausen,** Richard, *Treasures of Asia: Arab Painting.* Lausanne: Editions d'Art Albert Skira, 1962.
**Glubb,** John Bagot, *Soldiers of Fortune: The Story of the Mamlukes.* London: Hodder & Stoughton, 1973.
**Holt,** P.M., *The Age of the Crusades, The Near East from the Eleventh Century to 1517.* New York: Longman, 1986.
**Holt,** P.M., A.K.S Lambton and B. Lewis, *The Cambridge History of Islam, Vol. I.* Cambridge: Cambridge University Press, 1970.
**Irwin,** Robert, *The Middle East in The Middle Ages: The Early Mamluk Sultanate 1250-1382.* London & Sydney: Croom Helm, 1986.
**Leaf,** William, and Sally Purcell, *Heraldic Symbols.* London: Victoria & Albert Museum, 1986.
**Lewis,** Bernard, ed., *The World of Islam.* London: Thames and Hudson, 1976.
**Mayer,** L.A., *Mamluk Costume.* Geneva: Albert Kundig, 1952.
**Runciman,** S., *A History of the Crusades, Vol III.* Harmondsworth: Penguin Books, 1987.
**Ruthven,** M., and the Editors of Time-Life Books, *Cairo* (The Great Cities series). Amsterdam: Time-Life Books, 1980.
**Shaw,** M.R.B., transl., *Joinville and Villehardouin: Chronicles of the Crusades.* London: Penguin Books, 1963.

# ACKNOWLEDGEMENTS

The following materials have been reprinted with the kind permission of the publishers: Page 42: "Everyone had waited expectantly. . ." quoted in *The Future and the Past* by Jien (Brown and Ishida eds.): University of California Press, 1979. Page 44: "Sorry to see . . ." quoted in *The Little Treasury of One Hundred People, One Poem Each,* by Fujiwara no Sadaie transl. by T. Galt (ed.): Princeton University Press, 1981. Page 50: "At the New Year, ill omens. . ." and page 55: "Saiko, aged 85 . . ." both quoted in *Japan: A Short Cultural History* by G. Sansom, London: Cresset, 1946. Page 61: "They care only about raiding . . ." quoted in *The Middle East in the Middle Ages* by Robert Irwin, London & Sydney: Croom Helm, 1986. Page 80: "They brought up a ship. . ." and "The Franks . . ." and "When the Muslims stormed it . . ." quoted in *The Age of the Crusades: The Near East from the Eleventh Century to 1517* by P. M. Holt, New York: Longman, 1986.

The editors also wish to thank the following individuals and institutions for their valuable assistance in the preparation of this volume:
**Denmark:** Copenhagen – Marianne Poulsen, Danish National Museum. Ribe – Per Kristian Madsen, Antikvariske Samling.
**Eire:** Dublin – David James, Chester Beatty Library.
**England:** Cambridge – Dr. Christel M. Kessler; Dr. Phillip Lindley, St. Catharine's College. Cheltenham – Kate Fleming. Leeds – Stephen Turnbull. London – Marian Campbell, Department of Metalwork, Victoria & Albert Museum; David Carpenter; James Chambers; Nicola Coldstream; Jeremy Davies; Nikolai Dejevsky; Alistair Duncan, World of Islam Festival Trust; Ian Eaves, The Royal Armouries, H.M. Tower of London; Timothy Fraser; John Gillingham, London School of Economics; Dr. Lindy Grant, The Courtauld Institute; Christopher de Hamel, Illuminated Manuscripts, Sotheby's; Victor Harris, Department of Japanese Antiquities, British Museum; Clive Hicks; Gillian Hutchinson, National Maritime Museum; Beth McKillop, Department of Oriental Manuscripts, British Library; Dr. David Morgan, Department of History, School of Oriental & African Studies, University of London; Berwick Morley, English Heritage; Suzanne O'Farrell; Readers Digest Association Ltd.; Eugenie Romer; Kenneth Teague, The Horniman Museum; Brian A. Tremain, Photographic Service, British Museum. Loughborough – Dr. David Nicolle. Maldon, Essex – Lt. Cdr. Peter Kemp. Oxford – William Leaf; Nick Vincent.
**Japan:** Tokyo – Yuri Fukusawa.
**Poland:** Warsaw – Bogdan Turek.
**Spain:** Madrid – Jane Walker.
**Sweden:** Visby – Mrs. Gun Westholm, Gotland's Historical Museum.
**Wales:** Cardiff – Peter Humphries. Monmouth – Donald Jackson, Calligraphy Centre; Brodie Neuenschwander.
**U.S.A.:** Fort Worth, Texas – Dr. Emily Sano, Kimbell Art Museum. Washington – Barbara Shattuck, National Geographic Magazine.

The index for this volume was prepared by Ann Marangos.

# INDEX

*Numerals in italics indicate an illustration of the subject mentioned.*

# H



# I



# J



# K



# L



# M



# N



# O



# P

## Q



## R



## S



## T



## U



## V



## W



## X

## Y



## Z

# PICTURE CREDITS

*The sources for the illustrations that appear in this book are listed below. Credits from left to right are separated by semi-colons; from top to bottom they are separated by dashes.*

**Cover:** Art by George Sharp. **2, 3**: Maps by Chapman Bounford and Associates. **8**: National Palace Museum, Taipei, Taiwan. **10**: Map by Chapman Bounford and Associates. **12**: Mahzar S. Ipsiroglu, 'Wind der Steppe'/Akademische Druck, u.Verlagsanstalt, Graz 1984. **15**: Art by Roger Stewart. **16, 17**: Art by Tony Smith. **19**: Orientabteilung der Staatsbibliothek Preussischer Kulturbesitz, West Berlin, Diez.A. fol, 70, s.4. **21**: Réunion des Musées Nationaux, Paris. **22, 23**: Imperial Household Agency, Tokyo; National Palace Museum, Taipei, Taiwan – Edinburgh University Library, Edinburgh. **24**: Orientabteilung der Staatsbibliothek Preussischer Kulturbesitz, West Berlin, Diez.A. fol. 70, s.22. **25**: Master and Fellows of Corpus Christi College, Cambridge, MS.16, fol. 166r. **26**: National Palace Museum, Taipei, Taiwan. **27**: Robert Harding Picture Library Ltd., London. **28, 29**: Koji Nakamura © 1982 National Geographic Society. **30**: Bibliothèque Nationale, Paris – Map by Chapman Bounford and Associates. **32**: Kofuku-Ji, Nara. **34**: Map by Chapman Bounford and Associates. **36**: Hayashibara Art Museum, Okayama. **39**: Jingo-Ji, Kyoto/photo courtesy of Kodansha. **40, 41**: Art by Andrew Wheatcroft. **43**: Art by Greg Harlin of Stansbury, Ronsaville, Wood Inc. **46, 47**: Tokyo National Museum, Tokyo, except top right, Werner Forman Archive, London/Burke Collection, New York. **49**: Kamakura Kokuho-Kan. **52**: Hoshaku Temple, Kyoto. **53**: Kofuku-Ji, Nara. **56, 57**: Imperial Household Agency, Tokyo **58**: Nationalbibliothek, Vienna, Cod.A.F.9, fol. 42v. **60**: Maps by Chapman Bounford and Associates. **62, 63**: Chester Beatty Library, Dublin. **66, 67**: Trustees of the British Museum, London/OA 1281. 91-6-23.5; Trustees of the British Museum, London/OA 78.12-30.682. **68**: Réunion des Musées Nationaux, Paris. **71**: By permission of the British Library, London, MS.Cott. Nero E11, fol. 222. **72**: Picturepoint, London; Trustees of the British Museum/M&LA 1841, 6-24,1 – By courtesy of the Board of Trustees of the Victoria & Albert Museum, London. **73**: Courtesy of Sothebys, London; The Metropolitan Museum of Art, Gift of J. Pierpont Morgan, 1917. (17.190.985). **74**: Bibliothèque Nationale, Paris, MS. Arabe 5847, fol. 105. **77**: Bibliothèque Nationale, Paris, MS, Arabe 5847, fol.69v. **78, 79**: Art by George Sharp. **81**: Sam Fogg, Rare Books, London. **82, 83**: Royal Library, Copenhagen, GL. Kgl.Saml.4,2. **84**: By permission of the British Library, London, MS. Royal 10.D.V11, fol. 233. **85**: Walters Art Gallery, Baltimore. **86**: By permission of the British Library, London, MS. Add. 50000, fol. 9v. **87**: Painting by Brodie Neuenschwander/Donald Jackson, The Calligraphy Centre, Monmouth, Wales. **88**: Lennart Larsen/The National Museum, Copenhagen, 2nd Dep. **90**: Map by Chapman Bounford and Associates. **94**: Scala, Florence. **95**: Erich Lessing, The John Hillelson Agency Ltd./ Kunsthistorisches Museum, Vienna. **97-101**: Biblioteca Apostolica Vaticana, Rome, MS. Pal.Lat 1071. **103**: Erich Lessing, The John Hillelson Agency Ltd./ Culture & Fine Arts Agency, Vienna. **104, 105**: Art by Andrew Robinson/Pubbli Aer Foto, Milan. **106**: Foto Vuolo, Ravello. **108**: Niels Elswing, Copenhagen. **110**: Map by Chapman Bounford and Associates. **112**: The Institute of Art of the Polish Academy of Learning, Warsaw. **114-115**: Art by Graham Humphreys. **116**: Cercle d'Art/Artephot-Ziolo, Paris. **118**: Biblioteca Apostolica Vaticana, Rome, Codex Rossiniano 3, fol. 13r. **119**: Rokuharamitsu-Ji, Kyoto; Trustees of the British Museum/OA 1915.5-15.1. **120**: M. Babey/Artephot-Ziolo, Paris. **122**: Drawing by Ian Bott. **123**: The Institute of Art of the Polish Academy of Learning, Warsaw. **124, 125**: Art by John Howe. **129**: Réunion des Musées Nationaux, Paris. **130**: © Michael Holford, Loughton, Essex. **131**: Photo Jean Mazenod, from 'L'Art Gothique', Editions Mazenod, Paris. **132**: Clive Hicks, London. **133**: © Michael Holford, Loughton, Essex. **134**: Clive Hicks, London; M. Babey/Artephot-Ziolo, Paris. **135**: Clive Hicks, London. **136, 137**: Sonia Halliday & Laura Lushington Photographs, Weston Turville, Buckinghamshire. **138**: © The Pierpont Morgan Library 1987, New York. **140**: Maps by Chapman Bounford and Associates. **142, 143**: Art by David Bergen. **146, 147**: Bibliothèque Nationale, Paris. **149**: By permission of the British Library, London, MS. Harley 4751, fol. 36 – By permission of the British Library, London, MS. Royal 12 F.X11, fol. 45. **150-153**: Clive Hicks, London. **155**: By permission of the British Library, London, MS. Royal 7 F.VIII, fol. 54v. **157**: The Bridgeman Art Library/Victoria & Albert Museum, London. **158-161**: By permission of the British Library, London, MS. Add. 41230, folios 181v, 207v, 147v, 161v. **162, 163**: Maps by Allan Hollingberry. **164-167**: Art by Jonathan Potter.

Typeset by A.J. Latham Limited, Dunstable, Bedfordshire
Printed and bound by Brepols S.A. – Turnhout, Belgium
Colour separations by Fotolitomec, S.N.C., Milan, Italy